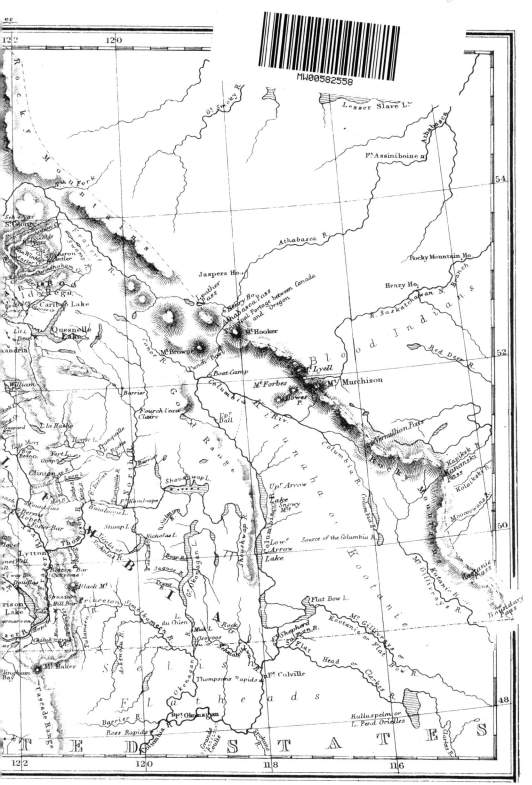

# POLICING A PIONEER PROVINCE

# POLICING A PIONEER PROVINCE

## The BC Provincial Police 1858–1950

*Lynne Stonier-Newman*

HARBOUR PUBLISHING

Published by
**HARBOUR PUBLISHING**
P.O. Box 219
Madeira Park, BC Canada V0N 2H0

Editor: Daniel Francis
Cover design: Roger Handling
Printed and bound in Canada

The author gratefully acknowledges the support of the Canada Council Explorations Programme.

Photographs and graphics on pages 12, 21 (bottom), 30, 39, 50, 57, 74, 79, 86, 95, 109 (bottom), 116, 127 (top), 136, 146 (bottom), 153, 159, 168, 174 (bottom), 181, 185 (top), 190, 200, 205, 209, 212, 221, 225, 229 (top), 232, 237, 240, 243, 246, 248, 253, 256 and 261 courtesy of the British Columbia Provincial Police Veterans' Association and first published in the *Shoulder Strap*.
Photographs on pages 127 (bottom), 174 (top) and 208 courtesy of the RCMP Veterans' Association and first published in *Off Patrol*.
Photographs on pages 12 (bottom) (PDP2898), 21 (top) (HP10501), 43 (HP24951), 64 (HP1096; HP6002), 102 (8919), 109 (top) (71346), 146 (top) (82954), 164 (HP99576), 195 (HP70521), 203 (HP8421), 229 (bottom) (HP70525) and front cover (HP74241) courtesy of the British Columbia Provincial Archives and Records Service.

**Canadian Cataloguing in Publication Data**


Stonier-Newman, Lynne, 1941–
  Policing a pioneer province


  Includes bibliographical references and index.
  ISBN 1-55017-056-2


  1. British Columbia Provincial Police – History.
  2. Police – British Columbia – History.   I. Title.
  HV8159.B7S76 1991      363.2'09711      C91-091677-2

# CONTENTS

*Author with her grandmother in front of her parents' home, Quesnel, 1942.*

# Preface

The British Columbia Provincial Police had a style as unique as the province itself. From 1859, when the first colonial constables patrolled the gold rush, to 1950, when the BCPP was absorbed by the RCMP, the Provincials helped to shape the course of British Columbia's development. They were often the first government representatives sent into an area. They explained the white man's laws to the natives, and British justice to the American gold seekers. As the province changed from unorganized wilderness to settled land, they patrolled immense geographic areas with little supervision and almost no support. When a Provincial found trouble, there were no reinforcements to call in.

As miners, loggers, railwaymen, fishermen and entrepreneurs flooded into BC, the reputation of the Provincials for innovative and effective policing was tested to the limit. Members of the force policed through two world wars, the Depression, bitter strikes and race riots. They marched in May Day parades, they lectured about safety to school children and they chased after murderers, bootleggers, and con men. Preserving law and order was just part of their job. They were also expected to collect licence fees, make weather reports, gather vital statistics, check cattle brands, test new drivers; in other words, perform any task the provincial government asked of them. In the process, Provincials became well-known members of the community, on a first-name basis with many residents.

My father was one of these men. When I was born, he was the highway patrol constable at the Quesnel detachment. Dad left the BCPP in 1943, but he continued to gather stories about the Provincials. When the family went on motoring holidays, Dad would pass the dusty miles relating anecdotes about the province's history and the history of the Provincials. He and I always intended to research the BCPP story further, but he died before we began.

In 1983, I started to write a series of articles about the force, and the material I gathered eventually grew into a book. *Policing a Pioneer Province* is an overview of the BCPP from its inception as a frontier constabulary to its incorporation into the RCMP. Most of the material in the book comes from old newspaper accounts, archival records and, most importantly, from many hours of interviews with former members of the force. Many of the men I interviewed wondered if their recollections were reliable. After all, almost forty years had passed since the force disappeared. But I found that the training these men had received in recording details and making observations made their reminiscences accurate and thoughtful. I appreciate their frankness in sharing their experiences with me.

Members of the British Columbia Provincial Police Veterans Association assisted me in many ways with the book. They provided me with copies of their quarterly newsletter, *Off Patrol*, published from 1980 to 1984 and full of stories about the history of the force. I also am grateful for the Association's permission to use photographs and information from the *Shoulder Strap*, the BCPP magazine produced between 1938 and 1950. As well, the BCPPVA executive provided me with the names and addresses of their membership, which gave me a broad choice of individuals to interview and often led me to former Provincials who were not members of the association.

Two BCPPVA members were especially helpful. Many thanks to Barrie Jones, secretary, for his patient assistance, and to Cecil Clark. In 1950, after Clark was summarily retired as deputy commissioner of the BCPP, he became a prolific writer about the force. The time, advice and information he shared with me helped greatly in finding research material.

Thanks also to the archivists at the British Columbia Provincial Archives and the Public Archives of Canada, to the patient librarians at Cariboo College, the University of British Columbia and Simon Fraser University, and to the curators at the many museums where I gathered information and contacts. I am grateful to the Canada Council's Explorations Program for a grant that supported my initial research, and to Senator Len Marchand, VCC history professor Andy Varmie and writer Joyce Dunn, who acted as my sponsors. Mike Rimmer gave me help as I made the transition from typewriter to computer, and Sheryle Kurta was a valued research assistant.

Joyce Dunn was the initial editor of the manuscript, and the support I received from her and her husband, Dan, encouraged me to persevere. A special thank you to Trudy and Wayne Montgomery, Shirley and John Stonier, my sons Garth and Ron Stonier, and my husband Brian Newman for their assistance, encouragement and perceptive comments, which sustained me during the past eight years. And last, but by no means least, many thanks for his valued assistance to my editor, Dan Francis.

# CHAPTER ONE

# "We enforce British law, Sir!"
# 1858–1870

O N A RAINY DAY IN 1858, the first chief inspector of the British Columbia Constabulary arrived in Victoria, the last stop before the new colony of British Columbia. Chartres Brew was relieved to get his feet on dry land again, having been delayed almost a month because of a shipwreck. "I embarked on the 4th of September last at Southampton in the steamship 'Austria' for New York to proceed across the Isthmus of Panama to Victoria," Brew reported in a note to Governor James Douglas. "The steamer burned at sea on the 13th of September, 4 days sail from New York. By this disaster, I lost all my property, all my money and all my papers." He went on to announce his arrival, request an appointment and explain he had borrowed £100 from British officials in Halifax to complete the journey.[1]

Later that day, as Brew waded through Victoria's muddy streets on his way to the Hudson's Bay Company's log fort, he passed hundreds of tents and ramshackle cabins surrounded by litter and piles of camping gear. He knew fewer than 400 people had lived in Victoria ten months ago, before the first prospectors found gold in the gravel bars of the Fraser River and a horde of gold seekers fell upon the town on their way up the river. The population now must be a couple of thousand, he calculated. The whole agglomeration looked grey and unappealing in the afternoon drizzle; Brew must have wondered if he had been right to come.

Brew eventually found his way to the Fort by requesting directions from a man in a top hat, and he was ushered in to meet James Douglas, Governor of Vancouver Island, Governor of British Columbia and altogether the most powerful British official west of the Rockies. Brew apologized that his official letter of appointment from Sir James Lytton, the British Colonial Secretary, lay at the bottom of the Atlantic with the rest of his baggage, but he summarized its contents, identifying Lytton's main directive: "You are to organize the British Columbia Colonial Police to carry out the general policing of the district, taking special care that drinking and gambling are as much as possible put down."[2] Brew told Douglas that he had devised a preliminary plan for developing a police system in the style of the Irish Constabulary. He explained that he could have 100 men hired and trained in approximately four months, well before the start of the gold rush's second season.

But the new chief inspector soon discovered that Douglas had other plans that did not necessarily conform to Brew's own, or to the instructions of the British Colonial Secretary. He also learned that Douglas did not allow his decisions to be questioned.

Chartres Brew was raised a gentleman. Born in Corsfin, County Clare, Ireland, in 1815, he started his career as a cavalry officer, served with distinction in the Crimean War and then joined the Irish Constabulary where he served for fourteen years. A burly man with impressive muttonchop whiskers, he was unmarried and in his early forties when the colonial secretary asked if he was interested in organizing a constabulary in the new colony. Since Brew felt responsible for his widowed mother and sisters and hoped to improve the family finances, he accepted. The salary was almost double what he received as the Irish Constabulary inspector for the City of Cork, and he expected to have a free hand in establishing a police force in British Columbia.

Brew had not counted on James Douglas's hesitation. The Governor was a formal man who had expected and received unquestioning obedience from employees when he was a Hudson's Bay Company factor. Impressively knowledgeable about New Caledonia, he had his own ideas of how it should be developed as a colony.

At their first meeting, Douglas announced that Brew was the ideal man to be assistant chief gold commissioner as well as chief inspector of police. When Brew doubted that he could handle both jobs, Douglas became annoyed. He explained firmly that massive gold-tax revenues were going uncollected. The new colony needed an improved collection system, which would combine well with law enforcement. And so, despite Brew's protests that he had no experience as a collector of taxes, and that revenue raising and law enforcement should not be the responsibility of one official, Douglas appointed him gold commissioner on the spot.

The governor then described his attempts the previous summer to establish a modest system of taxation and a temporary police force. He explained that neither was functioning very well but assured Brew that he would receive help improving that situation. Douglas added that he had hired some men earlier to police Fort Hope and Yale and he would be pleased if Brew maintained them in the same positions and salary levels. The governor then stressed that although revenues were limited, assistance with policing was now available in the form of 150 Royal Engineers arriving from England.

This last assurance must have puzzled Brew. He had been informed by the British Secretary about the Engineers, under the command of Colonel Richard Moody, who would also serve as lieutenant governor of British Columbia. But the Secretary had stressed that the soldiers would assist in policing only in emergency situations. They were there primarily to survey roads, build bridges and demonstrate to the United States government by their presence that the international border meant something.

Brew left the governor with many doubts. Not only had Douglas doubled his responsibilities, he seemed more interested in establishing a taxation system than a police force. There was no way Brew could have realized the importance of his dual appointment. Because of it, British Columbia became a jurisdiction where revenue raising was combined with law enforcement for decades to come, a rare combination in the British Empire.

Later that evening, Brew dined with Chief Justice Matthew Begbie and Colonel Moody at the Douglas residence. He learned that both of his fellow officials were also receiving directives from Douglas that differed radically from the instructions of the British Colonial Secretary. Moody did not expect his Engineers to be used widely for law enforcement. And Begbie agreed with Brew that taxation should be kept separate from policing. But Douglas was the governor, with authority to organize the new colony as best he could. Communication with London took a minimum of three months. It was obvious that for the time being, at least, Chief Inspector Brew of the British Columbia Constabulary was also going to be the colony's gold commissioner.

After dinner, Douglas described the circumstances of the miners wintering in the Fraser Canyon area. Most of them were unprepared for the freezing winter storms; many had run out of money and supplies. He expected a great number would leave the area in the next month or so, but he expected a large rush of newcomers when spring arrived. Approximately 25,000 prospectors had arrived in 1858 and thousands more were predicted to be coming in 1859.

As the conversation turned to the conflicts between natives and miners, Chief Inspector Brew learned that several thousand Indians inhabited the Fraser Canyon region. Today we know these people as the Nlaka'pamux, Lillooet and Shuswap tribal groups; then, there was little knowledge or interest about the various native cultures. Douglas and the

11

*Chartres Brew, the first chief inspector of the British Columbia Constabulary, forerunner of the British Columbia Provincial Police.*

*Victoria in 1860, much as Chartres Brew saw it when he arrived from Ireland. The watercolour is by Sarah Crease.*

others admitted that there had been amazingly few incidents of Indians turning on the whites who were intruding into their territory, but they expressed concern about a mass native uprising. Unlike fur traders, who needed to coexist as peaceably as possible with the Indians since they earned their livelihood trading with them, miners did not need to get along with the Indians. Most had no sympathy with native claims that the river and the gold belonged to them, nor with the Indians' need to retain access to their rich fishing grounds along the Fraser. For the past few years, some natives had been trading gold nuggets to fur traders; they did not intend to allow the miners to steal it. And even those who worked for the miners as guides, canoeists, cooks and labourers did not like the fact that white men were taking native women into their camps. All these circumstances made conflict almost inevitable.

James Douglas had received reports of warfare between miners and Indians earlier in 1858, and he had made two trips up the Fraser, supported by a force borrowed from the British Navy. At that time he lectured miners and native leaders on the necessity of obeying British law and appointed temporary officials to control the area. As Brew found out about these policemen and magistrates, posted at Hope, Yale and Hill's Bar, his concerns multiplied. The governor had ignored the issue of qualifications, instead emphasizing his recruits' "good connections." Most of the policemen were attracted to the work only by the hefty salary. Every time there was a major gold find, some of them resigned. As a result, the turnover was so high that it was difficult to say exactly how many men were still on the job.

Brew began to realize how few suitable men would consider becoming constables or revenue collectors in either colony. He recommended that Douglas request sixty men from the Irish constabulary, but the governor demurred, pointing out that the new colony needed more revenue before it created additional costs. Hiring more police was hardly a priority, particularly since the Royal Engineers were going to be working in the Fraser area the following summer. It was increasingly evident to Brew that Douglas and Moody had completely different expectations of the Engineers. Organizing a constabulary was going to take much longer than he had anticipated.

Brew travelled with the official party to Fort Langley for the ceremony proclaiming British Columbia a British Colony on November 19, 1858, and he was introduced to his domain when he, Moody and Begbie arrived to celebrate Christmas at the Royal Engineers' nearby camp at Derby. Two days after the holiday, Brew left for a tour of the area with a patrol of Royal Engineers, and shortly after their departure a plea for help arrived from the Yale magistrate: war was about to break out between two groups of miners.

One faction was led by Ned McGowan, a well-educated Californian who controlled the Hill's Bar area a few miles from Yale. During the California gold rush, McGowan had grown used to taking the law into his own hands and had even sat as a "judge." He had tried to establish a similar system at Hill's Bar, but was thwarted when Douglas had appointed magistrates and constables.

The "War" began when two of McGowan's men assaulted a black miner from Yale named Dixon. The victim promptly filed charges with the Yale magistrate, who directed the Hill's Bar magistrate to arrest the assailants. In a subsequent dispute between magistrates over the location of the trial, the Hill's Bar constable was thrown into jail in Yale. The Hill's Bar magistrate then deputized McGowan and gave him authority to arrest the Yale magistrate, who was brought to trial at Hill's Bar and fined $50 for contempt of court. The magistrate's friend, Dr. Fifer, paid his fine, and McGowan's friends assaulted Fifer as he left the court.

Now the Yale magistrate was asking for help. Colonel Moody and Chief Justice Begbie, aware that they could not easily contact Chief Inspector Brew, who was actually responsible for civilian law enforcement, both decided to go. "We quickly made our arrangements," Moody later reported to Douglas, "hired passages on the only River Steamer, embarked that night & long before daylight we were steaming away up the River. The Men (22 in number) of course delighted, looking up the locks of their Rifles and Revolvers — the Judge & myself grave & thoughtful . . ." The weather was severe, the river was freezing and the expedition became "all frozen in at a point from whence we could get neither up or down the river."[3]

After that rather comic start to the colony's first formal law-enforcing mission, matters improved quickly. A small party under Lieutenant Mayne was sent ahead to Hill's Bar and Yale, to make the trip up the Fraser by Indian canoe. He reported that the situation remained tense and might deteriorate at any time. Meanwhile, the weather improved and the steamer broke free of ice. When Moody and Begbie arrived at Yale, they were saluted with a volley from the miners' revolvers, the balls whistling directly over their heads, causing them to wonder if they were being welcomed or attacked.

Most of the miners chose sides in the dispute. When Moody, acting as lieutenant governor, dismissed the Hill's Bar magistrate, his decision met a storm of protest. He decided to order up the fifty Royal Engineers from Hope. Brew, having started up the river as soon as he heard about the dispute, arrived with them.

Once the reinforcements and the chief inspector had arrived, Ned McGowan was arrested for arresting the Yale magistrate, and a few hundred miners from Hill's Bar responded by gathering in Yale and demanding a public meeting. When Moody, Begbie and Brew appeared at the meeting, the miners first declared their support for the government of British Columbia, then made serious charges against the Yale magistrate. They accused him of regularly making biased judgements and of being particularly harsh with any Hill's Bar man appearing before him. Judge Begbie assured them that the charges would be investigated and that the law would be carried out impartially. After he invited them to attend McGowan's trial, they dispersed peacefully.

The next day, the small log courthouse was jammed to capacity, and those who could not fit in milled around outside. The miners were restless when Judge Begbie fined McGowan £5 for his attack on Dr. Fifer, but they cheered heartily when he acquitted McGowan for his seizure of the Yale magistrate. Judge Begbie used the trial as an opportunity to lecture on British law and to warn the miners, most armed with pistols or knives or both, that there would be strict enforcement of the law prohibiting bowie knives or guns. Once again the miners cheered loudly. Apparently they were prepared to conform to British law, as long as they felt it was enforced fairly and consistently.

The next day, when the officials accepted McGowan's invitation to join him and his men at the diggings for lunch, complete with champagne, the incident was considered closed.

"Ned McGowan's War" was the first major demonstration of the colony's new justice system. The standards that Begbie declared from the bench that day received much publicity. Miners discussed his speech at length and agreed with each other that British Columbia was going to be governed firmly by British law. Those who did not like it realized that they had better leave. As the story of the "War" circulated through the camps, the new administration of law became known throughout the region.

Chief Inspector Brew and a small detachment of Engineers remained at Yale when Moody, Begbie and the rest of the sappers returned downriver to winter camp at Derby. The Engineers who remained were left officially to survey the area, but their presence also helped to emphasize British control. In a letter to Moody, Brew reported that conditions were peaceful, though McGowan remained something of a nuisance.

> Sire, I have the honor to inform you that the 22nd Inst. was celebrated at Fort Yale by the citizens of the United States as the Birthday of Washington. At noon one hundred discharges were fired in imitation of one hundred Guns by exploding gunpowder between two anvils. The noise for each explosion was as loud as the report of the largest-size Gun. I am informed that they subsequently fired ten Guns as a salute to me, as they imagined that a young lad who was brought up before Captain Whannel for firing a squib out of a

15

pistol in the street and was discharged by him with a rebuke, was released through my interference.

In the evening, a ball took place at the house of a man named Campbell. I was invited but did not go. Mr. McGowan, Mr. Perrier and others promised me that they would exert themselves to have peace and order maintained during the night, and I particularly requested that no pistols should be taken in the room. The utmost harmony prevailed till the company went into supper, when some jealousy arose about precedence for seats. A Mr. Bagley, of Hill's Bar, abused McGowan and called him an old grey-haired scamp. McGowan immediately broke a plate on Bagley's head and Bagley in return broke McGowan's head with another plate. At once there was a general row and friends on both sides went off to get their pistols but when they returned to the scene the affair had subsided into a demand for "satisfaction" as soon as arrangements could be made [for]. . . a duel with rifles at 40 paces, to be placed back to back, walk to the mark, and wheel and fire at the word was to be held in United States territory.

If they were going to fight in this country, I should have had them arrested and bound to peace, but as they are leaving the Colony and are not English subjects, the propriety of interfering with them appears to me to be doubtful.[4]

Brew continued to be concerned about combining revenue raising with law enforcement. Though he tried to keep the two functions separate, he was often forced by lack of manpower to have his most reliable constables collect the gold tax since many miners balked at paying it. He did not trust some of the men hired the previous year and was pleased when the colonial secretary transferred all civil law enforcement administrative duties to him, including the right to hire and fire constables. He began to discharge the unsuitable collectors and constables and to hire others. But Douglas retained control of all expenditures and kept a tight rein on law enforcement spending unless it related to revenue collection. He also continued to send Brew well-connected but inept young men, as did other officials in both colonies. It seemed that the constabulary was the dumping ground for every young relative or friend newly arrived from Great Britain that nobody knew what to do with.

"I really do not know what to do with him," Brew complained about one of these raw recruits.

Recommended as he believes he was when he arrived from England, he hopes to occupy a more respectable position than that of constable, and if he is to be appointed to a higher post, I should be unwilling to order that he should be placed on constable's duty with the class of men who are constables here. The only duty I could put Mr. Moore to would be to collect duties on the river, but until I know more of him, I do not wish to trust him on a duty of this nature. He appears to have been while at Langley so very foolish. He left the place in debt, did not pay for his passage up river, and arrived here without one farthing in his pocket.[5]

Not all the men sent to Brew were inept. A few exceeded his expectations and they became the core of the law-enforcement system and gold-field administration. Some of the men who joined the BC Constabulary during the next years would not have joined a police force in Great Britain. They belonged to a higher social class than was usual for police constables. However, when young gentlemen such as Thomas Elwyn, John Hayes and William Cox arrived in the Fraser area, searching more for adventure than for gold, they were willing to serve as both constables and collectors. They came from respected Scottish or Irish families, and many of them had regular annuity incomes, a distinct advantage given a constable's inadequate salary. Men were paid £25 a month but since the cheapest boarding houses on the river charged £24 a month, someone without private means was pressed to make ends meet. When relatives and friends heard about the adventures of men like Elwyn, Hayes and Cox, some of them journeyed out to the colonies to join the Constabulary. These men created a standard that pleased even Brew, and the BC Constabulary began to be a credible organization.

Miners from around the world continued to come to British Columbia. When a bonanza like Barkerville or Rock Creek was discovered, thousands of prospectors headed into the wilderness to seek their fortunes at the latest strike. This required a special kind of administrative system, as distances were vast and communication was slow. With the development of each new gold region, a gold commissioner, who also served as stipendary magistrate, was appointed to take charge of the administration of law, claim registration and collection of revenues for that region. He arrived with a constable or two to organize a new area almost as soon as the miners started exploring it.

The gold commissioner collected mining fees and registered claims, often from a tent until a log cabin was hastily constructed for him. His constable travelled throughout the area collecting fees and announcing the arrival of the law. The commissioner also presided over court cases involving less than $250, directed public works, decided when the gold fields would be closed for the winter months and supervised law enforcement. Gold commissioners forwarded regular summaries to Gold Commissioner/Chief Inspector Brew, reports that helped to direct the development of the colony.

Commissioners sometimes ran into opposition. When hundreds of rebellious miners at Rock Creek (in the Similkameen, just north of the US border and about 500 km east of Hope) refused to purchase mining licences and to stop wearing revolvers and bowie knives, Gold Commissioner Peter O'Reilly sent for help. A week later, Governor Douglas, who had been examining the construction of the Fraser Canyon Wagon Road, arrived in Rock Creek with a red-coated troop of Royal Engineers. He lectured the miners bluntly, telling them that if they did not want to obey British law, they were welcome to cross back over the American border. He pointed out that Judge Begbie was fair, but that he imposed harsh sentences. Then he announced that construction would start immediately on a wagon road connecting the Similkameen with Hope and New Westminster. That resolved the miners' main complaint that they were isolated from the rest of the colony. Even before construction started, O'Reilly reported that the miners were co-operative and paying for their licences.

As each region became populated, a grand jury was organized, consisting of the gold commissioner, other local officials, the chief justice and invited community members, usually the owners of roadhouses, stores and saloons who were realistic about miners' behaviour and needs. Men wanted to bet, drink and dance when they came in from the camps. Control was maintained indirectly, not by banning these activities but by limiting the seating in each establishment and by closing down saloons accused of selling rotgut or using marked cards.

In the gold fields, a constable's most frequent duty was breaking up brawls. Fist fights were a common way to resolve disputes, but a personal fight often turned into a drunken melee. Then the police would be sent for, usually by a landlord who feared for the safety of his establishment. As soon as the constable arrived, he swore in a couple of hefty specials from among the spectators and they would bang a few heads together and drag the most belligerent rowdies off to jail. When the constable ended up with more prisoners than the tiny jail cells could accommodate, he chained the overflow to nearby trees to sleep it off. The next morning, the prisoners appeared before the magistrate, where they cheerfully paid their fines and any property damage, before heading back to the diggings, having had a "right good night in town."

In 1859, after supervising the second season of the gold rush on the Fraser, Brew moved from Yale to New Westminster. His administrative style and personality had won him many friends and before he left, eighty men from Hill's Bar paid him tribute at a farewell gathering:

> Your discriminating judgment and practical sagacity have been evinced in many exciting questions wherein the rights of miners have conflicted. In their settlement, honesty and common sense were the prominent characteristics of your decisions, and for them, sir, we desire to thank you.

The habits and customs of immigrants to new countries—particularly gold-bearing countries—are so diversified, that it is one of the most difficult things for those in power to mete out justice to all and not incur the enmity of some. To do so is the act of no ordinary mind, and evinces an intimate knowledge of human nature. You have done the first, and not only avoided the latter, but have retained the kind feelings and respect for all.[6]

Such flattering sentiments were probably questioned by some, including Governor Douglas. Brew objected to the system of miners' licences and regularly recommended an export duty on gold instead. He was also impatient that his superiors ignored his requests for a horse allowance and the agreed-upon reimbursement for travel and house expenses. Increasingly frustrated with the differences between what he had contracted to do and what his duties were, he appeared to some as a proper dour Irishman.

When Brew moved his headquarters to New Westminster, he became chief magistrate for the raw new capital of the mainland colony and for the New Westminster region, a geographic area stretching far up the Pacific coast. As well, he continued as chief inspector and gold commissioner. Because of his reputation for reasonableness and his knowledge of the colony, other officials sought his opinion on matters of policy, and in 1863, Brew became an appointed member of the first Advisory Legislative Council in British Columbia.

Some of the dilemmas of law enforcement must have been more amusing than worrying to Brew. After the Fraser Wagon Road was constructed, men began using all kinds of beasts and machines to reach the Cariboo gold fields. Constables got used to attending accidents, rescuing injured passengers from wrecked stagecoaches, shooting horses or mules with broken legs. But camels were a unique problem, and constables were stymied by the legalities involved. Impressed by reports that camels could carry four times the freight that a mule could, three innovative freighters imported twenty-one of them for use on the road. Chaos resulted. Horses and mules panicked as soon as they smelled camel, despite even the efforts of one owner who doused his camel in two gallons of imported wild rose fragrance. Some bolted up mountainsides, scattering freight and jeopardizing lives, while others plunged into the canyon to watery deaths. Yet as one constable complained, there were no laws against camels, so if the animals were not attacking or stampeding, what charges should be laid? In the end, the problem solved itself. Other animals continued to panic and the threat of civil suits and subsequent financial disaster caused the freighters to end their experiment.

Brew developed a close relationship with the Colony of Vancouver Island's police chief, Augustus Pemberton, and when Brew's sister married Pemberton, the friendship grew even closer. Both men were concerned about the potential for conflicts with the powerful west coast Indian tribes as settlers and miners encroached on their territory. They worried that a large, joint force of tribes might swoop down the coast in ocean canoes and attack either colony at any time. Pemberton agreed with Governor Douglas that the best way to control the natives was to continue intimidating them with the navy's big guns. Brew disagreed, arguing that in the long term only a strong constabulary, which explained as well as enforced the new laws, would effectively pacify the natives. He was convinced that for the good of the colony, they had to be given the same legal rights as whites, though he understood that the white man's laws were based on values exotic to native cultures.

Brew instructed his men to treat everyone with "firm dignity and respect, including Indians and Chinese."[7] He also emphasized to gold commissioners and constables that interpreters should be used whenever necessary; a man brought to trial had the right to understand what law he had broken. Brew sometimes argued with his good friend Judge Begbie about how severe a penalty should be imposed when the law had not been understood, but to little avail.

Despite the increasing number of charges laid against Indians, mainly for petty thievery when intoxicated, the actual crime rate in the colonies was surprisingly low. Judge Begbie summarized the situation in 1861:

> It is clear, however, that the inhabitants almost universally respect and obey the laws and voluntarily prefer good order and peaceful industry to the violence and bloodshed to which other Gold mining regions have been subjected and with such dispositions, the police force, scanty and scattered as it is, appears to have been hitherto sufficient not only to restrain from crime those who might otherwise have committed deeds of violence, but in general, to bring to justice the few persons who have been actually guilty.[8]

Of course, in the early days, there were few laws to be broken, and few charges to be laid. Constables dealt with an occasional murder or theft, but mainly they broke up drunken brawls, seized illegal weapons, inspected chimneys to prevent fires and sorted out disagreements over gold claims. But while Chief Inspector Brew agreed that the overall number of charges was low, he worried that the number of charges laid against natives increased annually. On the Fraser, he tried hiring native special constables and the crime rate did decline, though probably because most miners were departing for richer fields deeper in the interior. As more natives unsuccessfully fought the charges laid against them by blaming drunkenness, Brew tried to stop bootleggers on the coast by seizing their shipments. However, the practice could not be stamped out in a hurry. It was too easy to secretly load a sloop in the dark of night in

*Camerontown, near Barkerville, a typical mining camp in the Cariboo gold rush.*

*The first gaol built in BC, at Craigflower, near Victoria, in the 1850s.*

Victoria or New Westminster, then to slip away to some quiet bay where the cache was broken into smaller shipments to be sold to natives up the coast.

Brew was concerned more for the colonies' safety than the well-being of the natives. Officials were nervous about the Indians who congregated in increasing numbers at Victoria and New Westminster each spring. The native visitors often arrived in groups of a hundred or more, all dramatically painted, feather flags flying from their massive canoes, drums and chants echoing as they paddled into the harbour. In their camps at the edge of town, living conditions worsened, disease flourished and hostile groups skirmished with each other. Then, in 1862, a massive smallpox epidemic spread through the encampments like a prairie wildfire. Natives were ordered to leave Victoria and New Westminster. Evicted by military, police and other officials, they departed for home, spreading the virulent disease up and down the coast. Strong, self-sufficient tribes were almost wiped out within weeks: as much as one-third of the native population died. Many of those who survived the epidemic perished of starvation during the following winter because they'd been too sick to lay in food supplies.

Fear of smallpox was also widespread in white communities. When a case occurred, usually among the Chinese or Indian residents, the nearest constable was notified immediately. If no medical person was available, he became responsible for isolating the patient and for nursing him. There is no record of any constable catching smallpox during the great epidemic. However, in 1862, none of the twenty constables in British Columbia was stationed in the worst epidemic areas. That was Indian territory, and nobody gave much thought to what happened there.

In 1864 the Indian uprising whose spectre had haunted white colonials for so long appeared to have broken out. Terror swept the colonies when it was learned that road builders inland from the end of Bute Inlet had been murdered by Chilcotin Indians. The killings occurred on a wagon road connecting the head of Bute Inlet with the Fraser River via the Chilcotin Plains. Two hundred miles shorter than the Cariboo Road, it was touted by Alfred Waddington, its aggressive promoter, as "going to be the shortest and best route to reach the rich Cariboo gold fields!" As construction began for the third season, a group of Chilcotins had again been employed as labourers. At dawn on May 1, they attacked the sixteen white construction workers, killing thirteen of them; the previous day, they had killed a ferryman fifteen miles down the trail. Three workers escaped and fled to the coast where they were taken by Homathko Indians to the medical post in Nanaimo. The magistrate there sent a message to the new head of the Vancouver Island colony, Governor Arthur Kennedy. He notified Frederick Seymour, the new governor for British Columbia, a process that took three more days.

Seymour immediately requested a frigate and a gunboat from the Admiralty at Esquimalt and ordered Chief Inspector Brew to assemble a force of special constables to go to Bute. He specified that the approach was not to be overly aggressive, and that reinforcements would be requested only if necessary. He also conferred with his predecessor, James Douglas, who recommended that a mounted and armed force go in from Alexandria and that rewards be offered for each man involved in the murder.

The next day, Seymour, Brew and twenty-eight special constables (mainly former Royal Engineers), and also Waddington and Edwin Mosley, one of the three survivors, crowded onto the gunboat H.M.S. *Forward*. Before he left, Seymour directed his secretary to write to Gold Commissioner William Cox at Fort Alexander, authorizing him to organize a force, to offer rewards and to avoid "collision" with the Indians. He gave Cox "a very large discretion as to the number and race of the men you would employ and as to the course to be adopted but he suggests for your consideration that you should not be sufficiently weak to invite attack, nor your force so numerous as to form a heavy burden on the Colonial Treasury."[9] Cox was also informed that the expedition to Bute Inlet was "merely to assert the supremacy of the law. This strong body of men will follow up, in case of necessity, the Indians to their fishing grounds on the lake but the governor trusts that under the experienced management of Mr. Brew, the well-disposed Indians will be induced to capture and hand over the murderers."[10] Upon receipt of the instructions, Cox requested Donald McLean, a former Hudson's Bay man who had unsuccessfully tried to establish Fort Chilcotin years earlier, to be his second-in-command. Cox also assembled a group of seasoned miners and ranchers as special constables.

When the group arrived at Bute Inlet townsite, they learned that no one there had gone back up to the construction camps. Governor Seymour directed Brew to leave immediately, then returned to New Westminster. Brew began the arduous three-day journey up the Homathko River canyon with his second-in-command, Thomas Elwyn, Waddington, Mosley and the special constables. Qwhittie, a Homathko who had been cooking for the advance work crew and had been warned to flee as the attack began, accompanied them. At the ferry crossing, Waddington stayed behind to help get the mules across, much to Brew's relief as he found the promoter hard to tolerate.

At the first campsite, the twelve volunteers sworn in as a jury recorded they found blood-stained grass and tree stumps, drag marks leading to the river, destroyed tents and broken work implements. At the advance camp, they found three mutilated bodies. The inquest jury found "that William Brewster, John Clark and Jim Gaudet met their deaths by willful murder committed by certain Chilcotin Indians names unknown."[11]

The next day, the naval gunboat went back to New Westminster carrying five volunteers, Waddington and a report from Brew to Seymour. "No just idea of the Country or the Trail can be formed from Mr. Waddington's flattering description of it," Brew explained, describing the formidable geography, then added: "The Indians here are greatly afraid that the Chilcotins will come down and kill everyone, but the outrage was committed for the sake of plunder by a few men of a branch of the Chilcotin tribe and the main tribe will not become involved in war on their account."[12]

Meanwhile, up in the vast plateau country above the Bute and Bentinck Inlets, a Chilcotin killed William Manning. Manning and his partner, Alex McDonald—the only homesteaders at Puntzi Lake—had forced the Chilcotins from their freshwater spring and campground two years earlier. When Manning died, McDonald was in Bella Coola, unaware of the rebellion endangering him and the five workers he had just brought from Victoria to build Waddington's trail from Puntzi Lake to the Homathko Valley. Waddington was aware of it and he repeatedly requested that protection or at least a warning be sent to McDonald and the sixteen white residents of Bella Coola. But Seymour and Brew planned to be there almost immediately so did nothing, even when the Admiralty was slower to supply transportation to Bella Coola than expected.

McDonald, his five new employees and a young Chilcotin mule skinner departed for Puntzi Lake via the Bentinck Arm trail, accompanied by another packer, Peter McDougall, his purchased Chilcotin woman, two miners heading to Barkerville and forty-two mules. A small group of Chilcotins attacked them just twenty-two miles from Bella Coola and McDonald, McDougall, the woman and one miner died. The rest of the party, some badly injured, were allowed to escape. Some fled to Bella Coola as did a storekeeper from Canoe Crossing and his family. The residents and survivors, nervous about the unusual number of Chilcotin arriving and the increasing friendliness between them and the Bella Coola band, barricaded themselves in the general store.

Three weeks later, Seymour, Brew, Elwyn, a force of forty volunteers and seventeen pack horses arrived on the H.M.S. *Sutlej*, a large frigate. The Bella Coola residents, native and white, warmly welcomed the governor and his party; the Chilcotins disappeared. But the white residents and the former Royal Engineers volunteers were soon aghast. The governor accepted the native Bella Coolas' offer to help hunt the Chilcotins, emphasizing that this was not an Indian-killing expedition but a campaign to arrest the rebels on conclusive evidence. Brew provided them with thirty Lancaster rifles and uniforms and soon had his considerable party heading up the long mountain trail out of Bella Coola. On the trail, despite twenty of the native Bella Coolas deserting within days and taking three horses with them, Seymour and Brew continued to insist that all natives encountered be left as undisturbed as possible. Only the murderers would be taken into custody. Later, after a Chilcotin offered to act as a guide, led a search party into a wilderness area and deserted them, a volunteer wrote in his diary: "So much for Mr. Brew's maudlin sympathy for the Indians, and his orders that the Chilcotin rascal should not be treated as a prisoner."[13]

Two hundred miles away at Puntzi Lake, Cox and his party encountered Klatassine, a powerful war chief and a fugitive from Bute Inlet, and his band, but did not manage to capture anyone in a series of skirmishes. Nervously, Cox ordered the construction of a small fort, from which he could await the arrival of a powerful and friendly Chilcotin chief. He and his force were still in it when the force from Bella Coola arrived.

Brew and his men headed out into the wilderness where they searched for weeks, often close to their quarry but never cornering the Chilcotins. In exhausting conditions and on scanty rations, they grew increasingly fatigued, and the portly Brew became gaunt and grey. The Chilcotin bands they pursued suffered even more.

As fall approached, eight fugitives gave themselves up to Cox at Fort Chilcotin, realizing that they could not win against the white men in the long term. Led by the impressive Klatassine and prepared to make a treaty, they marched into the fort and were handcuffed and leg-ironed as murderers. Cox immediately bound his prisoners on horseback and started on the long journey back to Alexandria and Quesnellemouth.

When Brew's group returned to the fort at Puntzi Lake for provisions, they heard of Cox's success. But they rode out as planned, still hunting for the remaining fugitives on their way back to Bella Coola. As they travelled, Brew left messages with all the chiefs and natives he could contact, telling them that the guilty parties had to turn themselves in or pursuit of the Chilcotins would continue. Because of that threat, two more fugitives gave themselves up the following spring. Brew and his expedition returned to Bella Coola 103 days after their initial arrival in the tiny village. They left the next day on the *Forward* for New Westminster.

The five Chilcotins, Klatassine, Tellot, Tahpitt, Piell and Chessus, were put on trial before Judge Begbie. Prosecutor H.P. Walker succeeded in obtaining guilty verdicts against all, and they were hanged on October 26, 1864, after Governor Seymour refused to grant clemency. The so-called "Chilcotin War" was over.

Why did it happen? Theories and rumours abounded. Some reported that Chilcotins claimed that they had not been paid for their work on the road the previous year; that they objected to the route through their territory; that the road crew foreman wrote the Indians' names in his book, a serious taboo among the Chilcotin; and that the Indian workers wanted to avenge the victims of the smallpox epidemic. No definite cause for the murders was ever established. However, when Alfred Waddington claimed compensation for his unfinished road, Brew spoke against him, stating that the outbreak might have been averted if Waddington had done more to promote better relations between the natives and his white workers.

In gratitude for their work, the colonial government presented Brew and Cox with engraved silver tea services, each costing $2,000. Both men probably would have preferred an increase in salary. Brew joked to friends that he might exchange his gift for a supply of pistols and leg-irons for his constables.

By 1865, the British Columbia Constabulary was present in most areas of white population. Single constables lived at Osoyoos, Kootenay, Columbia, Cariboo, Quesnelle, Williams Creek, Alexandria, Bella Coola, Cayoosh, Lytton, Yale, Hope, Fort Shepherd, Douglas and Derby. Richfield and New Westminster each had four constables and Lillooet had three. Most constables lived in small log cabins that combined office, cells and living quarters. Each had a great deal of autonomy, a guaranteed salary, a varied and vast territory to patrol and mainly friendly and law-abiding residents to police—all in all, a pleasant life. As the number of miners declined and more government agencies were set up, constables had to collect fewer mining fees. Still, every time the government decided to impose a new licence on the population, the constable was expected to collect the fee, despite the chief inspector's ongoing protests about using his force as a collection agency.

Another frustration for Brew was the colonies' inability to provide adequate law enforcement along the coast. Constables were sent more frequently into the isolated coastal regions of both Vancouver Island and British Columbia to seek bootleggers or to investigate reported incidents, but emergency policing continued to be done by the Royal Navy. Enforcing the law became a naval manoeuvre, though a magistrate and a constable usually went along. The threat that the "big guns will come" protected many white men over the years, including the constables. Typically, naval guns shelled an Indian village, normally after the residents had been warned to leave, and destroyed homes, food supplies and canoes to demonstrate the white man's power. Or, when fugitives were captured in their home village, they were sometimes tried there. On at least one occasion, a man was hanged in front of his band and family after being found guilty. However, it was increasingly acknowledged that civilian law enforcement should replace such heavy-handed naval action.

In the interior, civil law enforcement was working to Brew's satisfaction most of the time. Sometimes a mining dispute became a courtroom battle and the decision was not always accepted amicably. Such was the case when the Grouse Creek "War" erupted, near Barkerville. A group of promoters calling itself the Canadian Company claimed that a twelve-foot strip of land was unstaked and proceeded to mine thousands of dollars from it. First the gold commissioner, then the chief justice, ruled that the property belonged to the Grouse Creek Bed Rock Flume Company, but the final legal decision took months. In the interim, hundreds of miners prepared to do battle with each other, regularly swinging picks and shovels and shouting threats. Newspapers in the colony, particularly the *British Columbian* in New Westminster, chastised the government for failing to control the miners, and the governor for "shillyshallying" in supporting the judicial decision. The editor lectured:

> In our most important gold field, the arm of Justice hangs powerless by her side, while a company of men, giving the most hollow and hypocritical professions of a desire to respect the law, are wantonly and openly trampling it under foot and taking gold out of the ground which the law had pronounced the property of others at the rate of $1600 a day.[14]

The region was normally policed by three constables who shared three revolvers and a single rifle. When the conflict first erupted, local constables swore in thirty specials from an enthusiastic assortment of Barkerville businessmen and miners. As the battle escalated, Governor Seymour authorized Chief Inspector Brew to hire five additional constables and to arm them with Lancaster rifles and Colt revolvers, despite the deep freeze on all such colonial spending. Seymour also decided to go up himself and requested that Brew accompany him. In Richfield, he decided that the area needed the chief inspector/gold commissioner's administrative talents and directed Brew to relieve Henry M. Ball, the Cariboo East gold commissioner, temporarily.

The crisis passed when Chief Justice Joseph Needham appointed commissioners to resolve the legal questions. But to maintain the peace, Needham recommended that Brew take over administration of the Cariboo district for a longer period. Brew resigned himself to a northern winter and, at the end of October, reported that the district was tranquil.

Chartres Brew remained in Richfield, his health gradually weakening. He died on May 31, 1870 and was buried in the Barkerville cemetery. Judge Begbie wrote his epitaph, perhaps the best summary of the man who first set standards of policing in British Columbia: "A man imperturbable in courage and temper, endowed with a great and varied administrative capacity; a most ready wit, a most pure integrity and a most human heart."[15]

# CHAPTER TWO

# "One constable is grossly inadequate!"
# 1870–1884

AFTER CHIEF INSPECTOR BREW'S DEATH, John Howe Sullivan, another veteran of the Royal Irish Constabulary, became interim superintendent of police. A tall, quiet-spoken man with intelligent eyes above a full black beard, Sullivan was the son of a lawyer. He joined the BC force in 1864 and served mainly at Barkerville, where he gained a reputation as an able, quick-witted policeman.

Shortly after his arrival in Barkerville, Sullivan became the first constable to apprehend a murderer by telegraph. On the trail of James Barry, a fugitive who had shot his travelling companion through the back of the head, then stolen his money and a distinctive gold nugget pin, the constable rode 120 hot, dusty miles from Barkerville to Soda Creek, only to find that his quarry had left on the stage for New Westminster. Sullivan remembered that the Collins Overland Company had just completed stringing telegraph wire as far as Soda Creek and persuaded the operator to try to contact Yale with a message for the constable there: meet the stage and arrest Barry. It worked, and Sullivan caught up with his prisoner the next day.

A few months later, he was involved in a second incident that almost killed him. He had arrested two natives, one Nicomen and one Lillooet, for the murder and robbery of a Welsh miner. After they were arraigned for trial at the assize court in Richfield, they were returned to the cell beside Sullivan's quarters. The Nicomen broke out of the flimsy cell and knifed Sullivan, plunging the blade deep into his back. It was three months before the constable returned to duty. By then, the escapee had been arrested in Osoyoos, this time by Constable Richard Lowe. The chief of

28

the Osoyoos Indians had given Lowe all necessary assistance during the pursuit and arrest, believing that the Nicomen was too dangerous to allow around his people. Lowe shackled his prisoner to a horse and they journeyed for one week to reach the nearest backup, located at Lytton. Later the Nicomen man was transferred to Richfield for trial.

Despite Sullivan's obvious qualifications, he only received a temporary appointment to head the Constabulary. Confederation was almost a certainty and there was much confusion about how the new province would be administered. After British Columbia joined Canada on July 20, 1871, Sullivan was officially appointed to head the British Columbia Constabulary but his duties remained unclear. Law enforcement was theoretically separated into provincial and federal areas of responsibility, but the BC constables continued to enforce almost all statutes and ordinances for years as there were few Dominion officials in British Columbia. The undeveloped territory between Canada and BC was a vast wilderness, inhabited sparsely by Indians, fur traders and American bootleggers. The North-West Mounted Police would not be established until 1873, and communication with Ottawa took weeks. But British Columbia's isolation was considered temporary and unimportant: surveyors were beginning to map the route for the railway!

Superintendent Sullivan and the Constabulary found that they actually experienced few changes after BC joined Canada. They now belonged to the Department of the Attorney General, which consisted of all the people involved in law enforcement and its administration, but the superintendent was to administer the Constabulary directly. The titles of the judges changed but the same judiciary remained: the two colonial judges were now called Supreme Court justices and nine magistrates (who were also the gold commissioners) became county court judges. The force carried on with day-to-day patrolling and law enforcement, including supervision of natives. The Navy remained available for emergency policing in coastal regions, though discussions about how to fund a vessel adequate for regular police patrolling continued.

The population of British Columbia had declined in the previous decade as the miners and many of the people who served their needs left when the gold rushes petered out. For the Confederation Agreement negotiations, every person was counted and apparently, if there was any doubt, counted twice. The native population could only be estimated as its actual numbers remained unknown. Administrators acknowledged that those numbers were declining because of smallpox, syphilis, measles and scrofula, a form of tuberculosis, but emphasized that BC still had one of the largest native populations in British North America. In the rural areas and unorganized communities, the constables were responsible for their region's statistics, which were then tabulated with the counts for New

*J.H. Sullivan, superintendent of the force from 1872 to 1874.*

Westminster and Victoria. It had not been an easy task. One frustrated constable explained in his report that the statistics had been gathered as accurately as possible, considering the handicaps: "a mining population is here today, gone tomorrow, so is hard to count."[1] The end totals found that as of December 31, 1870, British Columbia had a population of 5,782 white men, 2,794 white women, 297 colored men, 165 colored women, 1,495 Chinese men and 53 Chinese women. The Indian population was estimated at approximately 26,000.[2] The BC Constabulary, now the BC Provincial Constabulary, had 22 members, not counting clerks, toll collectors and gaolers, to patrol 250,000 square miles of land.

Constables became more involved with policing Indians every year as the white settlers spread onto lands formerly used only by Indians, and as more natives accepted employment in white settlements. Communicating with the Indians was an ongoing difficulty as the police explained new rules, investigated crimes and prepared for prosecution. Most constables learned to speak Chinook, a language that had been used by Indian traders for decades, but it had few words. A few constables became adept at native languages but, even after years of learning, their knowledge was limited: languages differed radically from one nation to another and each language was complex and full of subtleties. Many natives learned English but to a similarly limited extent, and constables frequently questioned the ability of some translators and the veracity of their translations. As a result, communication was limited.

Ever since his appointment as superintendent, John Sullivan had worried about the reports of increasing native drunkenness. In fact, he believed that Indians drinking bootlegged liquor was one of the new province's major problems, and he was determined to stamp out whisky smuggling.

Because of his dual role as head of the Victoria police force and the Provincial Constabulary, Sullivan was in an excellent position to pursue the local distributors supplying coastal peddlers with bootleg whisky. But he knew that arresting local warehouse owners would not stop the problem. He combed Victoria, searching for the San Francisco suppliers' second-in-commands. But they were difficult to identify, well-disguised by cloaks of respectability as they efficiently expanded the bootleg networks. Constables reported that not only were more Indians drinking, more were acting as couriers and salesmen. The superintendent decided to go after couriers.

For successful prosecution, police had to catch couriers in front of witnesses and with alcohol in their possession. This was difficult, as crews of the ocean-going canoes could see an approaching vessel in time to empty the whisky overboard. The liquor was transported in four-gallon containers — an ideal cover, since the same style was used for transporting molasses up the coast. Sullivan did not have the staff or budget to search each canoe leaving a Victoria waterfront warehouse stacked with four-gallon tins, or monitor traffic to control surreptitious warehouse-to-canoe transfers in the dead of the night. He had to find another way.

After conferring with Attorney General G.A. Walkem, Sullivan decided to travel up the coast to call on tribal elders and personally investigate what was happening. He left Victoria in a canoe in April 1873,[3] accompanied by Louis, a mixed-blood guide, who was also a respected interpreter. The superintendent wanted to talk to native leaders without any show of force or ceremony in the hope he would get some leads on who was behind the increasingly organized liquor distribution.

By coincidence, Sullivan and his guide arrived at Alert Bay in the aftermath of a tragic murder. The storekeeper, Frances McGrath, reported that he had killed Coma-Cow-Coma, a local Indian. He explained that he had thrown a rock at the Indian when he had discovered Coma and his woman stealing from the McGrath woodpile. The Indian had died from the wound just before Sullivan arrived. Although McGrath had, as Indian custom demanded, given blankets and other trade goods to the family as an apology, he knew that British law could not let the matter drop. He told Sullivan he was aware he would probably have to go to Victoria and face a murder charge. Sullivan postponed his tour in search of bootleggers and arrested the storekeeper, a completely co-operative prisoner. The three men set out on the 300-mile journey back down the coast.

As they cut through the choppy waves three days later, Louis pointed to five canoes far off their port side. Sullivan peered through his telescope, announced that the canoes were flying alcohol-to-trade flags and decided to intercept them. But as their canoe drew near the others and he shouted at them to stop, they sped past. Sullivan fired a shot into the water in front of the line of large canoes, then managed to intercept one of them by bumping into its bow. As he grabbed the side of the vessel, he yelled in Chinook that he was a police chief, and again ordered them to stop.

Three of the Indians began throwing blankets over the four-gallon cans piled along the canoe's broad bottom, while another pulled a pistol from a metal box and aimed it at Sullivan, who fired his own pistol. McGrath shouted a warning about another man with another rifle, and Sullivan turned and fired again. Two native men collapsed in the bottom of the canoe. Sullivan pushed his craft away from the canoes, but the ocean canoes followed and a volley of lead splattered into the water around them. But the pursuit ended suddenly as the natives turned seaward. Sullivan's canoe continued down the coast, its nervous passengers carefully watching behind them and staying close to the shoreline.

Superintendent Sullivan stopped in Nanaimo to report the incident to the magistrate there, then went to Victoria where he discussed it at length with the attorney general. They decided that since the Indians had been shot resisting arrest, and the chances of apprehending the native witnesses to the shootings were slight, there was little to be done. But when the political opposition and a newspaper owner heard about the battle, they challenged the government on the actions of its superintendent of police. "Outrageous, un-British, unacceptably high-handed," the editor of the *Daily Colonist* wrote.[4] Victoria's residents agreed, quickly forming opinions unencumbered by the facts. Amidst the growing furor and indignation over the superintendent's "despotic and tyrannical actions,"[5] Sullivan, sure that he had killed at least one native and possibly both, took the unprecedented step of ordering a constable to charge him with murder.

After the preliminary trial, the judge decided to go up the coast to investigate further, and he found witnesses in Alert Bay to corroborate Sullivan's account. When the court sat again and the judge explained his findings, the jury found that prisoner Sullivan had committed a justifiable homicide in faithful performance of his duty. One newspaper gleefully pointed out that Sullivan's chief witness in court had been his prisoner, McGrath, also charged with murder. The jury returned a verdict of manslaughter and, finding no malice aforethought, recommended mercy.

John Sullivan died on November 4, 1875, just before his forty-third birthday. Having survived multiple stab wounds and countless perilous trips through treacherous weather and currents, he drowned along with hundreds of other passengers aboard the S.S. *Pacific* when it collided with a sailing ship off the coast of Vancouver Island. Actually, at his death, he was no longer superintendent of police. Frustrated by the provincial administration's continuing cuts to the policing budget, he had resigned, pointing out that enforcing a growing list of provincial and federal statutes meant hiring additional constables, not cutting back on manpower.

In May 1875, Charles Todd was appointed superintendent of police. Todd was born and educated in England, studied law, then left before obtaining a degree and later served in the Australian Constabulary. He moved to Ottawa in 1867 and to British Columbia in 1872, where he was hired by Premier G.A. Walkem, an acquaintance, to pursue bootleggers.

Not everyone agreed that he was the right person for the superintendent's job. In the new province, suspicion about appointments was usual, partly because personal connections influenced hiring even more than they had in colonial times, and also because government positions were much desired in the unsettled economic climate. Administrations changed quickly: there were five changes of premier between 1871 and 1878. In the interval between Sullivan's resignation and Todd's appointment, two other men had been appointed acting superintendents, but neither was retained long, much to the frustration of their individual supporters. When Todd became superintendent, there were cries of political patronage, among them a lengthy article in the *British Daily Colonist*, which charged that he had vaulted over a number of better-qualified candidates: "Charles the Silent, surnamed the Todd...has dipped his spoon into the Government pap-bowl and pulled out a plum," wrote the editor. "Mr. Todd alights on his feet in the snug billet of Superintendent of Police with $1,752 a year, a residence and pickings galore."[6]

Despite the furor caused by his appointment, Charles Todd was in charge of the Provincial Constabulary for almost ten years. It was a difficult, "waiting for the railway" time for British Columbia. The survey of a suitable route through the Rockies took much longer than anticipated, partly because of political changes in Ottawa. The flood of immigration that Confederation was expected to unleash did not occur. The wealth generated for the province by logging, mining and agriculture did not keep up with the massive costs of administration.

British Columbia was a complex territory, geographically and climatically. It was difficult to keep transportation and communication systems open. Winter storms, spring floods and massive mudslides might close a transportation route in hours, and the damage could take months to repair. Vast areas of the province remained unmapped and unsettled by whites. Since the constabulary remained the most consistent government presence in the more isolated regions, some constables continued to have several titles and responsibilities, including assessor and tax collector, registrar of births, deaths and marriages, returning officer, government agent and notary public.

Yet a constable's life was usually pleasant. His workdays varied and although he was theoretically always "on duty," much of his patrolling was done by socializing — stopping in at a ranch house for a chat and a piece of pie, visiting over coffee at a cafe, calling on a native elder. A constable was expected to be a storehouse of information about his area, to have a good idea of potential trouble spots, and to know about strangers who were in his area or who had passed through. The Constabulary continued to consist mainly of young men from well-connected families in the British Isles who joined up for the adventure. Some married daughters of BC's most powerful men. The social stigma attached to being a "lowly" constable had not been transferred to BC from Great Britain.

It was a leisurely world of sing-songs, picnics, dinner parties, formal debates and parlour games. Young ladies, expected to behave with "proper decorum," were encased in corsets and dressed in yards of material adorned with bustles and voluminous sleeves. Most men were luxuriously whiskered, dressed in shirts with detachable stiff collars and cuffs to which they added waistcoats and long suit jackets, all strongly scented with sweat, tobacco and whisky. The Constabulary dressed similarly. Although there was no set uniform, a constable usually wore a dark suit, a vest and a tie. Then he added layers of outdoor clothes suitable to whatever he was doing. On the water, waterproof clothing was a necessity; a constable in the saddle needed chaps and leather outerwear.

It was also a hard world. People died quickly in great pain, as few medicines or surgical procedures had been invented. Many illnesses were caused by a general lack of sanitation. It was not unusual for drinking water to be obtained just downstream from a raw sewage dump. Cleaning wounds and bathing all of one's body were not yet considered necessary, and gangrene was common. Children frequently died of fevers and women of complications during childbirth. An abscessed tooth or a slashed foot was life-threatening. Constables were often involved in getting someone to a doctor or applying primitive first aid themselves.

In retrospect, it was also a world of droll duplicities. Although young men were warned that sex or self-indulgence would destroy their vigour in later life, bawdy houses were considered a necessity. They were generally ignored, except by clergy and matrons attempting to stamp out a "social evil." The Provincials patrolled them as they did any other business, usually encountering few problems. Sometimes a constable would receive complaints from some of the more "morally upright" members of the community about "those women" freely wandering about town. He usually solved the dilemma by confining "the girls" to a particular section of town for a particular period of time. Complainants offended by the "bawdies" could simply stay away during those hours.

Constables were occupied more with protecting individual safety and resolving neighbourly disputes than with murder or theft. One constable reported making three trips to neighbouring ranchers who disagreed about the ownership of a yearling. Each trip took him three hours each way, so on the last one he "firmly suggested that they butcher the animal and divide it equally."[7] Another constable queried whether he had the right to order a "greenhorn" going into the bush to prepare himself adequately. Apparently an enthusiastic gold seeker had arrived in Kamloops in October, rented a horse and, ignoring advice from both the stable owner and the constable, had insisted on riding out clad only in a business suit and raincoat. Neither the man nor the horse had been seen since. Yet another constable, this one at Savona, reported that he had arrested a man for cutting off a Chinese man's pigtail. The case was heard in court and the assailant was fined $125.

Of course, some cases involved more serious crimes. In 1876, two constables were sent to investigate reports of a series of murders in the Dease Lake area in the Cassiar, northeast of Wrangell, Alaska. They hitched a ride up the coast to the Stikine River on a naval vessel, then headed out by canoe. Despite warnings that the natives were dangerous, they were ordered to learn as much as possible about the tribes they encountered. One of the constables was adept at native languages, and it was hoped he would be able to communicate. The two men paddled up to Dease Lake without difficulty and later reported that they had found the natives independent and unsociable, but not threatening.

They located their suspect, a mixed blood, at a temporary mining community between McDames Creek and Dease Lake. As it turned out, they could not find any credible witnesses, and the stories people told them about the killings were contradictory. They knew that their chances of getting a murder conviction were negligible but decided to take their prisoner out anyway, partly to emphasize the power of the "white Mother's law." They started back on the 1,000-mile trip to Victoria, across lakes and down rivers, camping night after night on the mosquito-infested shore. Because of bears, a rifle was propped handily nearby, and one night their prisoner managed to slip his bonds and grab it. He fled into the dense, prickly bush with both constables in hot pursuit. There was no room to aim so he started swinging the rifle by the barrel. The stock connected with the nearest constable and broke his shoulder before his partner managed to bash the prisoner over the head. When they started out the next morning, the prisoner was bound hand and foot in the bottom of the canoe, one constable was in severe pain and the other had to manoeuvre the canoe downstream by himself. They found a doctor at Wrangell, then boarded a ship to Victoria. Their prisoner was tried and jailed briefly for his attempt to escape but, as the constables had expected, the murder charge was dismissed. The trip had taken the two constables more than two months and they had travelled over 2,000 miles.

Pursuing suspects into the United States became increasingly common as police forces set up systems to assist each other to find wanted men. It was usual to offer generous cash rewards and there were many part-time bounty hunters, as well as the serious full-time ones. Reward posters were exchanged regularly between most west coast police offices, and fugitives were often located far from where they had committed a crime. A private bounty hunter would cross back and forth across the international border without reporting to any official until he caught his prey, then turn his prisoner in to whichever government was offering the reward.

One reason for international police co-operation was that Chief Inspector Brew had actively sought the Americans' assistance in his pursuit of the major suppliers of bootleg alcohol, particularly in San Francisco. In return, he helped American law enforcers track opium smugglers in BC. (Although selling opium was not illegal in BC as long as the $500 vendor tax was paid, it was an illegal commodity in the US.) It was as difficult to stop the flow of opium south as it was to halt the liquor peddling up BC's coastline. Opium was actually manufactured in British Columbia from poppy cakes imported from Hong Kong, in quantities far above what BC residents could possibly use, and exported south of the border. Superintendent Todd regularly raised the issue with the attorney general but for some reason, possibly the revenues received from the poll tax, the situation was ignored.

Law enforcement agents on both sides of the border looked forward to the day when they would have adequate vessels for lengthy marine patrols. Each year it became harder to apprehend smugglers safely hidden away in an isolated inlet, exchanging shiploads of liquor for shipments of opium. However, the need for a marine patrol was near the bottom of the list of the government's concerns. As the economy faltered during the long wait for railway construction to begin, there were cutbacks in every area. Even the Constabulary was theoretically reduced in size to twelve men by 1878, though in practice, most of the other constables were simply given new titles.

The twelve "official" constables were posted at Nanaimo, Esquimalt, South Saanich, North Saanich, Burrard Inlet, Perry Creek–Kootenay, Yale and Kamloops; the Cariboo had one constable plus the only chief constable and the Cassiar had a constable at McDames Creek and another at Stikine River.[8] Each man patrolled a vast territory. For instance, the man at Kamloops was responsible for an area stretching from Ashcroft to Osoyoos, a distance of 220 miles. As well, he was responsible for law enforcement in the North Thompson, the Shuswap and the Similkameen regions. Constables were allowed to hire specials at a daily rate in emergencies, but only "if absolutely necessary."

On occasions when additional manpower was needed, the attorney general, through Superintendent Todd, ordered a municipal constable to report for duty. This meant that a constable from Victoria or New Westminster could be ordered anywhere in the province. Usually the man would leave immediately and be gone for weeks, leaving the city force shorthanded, the chain of command confused and the City Fathers protesting. The province paid a portion of all municipal constables' wages in exchange for the right to borrow them in provincial emergencies. But what exactly constituted a "provincial emergency" was never established.

Superintendent Todd, a taciturn man with a reputation for never using two words if one would do, was in his way as analytical about the Constabulary as Brew had been. After the gold-rush era, Brew's projections had considered the type of law enforcement required for a stable, developing colony. On the other hand, Todd's planning had to anticipate a potentially chaotic period when thousands of railroaders would enter the province. Many of them would be indentured Oriental workers, which Todd knew would create additional policing problems. The animosity toward Orientals was already a factor in maintaining the peace, particularly in mining areas. He was concerned that if the cutbacks continued, he would not have enough trained men to keep control. He pointed out again and again that his constables were spread thinly throughout a massive area and could not easily help each other out, as it "is not possible for one man to be in two locations at one time."[9]

The increasing number of charges being heard by the courts against Indians or mixed bloods, usually alcohol-related, also concerned the superintendent. Despite his efforts, a growing amount of liquor was being bootlegged and more charges were being laid against those who consumed it than those who distributed it. As Indians learned about British law, more of them asked constables for protection. Unfortunately, sworn evidence was often questionable, based as it was on translators who were often unreliable, and while some missionaries became adept at helping constables evaluate a complaint, others only added to the confusion. General differences in language and culture made it difficult to assess a complaint, a responsibility constables had to take seriously: native-settler disputes that appeared minor, for example, might be signs of serious conflict to come.

Government land policies complicated policing during the 1870s. The federal government took responsibility for Indian policy at Confederation, but attempts to create Indian reserves were thwarted by settlers and officials who desired to keep these reserves as small as possible. Indian dissatisfaction increased as governments not only failed to create adequate new reserves, but actually reduced the size of established ones in order to free up land for white settlers. Because the map of an outlying region was often very different from its actual geography, border disputes were common.

Many Provincials continued to patrol the natives as they had in pre-Confederation years. They arranged meetings between band elders and the three land commissioners charged with resolving land quarrels, and they helped everyone involved sort out the actual geography of their territory.

Superintendent Todd worried about the impact another phenomenon would have on the province: the transcontinental railway was finally making its way toward British Columbia. When construction began in BC, who would patrol the railway navvies? Policing rail construction was a federal responsibility on paper, but Todd knew that BC's geography and the precedent agreements would make it impossible to enforce the Public Works Peace Preservation Act in some areas. That Act prohibited the sale of liquor in a twenty-mile strip along the railway, a zone that was later increased to a forty-mile strip. But BC legislation took precedence over the Act, which meant that licensed saloons and hotels remained licensed

*Fifteen-year-old Archie McLean in leg irons shortly before he was hanged with his brothers for the murder of Constable Johnny Usher.*

to sell liquor, even if they were located in the construction zone. Many of them were in that very zone.

Premier George Walkem, who also held the attorney general's portfolio, agreed with the superintendent that policing would be awkward. He wondered if the North-West Mounted Police might be brought in, as they were assisting the Dominion Police to guard the railhead on the prairies. However, Ottawa informed him that the province was responsible: the Dominion Police would only be used to guard the actual construction sites and materials. Superintendent Todd was adamant that the provincial Constabulary had to be expanded to meet this new responsibility; as usual, he achieved no immediate satisfaction.

Then Constable Johnny Usher was shot down by the McLean brothers near Kamloops. In the subsequent publicity, many British Columbians became aware how understaffed their Constabulary was and demanded an end to the penny-pinching policies of the government.

Usher was a popular man in his region. His murder enraged local residents, particularly as his body had been mutilated after the shooting. The three McLean brothers were the sons of a former Hudson's Bay factor killed during the Chilcotin "War," and of a prominent Indian woman. Along with them was Alex Hare, a sixteen-year-old who had sometimes slept at Usher's to avoid being beaten by his violent father. When Constable Usher went after them for stealing a prize stallion, the McLeans killed him, then terrorized the area between Kamloops and Nicola Lake. They fatally shot a young shepherd and stole an arsenal of weapons and ammunition, bragging to petrified homesteaders that they would kill anyone who came after them.

Superintendent Todd took charge of the pursuit. He brought in all nearby Provincials, swore in specials and, with the help of knowledgeable Indian guides, organized a methodical search of the surrounding countryside. December blizzards blew and icicles formed on the men's beards and their horses' manes as they searched the massive area for the fugitives. Thanks to a tip from an informer, the police located the four murderers in a small log cabin. Thirty-seven heavily armed men surrounded the hideout and kept up a steady hail of gunfire, night and day. Finally, the posse pushed a smoldering hay wagon against the cabin and the smoke and heat drove the four out.

The McLeans and Hare were found guilty and hanged at New Westminster. Archie McLean, fifteen years old, was the youngest murderer ever to be executed in British Columbia. Alex Hare, his buddy, had turned seventeen by the time he stepped onto the gallows. In the aftermath, the public and the press worried over the case, seeking ways to make sure that such rampages did not happen again, ways to ensure the safety of rural residents and constables. Had the Provincial Constabulary been unwisely cut back in size, and thus in effectiveness? Some residents were adamant that if the province could not provide adequate law enforcement, the job should be passed to federal authorities. In Victoria, shortly after the McLeans were captured, the *Daily Colonist* editorialized: "MOUNTED POLICE FOR THE INTERIOR... it would be an act of supreme folly for the Government of any small Province to attempt to maintain such a force but the Dominion Government is amply able to do so, and in view of the recent deplorable circumstances at Kamloops would no doubt be willing to station at least one company there to maintain order and assure the public security."[10] The proposal was heard again and again during the next decades. Why should a small province attempt to do what the Dominion would be "so amply able to do"? However, the Dominion government remained firm that policing was a provincial responsibility and British Columbia must cover the cost.

On May 4, 1880, dynamite ripped into rock outside Yale, British Columbia. Construction was under way at last on the BC section of the transcontinental railway. In the beginning, almost 2,000 men laboured at the immense job of carving a railway through the treacherous Fraser River terrain. The construction army increased in size every week as any labourer willing to work from dawn to dusk, six days a week, was hired. Tough, experienced men, soft-handed store clerks and novice contract labourers from China came to work and live in the little town between the Fraser River and the towering canyon walls. With those men, Andrew Onderdonk, a professional engineer whose American syndicate had the contracts from Emory Bar to Savona's Ferry, initially had to blast fifteen tunnels through solid rock and move mountains of boulders to create a reliable surface for the rails through the canyon. If he did not do it on schedule, he would have to pay massive penalties.

Saloons reopened, prostitutes, gamblers and bootleggers settled in as Yale became once again the "wild and woolly" shack town it had been during the gold rush. Constable John Kirkup, the only Provincial posted in the Fraser Canyon, reported that Yale's main street was filled with activity day and night. During the day, teams of mules and horses hauled black powder, timbers and rails to the navvies. Dynamite explosions and the ring of thousands of sledgehammers echoed against the canyon walls. At night, Yale was a tawdry carnival, its long main street resounding with drunken laughter and raucous shouting.

Kirkup inquired of his superiors what long-term plans the force had for policing the region. Superintendent Todd replied that the government was considering his recommendation to hire three more constables immediately. However, Kirkup remained unassisted in Yale during the construction period. Two Dominion policemen patrolled the actual railway construction site and Canadian Pacific property, but they claimed their mandate did not let them assist in policing the construction workers, even as unofficial back-up. The lone Provincial was finding it increasingly difficult to keep order.

The situation at Yale was typical of the irrelevance of the Dominion Railway Construction Act and the Public Works Peace Preservation Act to British Columbia. The narrowness of the canyon made it impossible to keep townsites and construction camps separated. Saloon owners and bootleggers had a heyday. Establishments that had dispensed alcohol before the construction began expanded or sold their licences. Labourers had easy access to liquor, a problem unique to BC. John Kirkup became responsible for policing thousands of construction workers, while the legislature continued to delay authorizing the Constabulary to hire more men.

The editor of the *Inland Sentinel* in Yale pointed out in almost every issue that "one constable is grossly inadequate," although he complimented Kirkup's efforts. Since Sunday was the workers' day off, Saturday night continued for twenty-four hours and churchgoers listened to sermons delivered over the sounds of revelry. An editorial described a Sunday in May 1881:

> Yale was en fete that day, in a wild and woolly sense and the one long main business street, fronting on the river, presented a scene and sounds at once animated and grotesque, bizarre and risque. The shell-like shacks of saloons, whereof every third building nearly was one, fairly buzzed and bulged... Painted and bedizened women lent a garish colour to the scene. On the hot and dusty road-side or around timbers, rails, and other R.R. "construction" debris, men in advanced stages of intoxication rolled and fought in bestial oblivion.[11]

Kirkup found the liquor traffic particularly hard to control. Provincial liquor licences were in great demand, and licensed establishments exchanged owners regularly at escalating prices. As well, many enterprising individuals unable to obtain a licence went ahead and did business without it, considering the regular fines a cost of doing business. The maximum under the Liquor Act was $150, a pittance when measured against a bootlegger's profits.

A year after construction began, Constable Kirkup realized that he had a new problem: the growing animosity of some whites toward the Chinese. He was also concerned about the basic welfare of Chinese workers, for while the contractor supplied lodging and board to the white workers, Orientals did not receive any benefits beyond their wage. In 1880, independent Chinese men, experienced railroaders from the US and former indentured labourers who had become BC residents instead of returning to China, worked and lived with the hundreds of newly arrived indentured men. When a man signed a labour indenture, usually in China, he agreed to work for a set period for a set sum, which was often paid directly to relatives in China. All wages he earned subsequently went directly to the indenture-holder, who was to look after his basic needs and supply an allowance. Some did not.

As the number of indentured workers in Yale increased into the thousands, the protective influence of the independent Chinese weakened, and the level of care provided in some Chinese camps deteriorated. Kirkup reported increasing illness among the Chinese. He pointed out that their housing was not sufficient to keep them warm and their diet was inadequate, particularly considering how hard they were working. Many suffered from malnutrition. There were reports of smallpox in nearby Indian tribes, and Kirkup worried about an epidemic.

Kirkup was a brawny young man, capable with his fists which he used regularly to maintain the peace. He marched down the main street, breaking up brawls with his nightstick, then ordering the belligerents back to camp, arresting only those who would not go. He was innovative and

*CPR construction brought thousands of workers into the interior of British Columbia, and plenty of work for the police. Constable Kirkup often hitched rides on the construction excursion trains.*

persistent, proud of his reputation of getting his man – or woman. On one occasion, he arrested a madam who ran a gambling and drinking establishment and was selling liquor to mixed bloods. She asked to change her dress before being taken to jail, then she reappeared in the nude. Kirkup explained to the superintendent how he'd handled her: "I wrapped a quilt around the struggling woman and carried her across town to the lockup."[12]

Construction accidents were frequent. Premature explosions, slides, floods and rolling rocks all took their toll. Kirkup helped with injured or dead men whenever he was needed, assisting a Dominion constable or a foreman to take the victim to the small hospital or to help dig a grave. Chinese workmen suffered enormous casualties. They were fatalistic and desperate, prepared to do almost anything for additional wages. Most willingly took the cash bribes offered to attempt the most dangerous jobs. It was the indentured Chinese who set most dynamite caps and who dangled over the sides of canyon walls to drill blast holes. However, when a Chinese was badly injured or killed, there was normally no assistance from his countrymen, who believed it was bad luck to touch the victim, either to give medical aid or to bury him. Since many whites refused to have anything to do with a Chinese, Kirkup was called frequently. The number of Chinese men put into shallow graves along the track grew weekly, as did the number of white workers buried in Yale's cemetery. Then the bribes ceased, and Chinese workers were just ordered to set any fuses that whites refused to set. Occasionally, they rebelled. When one poorly set dynamite charge exploded too soon, killing and injuring several indentured workers, the Chinese stoned the powderman. He managed to escape, then filed a complaint. Kirkup arrested the "celestials" for assault and eight of them were sent to prison to serve three- and four-year sentences.

Smallpox continued to be a source of dread, particularly for Onderdonk, the CPR contractor, who feared the chaos an outbreak would cause with his construction deadlines. As a result, he wanted all smallpox victims sent out of the area quickly. However, when a prisoner developed smallpox, Constable Kirkup decided the choice was his, not Onderdonk's. "I have the honour to report to you that a severe case of smallpox broke out on a Chinaman who is awaiting sentence (under Appeal) for whisky selling without a licence," Kirkup wrote to the superintendent. "It [the smallpox] was first noticed by Mr. Roycraft. . . The Chinaman was at once removed to a cabin I purchased for $12 which is some distance back of the jail but in hearing. . ." When Onderdonk complained to the attorney general, Kirkup explained further: "If any persons have been in danger of catching the disease I think it is us who have been in close proximity with the prisoner. . . I consider that the Chinaman's life would have been in danger if he had been removed beyond the reach of infection and out of convenient reach of prison authorities . . . The man is still in close confinement for another week before removing him."[13] After the prisoner departed, Kirkup burned the small cabin and its contents to prevent the spread of infection.

Collecting the Poll tax, the annual provincial fee levied on all Chinese in BC, was another problem for Kirkup. One of his duties was to enforce collection of that tax; most paid it at the government agent's, but a few labour contractors did not pay until their representatives were contacted personally. When Kirkup disagreed with a camp foreman over the amount of payment required, "I was set upon by the gang and had to beat a retreat after laying out three of the gang."[14]

As British Columbia's revenues increased because of rail construction, the law enforcement improved. The first step was taken when the legislature passed "An Act Respecting Police and Special Constables" during the 1880 session. The new law outlined police responsibilities. It authorized Superintendent Todd to hire additional constables and re-establish a detachment at Lytton, the next centre for rail construction. Lytton had not had its own constable since the gold-rush days and its old jail had not held any prisoners for years. A young Provincial constable, Frederick Hussey, was assigned to the area and his first task was to repair the jail.

Although rail construction created the immediate demand for additional policing, other areas of the province also were in need of better law enforcement. The population doubled and doubled again as immigrants, some of them rich investors, continued to arrive. Farmers and ranchers were finally making as much money as they had expected, and miners and loggers earned large pay envelopes which they spent boisterously, fattening storekeepers' and saloon-owners' pockets.

Some newcomers settled in isolated areas and disrupted the Indian inhabitants, particularly along the west coast. Todd recommended that constables be sent to these areas to help prevent bootlegging and clashes between natives and white settlers. He and the newly elected government of Premier Robert Beaven agreed that liquor traffic could only be controlled with a fast, large police patrol boat, but in the meantime a constable or two would demonstrate the government's authority. The two constables posted to the upper Vancouver Island and mainland coast initially used a sailboat for their patrols.

Despite the superintendent's increased authority and budget, individual constables around the province experienced few changes. They did their duty as best they could under the circumstances. In rural areas, it was the weather and the terrain as much as the lawbreakers that made policing an ongoing challenge, as a report from Clinton demonstrates:

Constable Livingstone and Reid left here today to proceed to the head waters of Homathko River or elsewhere to arrest an Indian or Indians, supposed to be implicated in the Poole murders. I have taken two of the three horses from winter quarters for them...which they will take as far as Pinchbecks at Wms. Lake and leave them there for their return. They do not expect to be back for three weeks or more. There can be no doubt that their journey is a hazardous one, but they do not anticipate any trouble from deep snow so early in the winter.[15]

Superintendent Charles Todd retired in the spring of 1884 after almost ten years in charge of the provincial Constabulary. He had guided the force through the disorganized and disappointing years after Confederation and through four years of railway construction and economic boom. When the Dominion government offered him the position of magistrate to enforce the Peace Preservation Act along the transcontinental rail line, he accepted: the salary was much better, the demands fewer.

# CHAPTER THREE

# "Resolve conflict, do not start it"
# 1885–1896

I N JULY 1884, a messenger from the Skeena area informed the new superintendent of the Provincial Police, Herbert Roycraft, that Haatq, a Nishga chief, had stabbed a trader, Amos "Charley" Youmans, at Hazelton. The message explained that Billy, Haatq's only son, had drowned while working as a paddler for Youmans[1] at Kitselas canyon. Youmans had failed to go to Haatq and present the gifts necessary in Nishga culture to express sorrow and offer token compensation. Although he knew what was expected, Youmans had done nothing.

Billy's mother and many other powerful band members demanded that Haatq avenge his son; Youmans' death would be atonement for the loss of Billy. Pressure on the chief increased as he waited for the trader to come to him. Finally, days later, Haatq walked up to Youmans at dusk and stabbed him through the chest.

The white traders in the area recommended that the government send in an impressive force to arrest and punish Haatq at Hazelton, and stressed that it would take fifty to seventy-five men as both Haatq and the dead boy's mother were powerful within their clans. They believed that such a force would also help stabilize the area.

Roycraft knew the area was not stable. The previous winter had been hard, longer than usual, leaving the natives short of food. Smallpox had killed many more, particularly youngsters. And the elders in the area were unco-operative about proposed land settlement discussions. Roycraft and the government believed that Youmans' murder loosened their precarious hold on the area and that the safety of Hazelton's traders, missionaries and two settlers might be in jeopardy.

47

When residents of Victoria heard about the murder, many demanded that the government send troops to the Skeena to teach the Indians a lesson. Roycraft demurred. He agreed that Haatq should be arraigned in front of his own people to impress on them the power of the law, but he recommended that the arrest be made by a small force, as a large force would aggravate the situation. Because Roycraft's ability to placate natives and speak to some of them in their languages were reasons he had been chosen as superintendent four months earlier, the government accepted his recommendations.

Roycraft travelled to the Skeena accompanied only by Magistrate Andrew Elliott, a former premier of British Columbia, and Constable W. Hough, a boyhood friend of the murdered trader. The men planned to go up river to Hazelton by canoe, but coastal Indians, afraid of angering interior tribes, refused to transport them or to provide them with a canoe. Continuing north to the turbulent Nass River, the travellers managed to obtain a crew of Indians who reluctantly agreed to paddle them through the Nass' rapids and narrow canyons to the Skeena and Hazelton.

Roycraft and his companions arrived in mid-July, fishing season, and the village was almost deserted. The superintendent sent a messenger to find Haatq and request his return. Within hours, angry natives began gathering in the yard of Youmans' trading post. As Roycraft waited for a reply from the fugitive chief, he explained to the Indians that murder was against the "white mother's law" and that a person who murders another must be punished. He also pointed out that only three men had come to get the murderer because he knew the Indians understood the law. A few Nishga spoke, acknowledging Roycraft's position but stressing again that Youmans had to be killed. Haatq had no choice; the trader had not compensated the family for Billy's death.

Haatq appeared that evening, surrendered his knife to Roycraft and accepted arrest, ignoring the 300 natives protesting his decision. As the superintendent escorted his prisoner inside, he told the angry crowd that everyone could come to court the next day. The night passed without incident, and the next morning, the makeshift courtroom filled to overflowing with suspicious warriors. Constable Hough turned back all guns at the door but, as directed, ignored all knives.

Roycraft interpreted as Magistrate Elliott advised Haatq that he had the right to make his defence at a later trial and be assisted by counsel. But Haatq insisted on speaking to the magistrate and to his people: "When I heard my son was dead and Charlie Youmans had been in the place three days without telling me," he said, "an evil spirit entered my head. Then I walked down and stabbed him. I was like a drunk man . . . furious . . . I feel very sorry but it couldn't be helped. I will go with the police and see the white tyee. My friends tell me to kill myself but I don't do it." Haatq spoke at great length, ending on a note of quiet dignity: "I ask all my friends to let me go with the police."[2]

Magistrate Elliott formally committed Haatq to trial, and the two police officers escorted him and three Indian witnesses through the milling throng to the canoe at the river's edge. For a tense moment, the crowd rumbled with discontent, but the men were allowed to go through. Elliott stayed on at the village to safeguard the few whites there against reprisals, but no incidents occurred.

When Roycraft's canoe reached the treacherous section of the Skeena where Haatq's young son had drowned two months earlier, the Indian grieved deeply and tried to throw himself overboard. But they went on to Victoria, where Haatq was found guilty of murder and became the thirty-fourth person to be hanged in British Columbia since Confederation.

The white community did not recognize the tragedy of Haatq; they were grateful to Roycraft because their laws had been upheld successfully. The editor of the *Daily Colonist* in Victoria praised the government for having handled the incident "so wisely" and commended the decision not to send a force of excitable and inexperienced "white Victoria warriors" who wanted to massacre the whole tribe in retaliation for one man's death.

The incident helped Superintendent Roycraft gain support among British Columbia's legislators, even those normally opposed to the current government's policies and appointees. His recommendations for an expanded police force received assent, and the attorney general's department authorized hiring additional permanent constables.

Roycraft usually chose men whose abilities he knew of personally, men who had served as special constables under Superintendent Todd. They knew the residents in their area well, and they understood that charges were to be pressed only when absolutely necessary and when a guilty verdict could be obtained. He also hired a few men who had served on police forces elsewhere, choosing those offering rural experience and maturity. From twenty-six members at the beginning of the year, the BC Provincial Constabulary grew to a strength of thirty-seven men by the end of 1884, and with immigration on the rise, hiring new constables became a continuing responsibility.

Roycraft had many applicants to choose from. Being a constable was an increasingly desirable occupation: because many experienced constables were now occupying better-paid positions with the provincial and federal governments, young men saw the work as sound training. Consequently, a few Members of the Legislature pressured Roycraft to hire their relatives or supporters. Roycraft did not refuse directly; instead, he crossed those applicants off his list and complained to the deputy attorney general "about the unsuitability of political interference."[3] Occasionally, an offended politician or a disgruntled relative would try to create problems for the constable who was appointed, by arousing suspicions about his competence or integrity. Political patronage was much more blatant then, and a constable's powers were broad. But a constable's recommendations for liquor licences or government contracts had to pass muster with the community. So when a complaint was investigated by the attorney general's office, a constable usually had many more supporters than detractors.

As British Columbia's legislators tried to keep up with administering the flourishing province, they passed numerous laws. The Provincial Police became responsible for seeing that all gunpowder and other explosive substances were stored two miles beyond city limits. They had to sort out water rights disputes and check livestock brands. They had to issue more licences and collect more taxes, including the annual poll tax on all Chinese residents over age fourteen. As the railway neared completion and the government realized that many Chinese intended to stay, they taxed each $10 annually in the Chinese Regulation Act of 1884 and charged the Chinese $15 per year for miner's licences (all other miners paid $5).

They also prohibited the consumption and possession of opium, except for medical purposes. The legislation about opium appears to have had little effect: court records show that constables laid no charges of opium possession, despite the tons of opium consumed annually in the province. The manufacture of opium for local use and clandestine export to San Francisco continued unabated.

*A horse-drawn cutter was a constable's only means of winter transportation in some areas of BC.*

But the increasing number of laws sometimes left constables bewildered. If the charge was not correctly laid, a case could be thrown out of court. Constable Fred Hussey (Lytton) reported: "A rambunctious ram has on and off run at large and continues to do so. It is in the habit of knocking people over in the street, particularly children and women. . . I now scarcely know how to act since neither I nor the Government office at Lytton is supplied with any Acts bearing on the offence. I have expostulated with the man [the owner] in a friendly way, but without effect."[4] Hussey was directed to serve formal notice on the owner under a section of the Livestock/Rustling Acts wherein people were responsible for their animals' behaviour.

The question of jurisdiction was another dilemma for provincial constables. Along the railhead, there continued to be confusion over federal and provincial laws, particularly when liquor was involved. Anyone with a BC liquor licence could legally sell alcohol in the province – except to Indians and mixed bloods – but the railhead was theoretically dry. Licensed vendors naturally moved to where demand was the greatest. In July 1885, one of the liquor peddlers, Jerry Hill, touched off what has since been referred to as a constitutional war when he arrived in Farwell (now Revelstoke), his pack horses loaded with eight cases of whisky. Before it was over, two Provincial policemen were in jail, two NWMP constables were charged with assaulting and obstructing officers in the lawful performance of their duty, and a commissioner of the Dominion police was himself under arrest, as were three of his special constables.

Farwell had both a Dominion Police detachment, responsible in conjunction with the North-West Mounted Police for enforcing federal statutes in railway areas, and a BC Police detachment, responsible for provincial statutes and for general policing. When Jerry Hill showed up with his whisky, the local commissioner of the Dominion Police, George Johnson, directed his men to seize it, claiming that federal statutes prohibiting liquor took precedence over Hill's provincial licence. Johnson was temporarily in charge of policing the railhead in the absence of NWMP Superintendent Sam Steele. He apparently decided to enforce the Federal Department of Public Works' ban on the sale or consumption of liquor in the railway construction zone, and to ignore the fact that liquor distribution in Farwell fell under provincial jurisdiction.

John Kirkup, now senior provincial constable in Farwell, did not accept the decision of his federal counterpart. He sent Provincial Constable Miles to inform Johnson of Hill's right to sell his merchandise, and to suggest that he be released from jail and his whisky returned. The commissioner refused, sending a message to Kirkup that the whisky was being held under his supervision, guarded by four NWMP constables and three special Dominion constables hired for the purpose.

The situation became complicated. At Magistrate Malcolm Sproat's direction, two Provincials went to arrest the Dominion constable who had seized Hill's whisky. Instead, they were seized themselves and locked up in the Dominion barracks. Johnson immediately held a trial and sentenced the Provincials to fourteen days in jail. Kirkup and Sproat were enraged. Kirkup was ready to swear in enough specials to release his two men by force, but Magistrate Sproat insisted that the law must prevail. He issued warrants for the arrests of Commissioner Johnson and two specials, and wrote to the provincial attorney general, calling the situation "the pure outbreak against the law of Canada respecting the administration of justice."

"They threatened to arrest myself and every officer connected with the province," Sproat continued, "and marched into the chief street of this town like cowboys on a raid. Recognizing that this was a civil war and the situation created military, I arranged to take the barracks... where two Provincial policemen, one of whom is John Miles, are still in jail. A squad of mounted police troopers, it is said, are immediately expected... the future may somewhat depend on the good sense of their officer... I will not permit any obstruction of the law!"[5]

Kirkup managed to arrest the Dominion Police commissioner and his specials without violence, probably because Colonel J.F. McLeod, CGM, stipendary magistrate for the North-West Territories and former NWMP commissioner, conveniently arrived on the scene. Since two magistrates could legally hear a case without waiting for the assize court, McLeod and Sproat decided to join forces and convene a sitting of the court. Provincial Chief Constable Kirkup directed Provincial Constables Miles and Hubbard, recently released from the lock-up, to request that a vindictive penalty not be imposed but that the court make the rightness of their actions clear. Magistrate Sproat pointed out that the Dominion constables' offence of assault was punishable by six months in jail with hard labour, plus a possible fine of $100. But he and Colonel McLeod decided to be lenient. They remanded the NWMP constables to their new commanding officer, issued a warrant for the Dominion constables who had fled before the court convened and fined the inept Commissioner Johnson $10 on each of three counts of assault plus $9.75 in court costs. Johnson left Farwell shortly after.

Luckless Jerry Hill never did regain his confiscated property. The whisky had mysteriously disappeared! In fact, Hill ended up spending the winter, at least the nocturnal portion of it, in the Kamloops jail. The supplier of the whisky had not been paid so he charged Hill as a debtor. The Kamloops constable was sympathetic to Hill's plight, however, and he allowed him out during daytime hours, which the happy prisoner spent in the local saloon.

While Jerry Hill suffered from too much law enforcement, other British Columbians desperately wanted more. Granite City, a booming mining town in the Similkameen, was a typical example. Ever since gold had been found in the creeks near the sleepy little hamlet, miners had been flooding in and saloons opening their doors. Local ranchers liked to see the place prospering but they did not like the miners, and they especially did not like the saloons and dancing girls. The miners "have possession of the place and from nightfall till after midnight the yells and whoops and discharge of firearms and whiz of lead make night hideous," complained one resident to Judge Matthew Begbie. "Son of a bitch is the common word and drunkenness is the order of the day. Now we have a constable but he had neither handcuffs nor any other means. A sturdy lock-up is required as from 500 to 1500 men come . . ."[6]

Superintendent Roycraft received immediate permission to construct a jail and he dispatched a senior constable, equipped with handcuffs, and instructions to stay long enough to assist the inexperienced local man to establish order. Overnight the shooting stopped and the revelry quieted to a dull roar.

In the autumn of 1885, Yale once again became a lively place. Railway construction finished at Eagle Pass, and thousands of men came back to Yale to be paid off. One reporter wrote:

> The scene at Yale on Saturday last beggars description. A thousand white men lately employed on the railroad rushed out of cars and into the saloons. In two hours, the streets were full of lunatics; they roared and raved and attempted to force their way into private homes. Twelve hundred Chinese arrived on the same train and went into the woods and cooked their rice. It is amusing to see the difference between pagans and Christians.[7]

Many of the former railway builders decided to stay in British Columbia. Most settled in the lower mainland in the hopes of finding good jobs. But the economy was in a slump and work was hard to come by. White workers resented the competition for jobs from the Chinese who were popular with employers because they were hard workers, made no demands for benefits, seldom complained about safety and accepted low wages. This enraged the rest of the working population, and relations between the two groups grew explosive, particularly in Vancouver. The port city was enjoying a building boom, and cheap Chinese labour was in great demand.

Animosity toward Orientals erupted into violence in Vancouver in February 1887. When Chinese contract labour was employed clearing brush in the west end, discontented white residents, many of them unemployed, protested at a public meeting. There was lots of shouting but no clear resolutions, and after the meeting, about 300 people milled around outside the hall, listening to passionate pleas for "Action Now!" Many of them decided to evict all Chinese from the city. The unruly mob marched to the flimsy warehouses and shacks at the edge of Chinatown, manhandled the terrified Chinese out and set fire to their homes and possessions. The rioters were about to start their captives on a forced march to the city's borders when Vancouver Chief of Police John Stewart and Provincial Superintendent Roycraft arrived. They ordered the mob to release the Chinese and, as the *Daily Colonist* later reported, "the gallant front and unwavering pluck shown by them held the whole at bay."[8] Eventually Roycraft and Stewart persuaded the angry crowd to go home.

On March 1, as a result of the riot, the Provincial Legislature passed An Act for the Preservation of the Peace within the Municipal Limits of the City of Vancouver, suspending the city's charter and passing control to the lieutenant governor. Superintendent Roycraft took charge of Vancouver with authority to hire as many special constables as he needed to maintain order. He decided to bring in the specials from Victoria and ordered his chief constable there to hire thirty-four men, favouring those with a police or military background. One of the specials later recorded his early weeks in Vancouver after its charter was suspended. Charles Dickie, who applied for the job because he needed the money and was chosen because he had been a deputy marshal in northern Michigan, recalled:

> I took the required oath and was once more an officer of the law...in due time we arrived in Burrard Inlet, when we were mustered on deck and each was given a Colt .44 revolver and ammunition. Capt. Fitzstubbs in a short crisp address informed us that our guns should not be used unless wholly unexpected and unforeseen trouble should develop, but if he ordered us to use them we must let no scruples deter us from using them effectively... The dock and approaches were thronged when we disembarked but with the exception of cat-calls, jeers and scowls, we were unmolested..."[9]

Although the situation was tense, and the specials were harassed as they paraded through the muddy streets, there was no more rioting and the indentured Chinese proceeded to go about their work. As Dickie summarized, "the ambitious, rapidly growing City of Vancouver was told in unmistakable terms that it must not shirk or evade its responsibility for maintaining law and order irrespective of the merits or demerits, that mob rule must be nipped in the bud before it gained momentum and spread..."[10] By the time Vancouver's charter was reinstated by the Legislature, just over a year later, most of the special constables had been discharged.

Law enforcement was changing. Under Roycraft's supervision, and because a healthy economy allowed the government to spend more on policing, the Provincial Constabulary was becoming a well-equipped, cohesive force. Policemen in southern parts of the province moved about more easily as trains cut travelling time to half of what it had been on a riverboat or stagecoach. In the areas where telegraph lines were maintained, telegrams kept constables in constant contact with headquarters. In the main cities, telephones were coming into vogue and an individual could phone for a constable.

Investigative procedures were becoming more complex. When Kamloops' Chief Constable (and Government Agent) Hussey went to Spences Bridge to assist the constable there in organizing evidence after a railway section-man had been murdered, his report included a primitive ballistics analysis. He explained to the district attorney general why two Chinese were the prime suspects: "Their pistol is an old fashioned muzzle loading weapon, large bore with barrel about six inches long, a single shooter. Dr. Langis found in the body of Holloway a round piece of tin which exactly filled in the barrel of the pistol and had apparently been used for wad . . ."[11]

Often the police were dealing with suspects who spoke no English. In such cases, they put undercover interpreters into the next cell to try and get a confession. Such witnesses could not be used in court but once the suspect found out he had betrayed himself, he often pleaded guilty. As British Columbia had many residents who came from middle Europe, China and Japan, as well as native Indians, the Provincial Police worked frequently with interpreters to obtain details about crimes.

It was increasingly difficult for constables to keep abreast of the growing number of laws, especially when the courts disagreed about what the law stated. In June 1885, when Constable Hank Anderson arrested Robert Sproule for allegedly murdering another miner on the Bluebell mine property, the prisoner eventually hanged. But only after eight dates had been set and overturned for the hanging!

Magistrate Arthur Vowell held Sproule's first hearing and committed him to New Westminster to await trail. During that trial, Constable Anderson was chastised for unorganized evidence and a mistrial was declared. Then Chief Justice Begbie changed the venue and, in December 1885, Sproule appeared before the court in Victoria, defended by a lawyer named Theodore Davie and prosecuted by his brother, Attorney General A.E.B. Davie, both future premiers of the province. When the jury found him guilty, Justice J.H. Grey sentenced Sproule to hang, ignoring the jury's recommendation for mercy. Some Victoria residents and even some jury members vehemently disputed the verdict. Public furor grew, and spreading even into the US, Sproule's homeland.

The legal dispute that evolved centred on the Canadian Procedure Act of 1869: Sproule should have been tried in West Kootenay, the district where the crime occurred. The BC Supreme Court granted Sproule a reprieve to allow the case to be studied by the minister of justice in Ottawa, but the guilty verdict was upheld and the hanging rescheduled. Then many Victoria residents, including the mayor, protested Sproule's sentence at a mass meeting, questioning the constable's circumstantial evidence again and resolving to push for further enquiry. At the same time, the local US Consul kept his government informed; the Americans queried Ottawa on the matter, which delayed the hanging again. The case went before the Supreme Court of Canada, which found that Sproule should have been tried in West Kootenay.

Yet the prisoner was not discharged. The BC government questioned the Dominion's right to overturn its decision and threatened to appeal to the Privy Council in London. Instead, on September 1, 1886, a special session of the Supreme Court of Canada sat, and the court upheld Sproule's sentence, finding his trial constitutionally correct. A hanging date was again set, and inquiries from the US State Department and the British Colonial Office again delayed it. Finally, the verdict stood. Sproule must hang.

Throughout all the appeals and hearings, and on the gallows, Sproule claimed innocence. Even after he was hanged on October 29, 1886, public debate continued. "The hanging of Robert Sproule at Victoria, B.C. entails a fearful responsibility on the Canadian government," stated the *New York Tribune*. "Evidence of Sproule's innocence is so strong as to have convinced the public that he was wrongly convicted."[12]

Sproule's case had a lasting impact on police procedure. Constables were instructed to write down the details of their investigations, especially when they expected that a serious charge would be laid. Sometimes their notebooks were examined by their senior officer. As one junior man pointed out to Chief Constable Hussey, "one is not sure whether to give priority to proceeding with the investigation or to stop and write it all down to protect oneself against later questions."[13]

By January 1887, the Provincials had forty-four permanent members. As the Dominion government appointed more Indian Affairs and Custom and Excise men, the Provincials enforced fewer federal statutes. But in isolated areas, where the federal government did not yet have permanent representatives, and despite the province's complaints that they could not afford to fulfill federal responsibilities, BC's constables still enforced both provincial and Dominion laws. This was no easy task in some areas. The Kootenay valleys, for example, looked close to each other on the map,

*A constable on patrol usually led a second horse as a pack animal and spare mount.*

*A police constable visits a Beaver Indian camp at Moberly Lake in the northeast corner of the province.*

but were separated by high mountains, making it impossible for a constable in the west Kootenays to go quickly to the assistance of one in the east Kootenays. Some of those who did understand the geography involved questioned the expense of policing the east Kootenays: the area had less than 100 white residents but many Indians, a federal responsibility. Yet the only lawmen were Constable C. Hubbard and a special, who patrolled the vast area in the Columbia Valley.

The following spring, Chief Isadore and the Kootenai tribe created another rift in Dominion-provincial relations when they objected to the infringement of miners and settlers onto their lands. The articulate and intelligent Isadore charged that a provincial politician, apparently acquiring massive land holdings against the day a railway would be built in that area, was trying to change reserve boundaries to fit in with his speculations. Against this background of suspicion, the Provincial constable arrested a band member, Kapula, for the murder of two miners in the Sinclair Pass, and jailed him in the log cabin jail close to Wild Horse River. The constable was aware of possible reprisals and requested emergency help. He had been unable to hire special constables: the few qualified men in the region refused because they did not want to risk offending the Indians.

On March 20, before reinforcements arrived, Chief Isadore and twenty-five armed Indians broke into the jail and released the suspect. Premier William Smithe responded by declaring it a federal matter. He directed Superintendent Roycraft to order Constable Hubbard to Victoria to report on the escape, then telegraphed Prime Minister John A. Macdonald, pointing out that policing Indians was a federal responsibility and recommending that the North-West Mounted Police be sent in, "but the province cannot undertake the expense, especially as we consider the matter appertains to Indian Department, and information indicates incipient insurrection of Kootenay Indians."[14] Sir John promptly replied: "If absolutely necessary, will send Mounted Police force to Kootenay but there must be a requisition from your government...You are bound by Act to pay expenses. It is more especially proper now when force is asked to protect white settlers."[15]

Shortly after this exchange of telegrams, Premier Smithe died. But the difference of opinion continued between the prime minister and A.E.B. Davie, the new premier and attorney general. Davie emphasized to Macdonald that the BCPP constable had been compelled by the Indians to leave the district and it was too dangerous for him to return.

The debate continued even as NWMP Superintendent Sam Steele was instructed by the federal authorities to take a troop of seventy-five men from Lethbridge to Wild Horse River to assess the situation. Premier Davie pointed out that Steele's force was larger than the entire BC Provincial Police force and warned that the province would not help pay for the expedition. The incident reopened the issue of constitutional agreements about patrolling Indians. In the end, the Dominion decided to assume temporarily policing expense for the East Kootenay.

After Steele talked with Chief Isadore—"one of the finest Indians I have ever met," he wrote to Commissioner Lawrence Herchmer[16]—he reported that the situation did not appear dangerous and that the murder suspect would appear for trial. The suspect was eventually released for lack of evidence. Nevertheless, Steele recommended that his men remain in the area over the winter of 1887–88, and as the small provincial facilities were completely inadequate for his troop, he estimated the cost to construct and supply quarters at $30,000. At the end of August, Commissioner Herchmer recommended to the justice minister that Steele be authorized to build quarters, more because of the unsettled conditions after the North West Rebellion than because of a need for policing: "Messages are passing to and fro between the Kootenay Indians in British Columbia and the Bloods and other Tribes East of the Mountains," the justice minister explained to the prime minister, "endeavouring to arrange for concerted action with the Indians and Half-breeds South of the line in raiding Canadian Territory next Spring."[17] Steele directed his men to build log barracks, stable, kitchen and officer quarters. Fort Steele was built where they were camped, on a plateau a short distance above Wild Horse River, approximately 150 miles through the Crowsnest Pass from Fort McLeod in Alberta, 150 miles south of Golden and 75 miles from the US border.

White and Chinese residents were pleased to have the Nor-West troop for security and welcomed the new purchasers of food, hay and services. Steele's detailed reports that winter described his men's activities, health and discipline, the condition of the horses and the weather. He counted the population in the valley: 86 white men, 3 white women, 81 Chinese and 568 Indians. He assisted in negotiating a settlement, including payment for improvements, on cancelled reserve lands. When Chief Isadore and the Kootenai Indians at the St. Mary's Reserve did not meet with Indian Commissioners F.G. Vernon, J.W. Powell and P. O'Reilley as expected in November 1887, Steele became responsible. The commissioners wrote to Isadore:

> We have seen all your lands, and have increased your reserves to what we consider ample for your requirements. Major Steele will read this to you, and tell you what we have done. Before we tell you further about the Reserves, we want to talk to you about your conduct last winter in breaking the Government jail. Now when a man is a Chief, whether he be a white man or an Indian, he is responsible for the actions of those under him. The Government looks to him to help in preserving the law. They expect a Chief

to act as such, and if he cannot control his Indians, when they are inclined to break the law, his duty is to inform the Government Officer. . . When a Chief does not do his duty, another Chief is put in his place."

The lengthy letter went on to outline the revised reserves. "This is a final decision and will not be altered," was the firm conclusion. "We trust that in future you will be friendly to the white men who live amongst you. . ."[18]

In the two years that Fort Steele was operated by the North-West Mounted Police, no charges or summons were recorded. Five Mounties died there from typhoid. Inspector Steele supervised a new survey of Indian lands: "The Indians, as usual, have been as quiet and acting in as civilized a manner as any white community," he reported in July 1888, and he went on to explain why he recommended about ten men be left when the Nor-West Division withdrew.

Many people in the District desire to keep the Division here, chiefly from personal motives, and not from any fear of Indians. Twenty or thirty thousand [dollars] per annum is a great windfall. . . I think it extremely likely in the event of any slight misunderstanding between whites and Indians, in all probability brought on by the whites, such pressure might be brought to bear as to cause the Government to send in another Force. . . I had also been led to believe that the Hon. Minister and yourself were anxious to leave the administration of the District in the hands of the provincial authorities and any further remarks of mine on the subject would be useless, and be taken hold of by the public of B. Columbia. . ."[19]

The NWMP detachment was withdrawn in late 1888 and the facilities at Fort Steele were turned over to British Columbia. As mining exploration began to open up the area, the white population increased rapidly and the provincial government, represented by Gold Commissioner A.W. Vowell and Provincial Constable Dennis, resumed responsibility for all policing in the East Kootenay.

In other areas, the native question remained unresolved. In the spring of 1888, Magistrate Fitzstubbs wrote from the Skeena area, a region still as isolated as it had been at Confederation, to express his concern over the growing famine among the tribes. As well, a measles epidemic had claimed over 240 lives, many of them children. He reported to Superintendent Roycraft that there were "growing bad feelings" among the estimated 2,285 Indians in the area.[20]

Shortly after, Constable F. "Andy" Anderson wrote to Fitzstubbs to report that restlessness was increasing in the upper Skeena area; the Kitwancool were desperately short of food because of the extraordinarily long, cold winter and were also being devastated by a measles epidemic.

Anderson was also concerned about rumours that a native war might erupt over a recent murder. Apparently a truce had been broken by a murder somewhere between the headwaters of the Skeena and Nass Rivers and, although his information was scanty so far, he worried about the risk to the few scattered white men in the area. In the same week, Fitzstubbs received a message from Roycraft that the agent for the Hudson's Bay Company intended to ship goods into the Hazelton area by means of a pack-train, but he was worried by current rumors: "The Indians of that District, who are generally quarrelsome and very troublesome to settlers and others, are opposed and have threatened to shoot the horses."[21] The agent had requested that the government take prompt measures to remedy the situation, pointing out that it was March and shipments would have to start soon.

Then there was another murder, at the Kitwancool village above Hazelton. A woman whose Indian name translated to Sunbeam had recently lost two sons in the measles epidemic, and believed that they had died because of a spell cast by a shaman visiting from her birth tribe. She persuaded her husband, Chief Kamalmuk, to even the score by shooting the shaman.

Fitzstubbs sent in Constables Franklin Green and William Washbourn to bring out the murderer. But the chief tried to flee, and Constable Green killed him with what was meant to be a warning shot. Dozens of natives who heard the shot gathered at the riverbank, circling and threatening the constables as they nervously launched their canoe. When they arrived in Hazelton, Magistrate Fitzstubbs immediately raised the alarm, summoning the four white settlers in the Skeena area to move into the trading post. Believing that all whites might be in jeopardy throughout the region, he also sent messengers to locate the three traders who were moving through the area.

Superintendent Roycraft recognized the long-term and potentially dire consequences of the shooting of Chief Kamalmuk. The whole region could easily become inaccessible to both traders and settlers if the uneasy peace that had existed was not re-established. Roycraft decided to lead twelve constables to the Skeena on a peace mission.

Roycraft was the Superintendent who perhaps best understood the fragile limits to white influence in the North. In the lower coastal areas, the guns of the Admiralty maintained an aura of white power. But the various tribes in the Skeena and Nass areas had little contact with the British colonizers. They had no knowledge of the "Great White Mother" or her laws. The Indians were extremely possessive of their lands. They tolerated the presence of a few traders, policemen, missionaries and settlers but these newcomers had little impact on the natives. Roycraft knew that his authority had no relevance in the territory.

Roycraft and his Provincial constables travelled north aboard the supply ship *Barbara Boscowitz*, along with six sturdy canoes. Eighty men and officers of "C" Battery, Royal Garrison Artillery, followed on the naval corvette H.M.S. *Caroline*. They set up base camp at Metlakatla, just north of the mouth of the Skeena, as Roycraft insisted the navy not accompany his small troop inland. "We want to prevent a war," he said, "not start one."[22] He requested they have regular artillery drills, as he wanted the intimidating naval guns demonstrated to locals, who would then tell tribes in the interior.

Roycraft and his constables paddled for seven days up the Skeena to the Kitwang camp where the Indian community was riven by family feuding. Sunbeam, bereft of her twin sons and her husband, had reportedly returned to the winter camp of her birth tribe and offended the remaining shaman. Violence erupted and two more people died, the shaman and Sunbeam's father. Her uncle gave himself up to the police, claiming he had shot the shaman.

Roycraft and Fitzstubbs, both holding ex-officio commissions as justices of the peace, decided to hold court to sort out the situation. To get the necessary jury, Roycraft dismissed six of his constables, then swore them in as jurymen. As a result, six former policemen sat and listened to Indian witnesses describe how another policeman had shot one of their chiefs in the back. After due deliberation, the jury found that Constable Green was responsible for Kamalmuk's death and Green was arraigned for trial. The jury also decided that the death of the medicine man was justifiable homicide, and Sunbeam's uncle was allowed to go free.

While he was at Hazelton, Roycraft called an assembly of the thirteen chiefs of tribal groups in the area. "There is no doubt that this expedition has and will have a most salutary effect upon the Indians," he later reported.

> They seem now to understand our power. They have promised to keep the law and Chiefs will bring all offenders to Justice.
> There is no doubt that there was a great deal of sickness last winter in the villages... These Indians are exceedingly superstitious and believed, no doubt, that the whites had something to do with the epidemic. Consequently, when Green shot the Indian, the first one shot by a whiteman, they were very much excited and at that time the whites were undoubtedly in great danger [but] the excitement cooled."[23]

Roycraft warned that seven white settlers, particularly the two who had refused to obey Fitzstubbs' earlier request to move in, that the provincial government did not intend to continue the protection "hitherto enjoyed by the white population of Upper Skeena." Any who were apprehensive of further trouble with the Indians were advised "to retire to the Coast."[24]

Two months later, Magistrate Fitzstubbs was able to report from Hazelton that "an improved condition of affairs prevails here."[25] In Nanaimo that November, Constable Green was found not guilty by a jury of coal miners and tradesmen, who decided that the Kitwancool chief had been killed while escaping from lawful custody. Green continued as a member of the Provincial Police for a year, then resigned. Perhaps the other members and officers questioned the abilities of one who had shot so quickly. Traditionally, Provincials prided themselves on not needing to fire a gun.

Superintendent Roycraft's ability to negotiate with natives in their language led the federal government to offer him the position of Indian Agent for Skeena District in 1891. As the salary was larger than he could ever hope to earn as head of the Provincial Police, he accepted.

Roycraft's resignation as BCPP superintendent gave Theodore Davie, the new attorney general, the opportunity to implement a different system of administration. He directed the chief constable for each region to report directly to his office, and he assumed the duties of superintendent of police. The rationale for the new system remains a mystery. Perhaps Davie, who was also the new premier, wanted a more concrete idea of how the force could be reorganized. Or perhaps he wanted to save the attorney general's department some money: the superintendent received $1,800 per annum, whereas constables received $60–100 per month. Whatever the reason, the experiment did not last. Two years after Roycraft's resignation, Davie announced that he had appointed Frederick Hussey as superintendent of Provincial Police. Hussey knew the Provincials; he had been one of them for twelve years. As a rookie, he had patrolled along the coast for two years, "spending one year and ten months of that time cold and wet," as he later recalled. After a stint in Lytton during the railway construction period, he moved to Kamloops where he became the district officer for the Provincial Police as well as government agent and gold commissioner.

Hussey was a frugal man and somewhat concerned that his promotion was actually going to cost him money. His salary in Kamloops was $125 per month plus a residence supplied with heat and light and the right to use prisoners as labourers for household and yard chores. When he moved to Victoria as superintendent, his salary increased $25 per month, but he no longer received a residence. Hussey told the attorney general that he agreed to accept the financial loss, but expected an improvement after the long-awaited reorganization of the force.

Throughout his career, Hussey had helped to solve several puzzling cases. One of the most well-known occurred in August 1891, when a robber held up the Cariboo Stage just outside of Clinton. The masked

*Indians poleing up the Skeena River. In the summer, this was the only way for police to reach some remote sections of the interior.*

*Superintendent Frederick S. Hussey occupied this office at police headquarters in Victoria from 1893 to 1911.*

bandit stopped the stage, aimed his Winchester steadily at the driver and ordered the strongbox thrown off. After emptying the sacks of gold dust and nuggets, he disappeared. Posses found no trace of the fugitive, but Hussey was sure he must have remained in the area. A few weeks later, Constable Joseph Burr at Ashcroft reported to Hussey that a man named Rowlands had arrived there and staked gold claims on nearby Scotty Creek, murmuring about a rich placer find. Hussey instructed the constable to keep a close eye on Rowlands, suspicious that he was finding gold in an area that even the Chinese, known for their thoroughness, had stopped working. His hunch proved correct. Within two weeks, a wire arrived from Burr. Rowlands had deposited a quantity of gold with the Express for shipping and had booked a ticket to leave town the next day. Hussey boarded the next freight train going west out of Kamloops and arrived in Ashcroft that evening. He decided to obtain a warrant for Rowlands' arrest at once. He and Constable Burr burst into Rowlands' hotel room, pulled the suspect out of bed and handcuffed him. They discovered later that their surprise appearance had been wise; Rowlands slept with a loaded revolver under his pillow.

Rowlands spent the rest of the night in a cell, protesting his innocence and writing a long report about his gold finds. The report revealed to Hussey that Rowlands knew nothing about mining. Next morning, when the sacks of gold were examined, they confirmed that Rowlands had never been a miner. Gold from different areas is as different as fingerprints when it is examined under microscope. Rowlands' gold obviously had come from a wide variety of creeks, and none of it resembled a nugget previously found in Scotty Creek. Rowlands was tried and sentenced to five years for stagecoach robbery.

Demands for law enforcement remained much greater than the number of constables available. "Spreading the force out" became a challenge as new immigrants arrived to settle in all southern areas of the province. Hussey discovered that change was a slow process, open to political influence and patronage. Government agents in areas that desperately needed a constable first would hire a special, then lobby the local member of the legislature to ask the attorney general to hire the man as permanent constable "as he was already doing the job." Hussy told the attorney general that this was unacceptable. He was adamant that all new members be hired on ability and all applicants have equal opportunity. He continually pointed out that for maximum efficiency, the superintendent of police had to control all hiring and assigning of duties.

The number of charges laid remained low, although the amount of crime in British Columbia increased along with the population. The Provincial Police had a mandate to police anywhere in the province, including Victoria, New Westminster, Vancouver and some smaller municipalities which also had their own police forces. When a suspect was arrested within city limits by a provincial officer in the absence of a municipal one, he would be turned over to the city force.

As the population grew, law enforcement in British Columbia became more diversified, as reports to Superintendent Hussey indicated. The constable from Nanaimo wrote to explain how he had captured a Sailors Union sloop, detained its crew of three men and released five men, also found on the sloop, whom they had kidnapped to serve as labour on deep-sea ships. He reported that he planned to proceed with charges against the Sailors Union crew and their accomplices. There was a query from the Williams Lake constable, asking how to deal with an accusation that the hide inspector was in cahoots with some of the larger ranchers. The constable at Wellington reported further labour disturbances over Oriental and black labourers working in the coal mines. He then assured Hussey that the disturbances and fighting were not on the scale of February 1891, when the Riot Act had been read. The constable at 150 Mile House wrote that he would have to resign if he could not take a leave of absence because his wife was "loosing her reason"[26]

Health concerns also required more police supervision. As people settled closer to each other along rivers and on the outskirts of towns, it was necessary to keep water uncontaminated, plan cemetery locations and control garbage dumping to prevent the outbreak of disease. Although British Columbia had an established health department, a constable's report was often the first notification that a problem existed. For instance, Constable Stewart wrote from Nanaimo in 1894 that after receiving complaints from residents that bodies were not being buried deep enough in the Chinese burial grounds, he measured three: "[one is] between 12 inches in depth from the level of the ground, one 15 inches; one 6 inches, two 5 inches."[27] Another health-related problem was the increasing number of impoverished residents, many of them elderly, some who "had lost their right mind." The provincial constable often became involved when an elderly person could no longer look after himself, and sometimes it was the constable who took him to the Provincial Old Men's Home. Mentally disturbed people were also handled by the local policeman. One constable patrolling northern coastal waters requested instructions about what to do with a young mentally impaired man at Rivers Inlet "who appears to be growing more angry, hard to handle, but has not yet caused anyone damage." His mother wanted him left at home but others thought it was risky. The constable pointed out that because of the man's size and temperament, "it would not be possible for one man to take him in the boat alone, if need be. . . ."[28]

Hussey began a new procedure: regular policy directives to all detachments. In one, he instructed that each police station had to remain open between 9 a.m. and 10 p.m. every day and that it must be kept clean and in good order and not used for entertaining visitors. Although some detachments had enough manpower to staff shifts, many still had only one or two constables. Some police stations still contained the constable's living quarters, office and jail, and people were used to calling on the constable twenty-four hours a day.

New Provincial constables were hired annually, and by 1895 the force had seventy-two members. The newly hired Provincials were usually mature men in their mid-twenties with some related experience, though not necessarily in law enforcement. Hussey expected men to be able to function independently. He chose new constables by judging "their nerve, courage, horse sense and manhood."[29]

Not everyone understood the difficulties imposed on the force by British Columbia's demanding geography. One government agent wrote tartly to the attorney general, who had questioned his hiring of a special:

> I hired Bullock-Webster as a Special Constable until provisions are made for a regular constable. Even if on the map the locations appear geographically close, the district to be covered is from the foot of Okanagan Lake to the Boundary Line, including Penticton, Okanagan Falls, Osoyoos, Keremeos, Camp McKenny, Camp Fairview (where the mining population is now 300). The regular constable you refer to is McMynn who is at the mouth of Rock Creek and even if he was available, there is a range of mountains over 4,000 feet high between the two sections . . ."[30]

Even without the barricade of mountains, it was a distance of seventy miles and Constable McMynn was already working long hours in the middle of a booming mining area. However, the expense of policing the miners was a problem the attorney general tried to solve by increasing the size of the patrol area, rather than hiring more men.

The Provincials became the organizers during natural disasters, working with teams of volunteers and advising when the army should be called in. When the Fraser River flooded in 1894, massive property damage occurred all through the Fraser Valley. A man who rafted down from Yale described the whole area below Hope as a massive lake, the surface of the water studded with the roofs of buildings around which the corpses of cattle floated. Communication with the interior was on an emergency basis only; the CPR tracks had washed out; steamboats were endangered by debris. Constables, militia and volunteers worked around the clock to bring relief to devastated residents. The situation grew tense when a group of people living in Sumas decided to dynamite the log jams that were causing the Vedder River to overflow in their area, an action that would have flooded more land around Chilliwack. The police managed to maintain an uneasy peace until a government engineer arrived to take control of the dynamiting.

The revised Police Act, which Hussey had been working on since becoming superintendent, was ratified by the Legislature in 1895. The Provincial Police Act and General Regulations created cohesive rules and regulations for the British Columbia Provincial Police Force and formally gave the superintendent direct and exclusive jurisdiction over all Provincial constables, a major change. A government agent or gold commissioner could still direct law enforcement in an emergency, but the superintendent could then intervene if he wanted to. Seniority and duties were defined, as were the responsibilities constables had to each other and to the public. The intention of the new Act and Superintendent Hussey's expectation of "his" constables were best explained in two of the general regulations:

> 31. He must be particularly cautious not to interfere idly or unnecessarily. When required to act he will do so with decision and boldness. He must remember that there is no qualification more indispensable than a perfect command of temper; never allowing himself to be moved in the slightest degree by any language or threats that may be used . . .

> 42. Coolness and firmness will be expected in all cases, and in circumstances of peril all must be careful to act together and to protect each other in the restoration of peace and order. Whoever shrinks from danger or responsibility is unworthy of a place in the service and will be discharged at once.[31]

Under the new Act, all present appointments to the British Columbia Constabulary were cancelled as of June 30, 1895, then all members were sworn in to the British Columbia Provincial Police. Qualifications for constables were established. Each applicant had to be a subject of Her Majesty by birth or naturalization; a resident of the province for one year before application; able to read and write understandably and intelligently, in the opinion of the superintendent; over 21 and under 35, of good health with sound body and mind; equal to the performance of police duty; and of good moral character and habits. The Act also specified that constables had to accept transfers when and wherever assigned, an unpopular clause with constables who felt that they had been hired to serve in a particular district.

As well, the Act explained the responsibilities in taking a case to trial, formally detailing for the first time how a constable was to prepare for prosecutions. As the success or failure of the charges laid depended on taking the correct steps at the correct time, it was a relief for many constables to have formal guidelines at last. Record keeping was revised in other ways as well. Detachment daybooks had been used previously to record movements of officers and prisoners, giving only names and destinations, never the reasons why the movement was being made; now the day's events were also to be summarized on a monthly form—in only three lines. In a memo distributed with the forms, Superintendent Hussey stressed that constables were welcome to continue writing him letters about the details of events or about their concerns, as he needed such correspondence to enable him to do his job adequately.

The Act also directed the superintendent of police to prepare a report to the legislature annually. The Victoria *Colonist* reported at length on Superintendent Hussey's report for 1895. It explained that the reorganization covered all aspects of policing British Columbia, and it emphasized how quickly the Kootenays were expanding and how many more constables would be needed there and in other regions. Hussey also reported that coastal residents had written, pleading "for a better system of police protection; their property is more or less a prey to wandering whisky peddlers and smugglers, who constantly infest our shores." He discussed Indian issues: "Not withstanding the fact that the penalties for infractions of the 'Indian liquor act' are very heavy and are rigorously enforced. . . I am pleased to be able to report that in all other respects our Indians are peaceable and law- abiding and that breaches of the criminal law amongst them are rare occurrences. They are self-supporting and industrious." But bootleg alcohol and home brew were creating havoc in many native villages, and the traffic could only be controlled with adequate patrol ships. Hussey recommended that the Dominion government equip a steamer as a revenue cutter: the Provincial force needed another steamer immediately, and an agreement to share patrols would benefit both levels. Hussey then voiced his concern about the number of unsolved crimes. "There should be attached to the department at headquarters," he recommended, "one or two thoroughly experienced detectives for the investigation of important criminal cases."[32]

Hussey's report included details about who was serving where, what salaries were being paid and what changes were necessary. For instance, he recommended moving the Comox district headquarters to Union and putting Constable W.B. Anderson in charge of the three constables posted there: "[Union] is an important mining centre, with a population of about 2,500 persons," he explained. "The necessity of a proper court house for the use of the stipendary magistrate and the local justices of the peace is very badly felt in this town. The room at present used for this purpose. . . is the police office in the lock-up, which is too small and altogether unsuitable."[33]

Superintendent Hussey's report was printed in full in many newspapers. In an editorial in the Victoria *Daily Colonist* on March 16, 1896,

Hussey was praised for his work directing the force, and for his astute observations on policing concerns. The editor pointed out that the seventy regular constables, under the supervision of Hussey and Sergeant John Langley, plus specials when required, made the force an organized body of capable men, able to maintain law and order. He declared that the British Columbia Provincial Police had come of age.[34]

CHAPTER FOUR

# "Coolness and firmness is expected"
# 1893–1911

EVEN AS THE BRITISH ADMIRALTY moved its main base to Hong Kong in the late 1880s, ending their assistance with policing the coast, many provincial politicians remained adamant that to create a BC Provincial Police marine branch was an unnecessary expense. They argued that patrolling the coast was a federal financial responsibility since most incidents were Customs and Excise or Indian Affairs matters. However, in the 1890s, a pair of murders caught the public's attention, encouraged joint federal-provincial patrolling and hastened the purchase of a provincial police motor launch.

The first victim was Old Jack Green who ran a store on Savary Island, trading supplies and liquor with people passing through. One day in the autumn of 1893, a couple of customers arrived at the cabin and found Jack Green and his occasional helper, Tom Taylor, lying dead in pools of dried blood. When Provincial Constable Walter Anderson, the coroner and the doctor arrived at the scene, they agreed that the men had been shot to death, and that their guns had been placed beside them to make it appear that they had killed each other in a gun fight. But neither gun had been fired, and Taylor had died clutching a pipe in his right hand. It was clearly premeditated murder.

As the investigators reconstructed what had happened, they noticed that the walls were splattered with bullet holes. By inserting cedar sticks into each hole, Constable Anderson showed that the murderer had blasted off his fusillade from the centre of the cabin, killing Taylor as he lounged on his bunk and Green as he sat in a chair by the door. Anderson and the coroner concluded that the murderer was someone whom Green and

Taylor had expected and trusted. When the constable examined the island, he found no other clues except for pieces of birdshot outside the cabin door and down on the shore.

The brief inquest ruled the deaths had been caused by a person or persons unknown and that several days had passed before the bodies were discovered. After questioning people on the mainland and nearby islands, Anderson discovered that Hugh Lynn had been drinking with Taylor and Green the week before at the pub in Lund, on the mainland across from Savary. Lynn was well-known up the Georgia Strait and respected by few, though his father, a former Royal Engineer, was a respected homesteader on the north shore of Burrard Inlet. The pub owner said that Lynn had returned the next day for seven bottles of whisky which he charged to Green's account. Anderson put out a wanted bulletin on Lynn.

Some locals decided that passing Indians had murdered the men, but Constable Anderson searched for Lynn. Weeks later, after a big storm, Lynn's skiff washed up on a beach a few miles from Savary and was towed in to Anderson, who happened to be at Lund. When he found birdshot spilled in the bilge, he was more certain than ever that Lynn was the murderer. Anderson had little to go on except for the trail of birdshot and a strong hunch, but he kept hunting for Lynn, questioning people up and down the coast. He found out that the fugitive was travelling with an Indian woman and child, but he could not catch up with them.

Finally, a reliable report came in that Lynn was on a small ranch on Shaw Island, in American territory. Superintendent Hussey went in with two constables and a United States sheriff to arrest the suspect. Lynn reportedly had an arsenal with him, so the police took all precautions. They crept up to the log cabin unseen, then entered both doors at once and had Lynn handcuffed before he could get to his rifle.

The woman, Jenny, and her seven-year-old son were also on the island. Jenny had become Lynn's prisoner and was relieved to be set free. She and the boy became witnesses for the prosecution, identifying Lynn as the murderer and as a thief. He had taken various merchandise, including a broken bag of birdshot, from Green's store. Apparently he had actually been after the treasure that everyone said Old Man Green kept on Savary. (For years afterward, the ground around the abandoned cabin was well dug up by treasure hunters, but nothing was ever found.) After a lengthy court case, Lynn was sentenced to hang in New Westminster, primarily because of testimony given by Jenny's son. The young native boy told the jury how he had seen Lynn shoot the men when he had gone up to Green's place to tell Lynn that Jenny was sick.

Soon after Hugh Lynn's trial, another murderer claimed a victim on an island in the inside passage. In October 1894, a man's body was found in a rowboat floating just off Read Island and was identified as Chris

Benson, a partner in the combination store and hotel. The nearest justice of the peace, Michael Manson of Cortes Island, took the body to Vancouver for an autopsy; the coroner found Benson had been murdered by repeated blows to the head. Superintendent Hussey directed Constable Anderson to investigate. Benson's partner, Ed Wylie and his wife, and their neighbours, John and Laura Smith, assured Anderson that they had no idea who had murdered their longtime friend. But as Anderson chatted with residents living on nearby islands in Georgia Strait, he became increasingly suspicious of the Read Island residents. He decided a detective might learn more. Hussey agreed and with Magistrate Manson's assistance, the Provincial Police hired a young fisherman to move to Read Island and investigate. The undercover agent found out little until Laura Smith confided to him, as she tried to seduce him, that she had to find a way to escape from the Island. She confessed she was terrified that her husband would murder her as he had murdered Benson when he had found them in bed together. John Smith was charged with Benson's murder.

However, when the case went to court, it turned out that there were mitigating circumstances and a very sympathetic jury. Judge G.A. Walkem became so enraged when they declared Smith not guilty that he ordered all of them to leave his courtroom. Smith returned to his island home a free man, while the undercover man went back to fishing and Constable Anderson returned to his coastal patrol, more than likely hoping that he would not soon have to return to Read Island.

During the investigations of the Read Island and Savary Island murders, newspaper editors decried the lack of a proper marine patrol in the province. It was a disgrace, they wrote, that Provincials had to patrol "our coastal waters" in hired boats, or by hitching rides with fishermen or missionaries, or by using the ferries, which ran only once per week. With two sailing sloops, three skiffs and six rowboats, the BCPP patrolled thousands of miles of coastal waters as well as the immense inland waters. Superintendent Hussey's repeated recommendation for a Provincial Police marine patrol gained supporters, and in 1896, purchase of a patrol steamer received government approval. The first vessel arrived two years later and was also used as a revenue cutter for the federal government.

The Provincials differed from many police forces, as each constable was expected to act as an independent agent, within the BCPP standards. Even in an emergency, the force seldom had more than four or five members in one place at one time. A constable in a rural or coastal location often went weeks without seeing another member of the BCPP. Superintendent Hussey chose all new constables, hiring men "who sounded like they could get on with people and could quietly give orders which would be obeyed."[1] He expected each Provincial to know what was happening in his patrol area and be acquainted with most of the people there, despite the number of new arrivals. "Hussey influenced many of us for years," one former Provincial recalled. "He died two years before I joined the force but I had a crusty chief constable who used Hussey as a reference. He had some doubts about whether my ability to reason a situation through would ever improve enough to be acceptable by Hussey's standards."[2]

British Columbia now had over 150,000 residents, not including natives. Though the size of each patrol area decreased, the number of inhabitants in it increased. A constable looked after his region, conferred with magistrates about local problems, asked BCPP headquarters about procedures or dilemmas and recorded few incidents. The constable who had policed the Quesnel area recalled:

> The unreported things took a lot of time. Sometimes neighbours needed a little help settling a dispute — I tried to prevent bad feelings from building into spats. Then another job was bringing accident cases into hospital, often over a poor trail or bad side road. When I needed assistance, which was not too often, another constable arrived on the next stage.[3]

Superintendent Hussey's pride in and protectiveness of "his" men became legendary. Newspapers began referring to the Provincial Police as "Hussey's Pets," a nickname gleefully picked up by some members of the public. Hussey ignored it completely, even as he told the public that they could expect truthfulness and consideration from his Provincials. He was impatient with politicians who questioned a constable's ability or honesty without backing it up with fact, but if criticism was supported by

*Beaver Indians near Fort St. John. Second from the right is Mannie Gullion, an interpreter used by the police. Not many constables spoke Indian languages, which added to the difficulty of policing the native population.*

evidence, the constable was dismissed. Hussey did not tolerate dishonesty or laziness, though he defended his constables' right to make occasional mistakes. Above all, he prized the men's right to act independently. In police forces modelled on military organizations, patrols were made by at least two men, but Hussey believed that most BCPP constables should work alone. "Why send two men when one can do the job?" Hussey asked new constables, teaching that reasonableness could accomplish more than force.[4]

However, he was the first to agree that some areas were harder to control than others. Particularly difficult were the mining districts in the Kootenays and on Vancouver Island, where demonstrations against cheap labour and dangerous working conditions were becoming increasingly unruly. After policing a confrontation at a small mine in the Kootenays, where workers tried to stop contract workers from going out to the camp, one young constable wrote to his sister: "I hope and pray that I will not be stationed here for long." He thought the government was wrong in allowing cheap contract labour into British Columbia, yet he was determined that no harm come to "those poor souls." He continued: "Sometimes I feel that the government should not keep letting contract workers in but there is much space and few people."[5]

In the clashes among workers, constables were caught in the middle. Often protestors assaulted the workers being imported as replacements. It was the constable's job to prevent the new workers from getting battered while he persuaded the old workers to maintain the peace and return to their homes – even though he was aware that sometimes the company was evicting them from those homes to make room for the new workers.

One such incident ended up as a complaint on the desk of the attorney general. In August 1902, at Michel in the aftermath of a protest against the Crows Nest Mining company, strikers threatened to drive Joseph Horne, a European-born strikebreaker, out of town. Two of the strikers had previously been arrested for assaulting Horne, and the night before their trial, about twenty others gathered outside Horne's residence, threatening to beat him up if he gave evidence the next day. Three Provincials arrived from Fernie to back up the Michel constable and decided to take Horne to the lock-up overnight for his own protection. Horne could not understand why he was being jailed instead of the men who were threatening him, so the senior constable got the local priest, who had great influence over the Slav community, to explain to the indignant witness. But it was to no avail. A frightened Horne refused to testify the next day, so the magistrate jailed him for another twenty-four hours. The priest decided it would be best for Horne to go back to his family in Washington, and safest if he accompanied him on the trip. But when Horne was released from jail, he refused to go with the priest and fled back to the mine at

Michel, where he complained to management that the constables had locked him up for being a strikebreaker. Management in turn complained to the attorney general, and the chief constable in Fernie ended up trying to explain the circumstances to Hussey." You will see," he concluded, "that we are in an awkward position as both sides think we are favouring the others. I also enclose a letter from Constable Cameron at Michel in which he says Mr. Evans, the superintendent, wished him to shoot the men."[6]

Mine owners and managers, powerful men in provincial political affairs, regularly complained to the attorney general. They wrote letters, indignantly explaining that a constable had permitted the miners to harass new employees. According to management, this showed that his sympathies were with the strikers and that he must be brought to task for his biased policing. On the other side, miners lodged protests that the constable sympathized with the owners, who were bringing in immigrants to work at lower wages: "the Constable is ready to jump however high the company's boss wants."[7]

British Columbia's extensive advertising campaign in Europe attracted many miners and their families from Italy, France, Portugal, Greece and the Slavic countries. The immigrants often became angry at the conditions they found. They had come in good faith, expecting to find better working and living conditions than in their homelands. They expected education for their children and opportunities for themselves. Instead, they discovered that the advertising had been a gross exaggeration. They found that they had to work longer hours in worse conditions than they had left behind, barely existing on miners' low wages. Many hated the drab rows of one-room cottages provided for them in Coal Creek, Morrissey, Hosmer, Natal and Corbin; they missed the gardens and public parks they were used to. And many hated the long cold Rocky Mountain winters. Constables reported some European immigrants were sullen, simmering with rage; others were restless, impatient; some requested help to return home. But no subsidization was available for return fares.

The language barriers created new problems for constables in the east Kootenays as did many immigrants' ingrained distrust and fear of police. It was hard to communicate. "I am having great difficulty obtaining factual information as not many speak English," one constable in the east Kootenays complained, tired of his various recorder duties. "I do not propose to go canvassing from house to house asking if anyone had died or if a baby has arrived. I beg to assure you that there is no desire to impertinence or disrespect in the foregoing but I believe it is time to call a halt to having work piled on me for which I do not even receive thanks."[8]

Issuing reasonable orders and expecting obedience had been a Provincial constable's primary method of policing previously, but it was ineffective when he could not talk to the individuals involved. The larger centres in the Kootenays divided into ethnic districts — Slav Town, French Town and Italian Town — and fights broke out among residents of the different districts. Hampered by his inability to speak the newcomers' languages and by a scarcity of manpower, a constable had little choice but to ignore most brawls, except for attempting to confiscate illegal knives or guns.

Policing the Kootenay area was exhausting work for Provincials and some resigned after a few months of it. In the smaller settlements, the constable was often the only government official available. He gathered statistics for health and school officials, assessed the need for repairs in rural areas after floods and road damage, and reported on all accidents and natural disasters. When a forest fire scourged the area or when a mine exploded, the constable provided the first report of casualties and damage.

Mining accidents were especially horrendous. On May 22, 1902, the Number 2 colliery exploded at the Coal Creek mine, six miles from Fernie. Eight hundred miners were below ground when it happened. As the explosions reverberated, some miners made it to the surface, dragging and carrying others. But many more were trapped underground. The four Provincials stationed in the Fernie region commandeered wagons, carriages and horses and rushed to the site. They tried to organize the rescue effort, but as one of them reported later: "Some men were so burnt that it was almost impossible to move them without them falling apart. The smell of burning flesh was awful. Desperate relatives searched through the carnage for loved ones, crying and shouting. We began the endless cortege from mine to town, first taking the injured, then the dead. It took days."[9]

Of the 128 men who died in the explosion, many were buried unidentified. For months after, the BCPP detachment in Fernie answered inquires from people trying to find missing relatives. The constables wrote letters and forwarded valuable possessions to the relatives of victims who had been identified.

There were other challenges for constables posted in the Kootenays. The wealth in the area attracted professional card sharks and con men, many of them Americans. After receiving a complaint from a concerned resident in Sandon, Hussey queried why the constable responsible for policing the boom town was not able to keep such people out. "[There] are now twenty-four hotels and twenty-three saloons at Sandon," replied the chief constable for East Kootenay. "One Constable cannot sort out and keep track of who is a resident and who is suspicious, even though he watches all arrivals and departures of the train."[10]

Despite co-operation between the Provincials and the state police in Oregon, California and Washington, it was difficult to pursue lawbreakers travelling back and forth across the international border, so Hussey began to hire private investigators. "When Mr. Hussey was here yesterday he requested us to write to you, relative to the east Kootenay murder case," explained the Thiel Detective Service manager in Seattle to Provincial Police Sergeant Atkins in Victoria. "He states that information was liable to reach you any day, from some of the parties concerned, and if so, to ask you to take the subject up with Mr. McLean, and get his authority to engage our services to boost the fellow across the line, which we think we can do very neatly, and without causing any international complications."[11]

During the same years that the Kootenays flourished, the Klondike boomed. Hundreds of Americans cut through northern British Columbia on their way to the gold fields, causing some concern that the United States would have expansionist ambitions along the unsurveyed border between Alaska and BC. Directed to take charge of the area, Hussey instructed Chief Constable William Bullock-Webster to establish a Provincial Police district in the north and to open detachments as required.

Many of the Klondikers were greenhorns, inadequately prepared for the fierce weather conditions. They arrived with tons of freight to take into the gold fields, much of which was impractical and had to be abandoned. Most of the miners travelled by ship up the coast, then crossed the Alaskan panhandle and hiked or floated into the Klondike. Others crossed in northern British Columbia. New settlements developed within weeks because of them; some became ghost towns just as quickly. Glenora grew into a town of 2,000 and Telegraph Creek, Teslin and Dease Lake also became centres because of the Klondikers of 1897. The BC Police and North-West Mounted Police had the awesome task of ensuring that gold-seekers took in adequate supplies to survive the cruel winter and treacherous spring break-up. Both forces monitored would-be miners' equipment whenever possible, not only to save lives but also to prevent the chaos that occurred when men starved.

Bullock-Webster had eleven men under him to patrol the 80,000 square miles between the Skeena River and the Yukon border. He initially stationed four constables at Glenora, two at Telegraph Creek and one man each at Teslin, Lake Bennett, Echo Cove, Fort Simpson and Port Essington, then moved them around as population shifted. The BCPP and NWMP shared information as much as primitive communication and transportation systems allowed. Although telegraph lines were functioning in a few areas, in most northern regions messages had to be hand-delivered, a slow and somewhat sporadic process.

During the peak of the Klondike gold rush, the Log Cabin Detachment was also established by the BCPP as a roving clearinghouse for the thousands entering the Klondike by way of coastal British Columbia.

*The BCPP detachment in Atlin, 1898. Group includes Constable E.W. Bickle, far left, Constable Harry Heal, third from left, and Constable W.H. Vickers, fourth from left, along with the detachment's dog team.*

*A collection of handcuffs and shackles decorates the interior of the Atlin detachment. From left: Constable Harry Heal, Mrs. J. Clay, a well-known mining woman, and Chief Constable E.A. Desbrisay.*

Provincial Constable Walter Owen reported to Superintendent Hussey that they had cleared 25,000 people for Dawson and 12,000 for Atlin through Log Cabin in less than two months. The detachment was considered part of the Nanaimo District, which encompassed all the territory from Shawnigan Lake on Vancouver Island up to the Chilkoot Pass.

Gold attracted more than miners: thieves and the occasional murderer also arrived. Early one spring, a packer reported an abandoned tent half-buried in snow about thirty miles out of Glenora. Bullock-Webster and a constable set off to investigate. They found two men dead in the tiny tent, one shot through the head, the other savagely battered. The constable recognized them as two of six men whose supplies he had inspected at Glenora a few days earlier, except now the murdered pair's money was missing. As the Provincials searched the area, they noticed a rifle that had been thrown into the partly frozen Stikine; the constable retrieved it by removing his clothes and plunging into the icy water. Then he and Bullock-Webster loaded the frozen bodies onto a sled and hauled them thirty miles through slush to Glenora.

Once the victims were thawed out beside a fire, Bullock-Webster proceeded to do the post-mortems, there being no medical person in the area. Partly digested food in the stomach suggested that the men probably had been murdered about two hours after their evening meal, and Bullock-Webster concluded that they had been awake. When he removed the bullet, he compared it by weighing it on a miner's scale with the unfired bullets in the rifle and found it to be a matching calibre. Then he organized a jury of miners who ruled "Murder by person or persons unknown." Late in the evening on the day after he had gone to check out the tent, Bullock-Webster conducted the burial service.

In the course of a manhunt for the missing partners of the dead men, the three Vipond brothers were intercepted up the trail. They knew nothing of the murders and had none of the stolen goods. They explained that the group had separated the first night out of Glenora because Claus, the sixth partner and a friend of the dead men, was being so obnoxious that they did not want to continue travelling with him. Hearing about the murders, they immediately suspected Claus. When Claus arrived at Teslin Lake, a constable was waiting for him. The suspect was carrying $1,000, though he had been almost penniless a few weeks earlier. He claimed that he had killed in self-defence and that he had taken the money for safekeeping, fully intending to turn it over to the first policeman he met. However, he could not explain why he had not returned the thirty miles to Glenora instead of travelling hundreds of miles farther north.

It turned out that Claus could not be tried in Glenora, for reasons that were symbolic of the complexities of law enforcement in the province. First of all, the judge could not legally travel through Alaskan territory to reach the Stikine area because it contravened the British and American immigration treaty. Second, even if the court had been able to get to Glenora, there were not enough registered voters there to empanel a jury. Temporary residents who moved with the gold rushes could not perform legal functions as they were not registered voters; neither could most of the permanent northern residents because they were Indian. Claus was taken to Nanaimo, found guilty by a jury and sentenced to hang, but he escaped the noose. He committed suicide by taking poison, which his wife may have brought to him in the family Bible. She was not charged.

Despite the wealth in the Klondike, the riches being discovered in the Kootenays and the flow of immigrants, British Columbia was in an economic depression by the turn of the century. International investors hesitated to invest further money, the government changed four times between 1898 and 1903, Prime Minister Wilfrid Laurier was forced to dismiss Lieutenant Governor T.R. McInnes, whose unpopularity with legislators was making stable administration impossible, and numerous strikes dampened the economy. Investors were also nervous about British Columbia's trade union movement—the province had approximately 100 unions in December 1900 and 216 unions by July 1903.[12]

The growing trade unions also affected the BCPP. In less than two years, they policed major strikes involving the Fraser River fishermen, the Vancouver Island and Rossland coal miners and the CPR trackmen, and they patrolled numerous smaller confrontations over contract labour, wages and safety issues. Many administrators felt that more permanent constables were needed. Superintendent Hussey, increasingly frustrated with the disorganized provincial administrations, hoped that the election of James Dunsmuir and his party in June 1900 would provide stable management. But as the Dunsmuir government moved into their offices, the fishermen went on strike. By autumn, Hussey's cost estimates for policing during 1900 bore no relation to the actual expenditures, much to the displeasure of the new government.

The Fraser River strike, a conflict involving the fishermen, cannery owners and cannery employees, began in late June and escalated through July 1900. Two unions representing over 4,000 Japanese fishermen, 500 white fishermen and numerous Indian fishermen disputed the price per fish being paid by the canneries. Just before the fishing season started to peak, the strike closed the canneries, putting hundreds out of work during the few weeks when they made most of their year's income. Hussey directed five constables to help the Steveston constable patrol the turbulent waterfront and protect the canneries and fishing boats from sabotage.

When the cannery owners offered a higher price per fish, a large number of fishermen rejected the offer but the majority voted to accept it. Some 3,000 fishermen attempted to begin fishing and others picketed the river in patrol boats, harassing and threatening them. Frantic not to miss harvesting the peak salmon run, cannery owners – among them the new minister of finance – demanded the provincial government protect those wanting to fish with more than a few Provincial policemen.

The government authorized hiring special constables, but when Hussey advised him that still more manpower was required, Premier Dunsmuir called up 200 militia. The combined force patrolled the waterfront as negotiators debated the price of a salmon. The strike ended on July 31 after the major salmon run had passed. The militia were withdrawn but the Provincials and special constables continued to patrol in force for the rest of the season. Despite continued animosity and verbal threats among the factions, few incidents and little damage were recorded that year.

In the aftermath of the expensive strike, the new government made radical cuts to the costs of administering the province. One measure was the annulment of the Provincial Police Act of 1895 and the transfer of police administration to the attorney general's office. Hussey, instructed to act as a consultant to Attorney General D.M. Eberts, suddenly had little authority and no power to prevent the subsequent directives that temporarily changed how BC was policed.

When Hussey had developed the Provincial Police Act, he expanded on the regular BCPP procedures – the informal guidelines that Brew, Todd and Roycraft had used to shape the force since its inception. The Act gave a constable a written definition of his responsibilities, but it made few changes to how he policed. Mobility was crucial to that system of law enforcement: each constable moved about his patrol area to stay informed about what was going on, about who lived where and what problems might be developing. He also tried to prevent lawbreaking. A provincial constable warned and lectured much more frequently than he laid charges. Hired for his ability to act independently and to use common sense, he was expected to try to resolve problems and prevent conflicts as much as possible.

The BCPP system was thrown into chaos when the new government decided that the ninety provincial constables were not to travel except in an emergency. Each constable was directed to remain at his office until summoned, which prevented him from performing his normal duties. As well, travel vouchers for trains and lake steamers became almost unavailable and horse allowances were abruptly cancelled, making it difficult to respond to emergencies. Regularly borrowing a horse was not feasible, and some stable owners were reluctant to rent to a constable on a daily basis, as pursuing a suspect could take longer than expected, and the government paid accounts slowly. The order to stay in one locale immediately hampered police effectiveness. The one or two men responsible for a detachment with a large geographic area no longer knew what was happening in their district, as they were unable to visit certain areas until an emergency occurred.

In March 1901, for example, the constable in Grand Forks was notified early one morning that some draft horses had been stolen from a farm about fifteen miles outside of town. Unable to obtain a horse, the constable had to take the stage the next day. By then, the thief and the valuable horses were long gone and the farmer was as angry at the constable as he was at the thief. Such incidents, occurring throughout BC, aroused public opinion about the policing situation; residents and news-paper editors demanded that law enforcement be restored to its previous effectiveness.

Superintendent Hussey became increasingly frustrated. Two issues in particular dismayed him: patronage and administrative confusion. With each change of government, new favours were owed, and many secret trade-offs were made over projected railway rights. Hussey had been careful not to allow positions on the force to become payment for such debts, so when he learned two men had been appointed to the BCPP because of a political connection, he was enraged. Then a constable was dismissed because he had offended an MLA. To make matters worse, Hussey realized that the responsibilities of the chief constables, who ran the districts under the superintendent's direction, were being undermined: "I do not doubt that my being left in ignorance of dismissals and appoint-ments of constables is only an oversight," the Chief Constable at Nelson complained to Hussey and the deputy attorney general, "but I venture to point out that I am placed in a most unpleasant position in consequence. I cannot give instructions to, and expect reports from, constables of whose existence I am unaware."[13]

In December 1902, Hussey took an extended leave of absence. He and his family went to San Francisco, supposedly to have his eye condition studied by specialists there. Shortly after Richard McBride formed a government in late 1903, Hussey returned and was asked to report on the condition of the force. He reported much confusion in the detachments and disorganization in the attorney general's department. In the next legislative session, the 1904 Police Act was passed, which basically cancelled the annulment of the 1895 Police Act, and Hussey began rebuilding his force. Constables were authorized to recommence patrols, travel vouchers were reissued and the horse allowance of $17 was reinstated. However, despite general agreement that the force needed to be better equipped, low provincial revenues kept the BCPP functioning under tight financial restraint for a few years.

The recommended purchase of one new invention, the automobile, was delayed even though it was coming into growing use by the public.

At the end of 1905, there were 565 registered vehicles in the lower mainland and on the island. The lack of suitable roads and laws affecting the automobile meant that drivers of horse-drawn conveyances were often endangered by a new driver's complete inability to control his machine. Nonetheless, Hussey forecast that the day would come "when those smelly machines will replace horses, just as surely as there are white hairs coming on my head."[14]

During the four years between the annulment of the Police Act in 1900 and the new Act being passed in 1904, some experienced constables had left the force. The Provincial Police consisted of the superintendent, seventy-eight regular constables, Sergeant F.R. Murray at Headquarters and six chief constables: William Bullock-Webster at Nelson, John McMullin in Fernie, Colin Campbell in Vancouver, Stanley Spain in New Westminster, Walter Owen in Atlin and Joseph Burr in Ashcroft.

As the provincial economy improved, the force added new members but did not increase salaries. In 1906, chief constables received between $80 and $100 monthly, while constables received from $50 to $80, with no additional benefits except in the few detachments where the office/jail included living quarters. Constables regularly requested a clothing allowance, as the force was not in uniform and policing was hard on clothes, but decisions on that controversial subject continued to be postponed as administrators debated the issue of a uniformed force. As wages for millhands, labourers and construction workers rose to between $3.50 and $6 a day, BCPP members found their salary inadequate. "I respectfully submit that my eight years' experience in the RNWMP and ten years' police service in this province should make my services to the Government of as much monetary or commercial value as is paid to the very ordinary unskilled labourers in this district," wrote the newly appointed chief constable at Nelson.[15]

Though the population had changed radically during the past decade in some regions, it had changed little in the Ashcroft area, which included Spences Bridge, Clinton and Merritt. Chief Constable Joseph Burr was responsible for policing a population made up of railroaders, stagecoach drivers, cowboys, Indians, Chinese and a number of well-established expatriates from England, many of whom had lived there for years and were used to much freedom and little government. The popular Irish Provincial was kept busy cleaning up after accidents, chasing the occasional rustler and controlling the fist fights that broke out frequently on the main street of Ashcroft.

He also had to keep the peace in Ashcroft's extensive Chinatown, a complicated job because of the existence of secret societies, called tongs. On one occasion, a Chinese resident complained to Burr that his friend had been killed in a fight between the powerful Lee Tong and the Chee

Kong Tong. Burr was convinced it was murder. He arrested two suspects on other charges to prevent them from leaving town, then began searching for a body. Unable to come up with any evidence, Burr eventually took the two men before the court on the minor charges. They were fined, then released. But as they walked out, the chief constable re-arrested them on other charges. Burr hoped that a $500 reward and the search for information in New Westminster's and Vancouver's Chinatowns would produce some evidence before he had to take them to court again.

Three months after the original complaint, the victim's decomposed body washed up on a bank of the Thompson River just outside Ashcroft. Finally Burr had his evidence and could schedule his prisoners for trial at the spring assizes. However, all his work went for nothing when the judge dismissed the jury on a technicality. At the fall assizes, the accused were retried but a different judge refused to admit certain key evidence linking them to the murder, and the jury found them not guilty. Much to Burr's frustration, the defendants were discharged and disappeared from the area.

It was a rare case that Joseph Burr lost. He developed quite a reputation over the years for astute judgement of people and for well-organized prosecutions. In another of his cases, a CPR night operator at Spences Bridge named Webber brought Jonah, an old Indian, into the Ashcroft jail and charged him with theft of gold dust from the Express office. Jonah admitted that he had walked into the Express office and stayed for a while the day of the robbery. Although Burr had known Jonah for years and the charge did not ring true, the CPR investigators from Vancouver decided that Webber's testimony was adequate and the case went to court.

During the hearing, Burr surprised everyone by suddenly presenting the magistrate with a warrant for the arrest of Webber. Burr had discovered that Jonah had made his first-ever trip to the Express office to view Webber's elaborate moustache. After viewing it for some time and being most impressed, he had described the moustache in detail to a friend who was waiting for him. Burr informed the court that Jonah's friend was prepared to testify. Burr also discovered that Jonah always wore moccasins, which made no footprints. Yet Webber claimed that Jonah had left a footprint. These were small points but they were enough to force a confession from Webber. Jonah was a free man.

Criminal investigations were only part of a Provincial's duties. During the Depression years, the province had dismissed many health care workers and licence inspectors so constables were again enforcing quarantines and other health regulations. Quarantines sometimes created acute problems as many families did not have enough money to cover rent and food for the length of the quarantine and the constable would often become

*Bill Miner, the famous train robber, in 1906 after his capture by the BCPP.*

*A stagecoach leaves Ashcroft for Clinton in 1890. Constables frequently travelled the Cariboo Road by stage, sometimes with a handcuffed prisoner on the way to court, or gaol.*

responsible for their well-being. Whenever possible, churches or relatives were called on. Otherwise, the constable would get funds from the public purse, then arrange for grocery deliveries and other necessities.

Provincials were also responsible for enforcing the Lord's Day Act and the new laws prohibiting gambling, which left them vulnerable to the wrath of hotel owners. An efficient constable was liable to find that complaints about his honesty or ethics had been made to the attorney general and that he was under investigation. One typical case involved the young constable at Stewart, Charles Taylor. Letters published by the Victoria *Colonist*, the Vancouver *Province* and the Vancouver *World* in 1910 accused him of graft. He immediately requested that Hussey hold an official inquiry: "I consider in fairness to myself I should not be driven out of my occupation by men of low reputation and prostitutes who I have often had to take proceedings against."[16] The newspaper stories, all published under the headline "A Constable's Graft," generated a great uproar in the legislature.

Then Senior Constable George Dinsmore, who supervised the Stewart detachment, reported to Hussey: "A new complaint was made to me last Saturday that Constable Taylor collected $10 from another tenderloin woman, and yesterday while at her place, I worked it from her that a scavenger induced her to tell this story so as to try and get Constable Taylor discharged from here as he was too severe on law breakers and they had to get him out of here. I find him a good officer and get along with him fine but these reports make a man feel blue at times, thinking there is something in them for there is so many, but I have tried to show you the type of parties making the complaints."[17] After Dinsmore's report, Hussey considered Taylor exonerated.

As the economy improved, labourers were needed again to mine ore and coal, to fish, to log and to build railways. Thousands were immigrants from Japan, China and South Asia, and demonstrations against them increased in frequency in Vancouver, Victoria, Nanaimo and in the Kootenays. The chief constable at Nelson, for instance, reported that he had hired three special constables to accompany him to Ymir to protect 20 Japanese and 12 Chinese from about 250 men armed with clubs and axe handles. Even in distant Cassiar, the Riot Act had to be read when miners tried to prevent new Japanese workers from reaching a mine. As owners demanded more labourers, Canadian agreements with Japan, China and India allowed for greater immigration, even as many British Columbians lobbied their MLAs to limit entry of nonwhite immigrants. The legislature passed an ordinance to make all would-be immigrants pass an English test; however, the federal government promptly disallowed it.

Anti-Asian agitation peaked in Vancouver in September 1907, when the Asiatic Exclusion League sponsored a parade and speeches. A crowd of about 2000 people gathered outside City Hall, observed by Vancouver city policemen and a few Provincials. During an address by the secretary of the Seattle Exclusion League, simmering passions exploded into violence. A shouting mob swept past a police cordon into Chinatown, where they smashed windows and destroyed merchandise. When they moved on into the Japanese district, they were met by an angry group of Japanese, armed with sticks, knives and a few guns. Open fighting broke out and it took every available policeman in Vancouver and the district to regain control and start to clear the streets. The police bundled two dozen prisoners off to jail and transported the injured to hospitals. Several people were badly cut by knives, and fifty-six businesses were damaged. A wire sent to Superintendent Hussey reported that things were quiet by Sunday but that Chinese workers had not returned to work and demonstrators might try to interfere with the 800 Japanese and 900 East Indians scheduled to disembark that week. When the Japanese elementary school burned on Monday night, Hussey prepared to order more Provincials into the city, but it turned out to be an isolated incident. An uneasy peace returned to Vancouver.

In the aftermath of the riot, the federal government sent Commissioner William Lyon Mackenzie King to investigate: the incident was considered an international embarrassment, as Japanese diplomats had been touring Canada when it occurred. Prime Minister Wilfrid Laurier directed King to find out why the riots had happened and to validate claims for losses. King reported that the influx of 8,125 Japanese in the previous ten months caused alarm and unrest, combined as it was with the ongoing arrivals of Hindus by the hundreds and Chinese in larger numbers than in recent years. Part of the problem, he thought, was a clash of values between Orientals and whites, particularly the willingness of Japanese and Chinese to accept low wages. This discord was aggravated by agitators.

Other investigators discovered that many of the injured and a few of those arrested had "gone along with a friend who asked them to the parade"[18] and they were unable to say why they had started running through the streets with their friends. Authorities realized some of those involved had actually attended to see the parade and other entertainment offered, not to demonstrate against Orientals.

Investigation of the riot accentuated Hussey's warnings that the BCPP had to learn to police the growing number of non-English speaking residents more effectively. He believed that many European and Slavic immigrants were easily influenced by agitators because of their general distrust of all authority. Constables who spoke their languages would be much more effective; part-time interpreters made for unreliable communication, he pointed out, recalling the story of one young constable who discovered that he had hired an undercover agitator to act as an interpreter.

Given the number of recent arrivals from China and Japan, the superintendent directed chief constables to find qualified interpreters in those languages as well as the Slavic languages.

Hussey was also authorized to form a BCPP mounted troop, a decision that was a turning point for the BCPP. Previous provincial police organization had focussed on the individual — one constable, responsible for a set area. Emergencies had been handled by hiring special constables and, occasionally, with assistance from the British navy, the BC militia or the NWMP. But as the need to keep public order grew, Hussey recognized that a show of police strength was becoming necessary and recommended a small mounted troop of ten mature and experienced men.

Another consequence of the riot was a new federal Opium and Drug Act. When Mackenzie King was presented a list of claimants for damages suffered through the melee, he found it included owners of two opium factories. Each claimed damages of $100 a day for the six days that their factories were closed because of street disturbances. Investigating further, King was stunned to discover how much opium was legally manufactured in the fourteen factories in the Chinatowns in Vancouver and Victoria. Tons of poppy-seed cake imported from the Orient was boiled into syrup in massive copper cauldrons, then smuggled into the US, although an impressive amount was smoked in British Columbia. Not only that, but government profited handsomely in the traffic. The federal government collected duty of $160 a case on crude opium and the BC government charged manufacturers a $500 annual licensing fee. As soon as he returned to Ottawa, King had his fellow parliamentarians pass a law ending the opium industry. The new Opium and Drug Act of 1908 imposed heavy penalties for illegally possessing opium as well as manufacturing it. Sources of opium dried up quickly. Factories closed and cases of crude no longer arrived from Hong Kong. Smuggling into the US declined drastically as Canada joined with other nations to fight the world drug traffic.

In BC, opium use went underground. Many Chinese were willing to risk heavy penalties and jail to continue using the drug, and illegal opium dens became profitable businesses. The Provincial Police were given the responsibility of stopping the opium trade. In fact, they pressed few charges under the new Act. Given that the use of opium resulted in very little other crime, especially as compared to alcohol, many people doubted the wisdom of the new law and it was not enforced with much vigour.

During Hussey's last five years as superintendent, policing changed with the rapid growth of BC's population and economy. Additional police motor launches were purchased as well as the BCPP's first automobiles. Construction of new facilities and upgraded equipment made policing easier. Though the number of labour confrontations continued to increase every year, particularly in the Kootenays and on Vancouver Island, owners settled quickly, anxious to maintain a share of the wealth being generated by massive railway construction. Demonstrations against ethnic groups working cheaply continued. Courtroom procedures became multicultural as the law's representatives and interpreters tried to sort out who was guilty and who was innocent. The Provincials' investigations and prosecutions grew in variety as well as in numbers. Though drunkenness, bootlegging and petty theft remained the most common charges, there were more murders, extortions and swindles. During that period, a man in the interior and another in the Skeena became involved in crimes that have become well-known legends in BC.

In 1906, Bill Miner and his two companions robbed the Vancouver-bound Canadian Pacific Imperial Limited Express #97 train, expecting to scoop the relief funds being shipped to victims of the San Francisco earthquake. After a water stop at Duck's Station, about twenty miles east of Kamloops, two masked men jumped aboard the engine, flourished pistols and ordered the engineer to bring the train to a stop, and the express man to open his car. The trio took the mail and express bags, thanking the engineer and express man as they left. But Miner picked the wrong train. When the robbers eventually stopped high up on the tumbleweed plateau to count their haul, they discovered they had only $15 and some registered mail.

At age fifty-two, Miner had a long history as a train and stage robber. He robbed his first train at sixteen, spent two-thirds of his life behind bars and escaped from jail twice. Eventually, he moved to the Tullameen Valley, where he called himself George Edwards and became a popular resident. He played the fiddle, cobbled shoes for neighbours and charmed the ladies and children. Even when he was prosecuted for robbery, he continued to have many supporters. "The attitude of those times was 'oh, Bill Miner is not so bad'," explained one of the men who helped Constable Fernie search for Miner. "He only robs the CPR once every two years but they rob us every day."[19]

As soon as the BCPP constable in Kamloops, William Fernie, was informed of the hold-up, he organized search parties and hired native trackers, familiar with the suspected hide-out area. Aware that the three men would be trying to slip through the wilderness and flee to the US, Superintendent Hussey sent out additional special constables when he arrived two days later. The BCPP posses were assisted by an RNWMP patrol from Calgary and by CPR detectives. Fernie, who had gained a reputation as a tracker during the Boer War, and the Mountie patrol went into the Nicola Valley toward Quilchena, where they picked up the fugitives' trail. When they lost it, Fernie decided to ride back and get more searchers, and he happened to locate the Miner gang on the way. He returned for the Mounties, then the five policemen closed in on Miner and his two cohorts, Shorty Dunn and Bill Colquhoun. Miner tried to bluff his way out, feigning innocence and protesting that they were prospectors who had not been to town for over two weeks. When RNWMP Sergeant J.J. Wilson replied that since they fit the description of the train robbers, they had better come along, Shorty Dunn panicked. Grabbing his pistol, he plunged toward the creek, firing as he ran. The police took aim and several shots rang out in unison. Shorty fell to the ground with a bullet in his knee, still shooting wildly until he emptied his pistols. Miner and Colquhoun gave up without a fight.

Because of legal technicalities, it took two trials to obtain convictions of Miner and his comrades. Both trials were covered dramatically by the newspapers. Though all three men received lengthy sentences, Miner served less than two years before he escaped from the BC Penitentiary and disappeared. He remained free for five years, until he was caught robbing a train in Georgia. Colquhoun died in the BC Pen of tuberculosis in 1911; Dunn remained inside until he was paroled in 1918.

The same spring, another legend began when Simon Peter Gun-an-noot, a hard-working and respected Kispiox chief, fled into the Skeena wilderness. He had been found guilty by a coroner's jury of willfully murdering two mixed-bloods, McIntosh and LeClair, after a brawl in a Hazelton hotel bar. Their bodies had been found the morning after the fight on the trail just outside of Hazelton. McIntosh had been shot through the heart while galloping along the trail on his horse, a shot that only an expert marksman could achieve, and slightly farther on, LeClair lay dead from a similar shot. The jury decided that Gun-an-noot was the prime suspect as he was one of the best riflemen in the district, and witnesses said that as well as fighting with the two men, he had threatened them after they continued to malign his wife and other Kispiox women. A warrant was issued for his arrest and also for the arrest of his brother-in-law, Peter Hi-ma-dan, who had also been in the bar fight.

Provincial Constable James Kirby was sent to arrest them. But when he arrived at the Gun-an-noots' ranch, he was informed that Simon had left on a hunting trip with Peter. His family claimed to have no idea when Gun-an-noot would be back, which made Kirby even more suspicious as the chief was a considerate and protective family man, unlikely to leave for an indefinite time.

The search was intensive during the first year. To keep a close watch on Gun-an-noot's family and relatives, Hussey authorized Constable Kirby to hire specials and guides as required. Expert trackers were sent in, then when a reward was offered, many bounty hunters also stalked the pair in the vast Omineca country. That winter, temperatures fell to 50 below zero and stayed there for three weeks. Many were sure that the Kispiox fugitives had died from exposure, weariness and hunger.

For thirteen years, searchers hunted for the bushwise suspects. The original reward of $1000 was gradually increased to $8000; each increase attracted more bounty hunters and private detectives. Whenever new clues about Gun-an-noot's whereabouts were reported, another search party would head out. Gun-an-noot eluded all of them, and became one of the British Columbia Provincial Police's most famous fugitives.

But if he was free in the wilderness he knew so well, he was also a prisoner to that wilderness, a fugitive who could only live with his wife when she joined him in hiding. It was an increasingly heavy sentence for a man who had been proud father to his children, thoughtful son to his elderly parents and friend to his tribesmen, particularly after Hi-ma-dan surrendered and proved his innocence.

Gun-an-noot finally decided to give himself up, and was held at the Hazelton jail before being transferred to Vancouver. There he and Provincial Corporal Sperry Cline began what was to become a lasting friendship. After so many years in the open, Gun-an-noot suffered severe claustrophobia in enclosed places, so the corporal left the cell unlocked and Gun-an-noot was free to go outside. Some residents found it strange to see the man charged with murder swinging an axe and a few questioned the corporal's wisdom; the former mule packer replied that his prisoner was in jail by choice so why should he be locked in?

Gun-an-noot was escorted to Vancouver for trial by Deputy Inspector Tom Parsons, along with witnesses to the events that had occurred years earlier. Gun-an-noot swore in court that he had not shot the men, but because he had threatened to, he did not know how to prove that he had not killed them. So he had run, hoping that the murderer would be found. Then there was nothing to do but to keep running. The witnesses' garbled testimony was considered useless, and after brief deliberation, the jury found Simon Gun-an-noot not guilty. He finally could return to his people, a free man.

The long pursuit was estimated to have cost British Columbia over $100,000. Speculation continued for years about who had shot McIntosh and LeClair. Gun-an-noot's father was considered the prime suspect by some, which would explain why Gun-an-noot had run for so many years. Then Hi-ma-dan's wife confessed on her deathbed that she had committed the crime, but no one believed her. No further charges were laid for the murders of McIntosh and LeClair.

CHAPTER FIVE

"You are to hire additional specials"
1911–1916

IN SEPTEMBER 1911, Colin Smith Campbell was sworn in as the new
superintendent of the BC Provincial Police. Originally a farm lad from
Ontario, Campbell once said he had been brought up to start work at
daylight and quit at dark, except in emergencies where he just worked
through. He didn't drink, didn't smoke and didn't swear. A taciturn
administrator, he said little, but when he spoke, his men listened. He had
been a member of the Provincials for fifteen years, serving in the
Kootenays, then in Victoria where he helped organize coastal patrols
against bootleggers. Before becoming superintendent, Campbell was
chief constable for the Vancouver District and had been assisting Hussey
with plans for Oakalla, the new provincial prison farm. He had expected
to be the first warden but agreed to accept the superintendency when
Hussey's health forced to him to retire in the spring of 1911.

Hussey died shortly after retiring. At his memorial service, Attorney
General William Bowser praised Hussey's twenty years of service to the
Provincials, recognizing how much he had shaped provincial policing by
developing the 1895 Police Act. Bowser also emphasized how BC had
changed; when Hussey was hired during CPR construction, the population
numbered in the thousands, whereas now "we count our residents in the
hundreds of thousands."

Campbell's reputation for brisk efficiency was quite a change from
Hussey's well-known patience. On one occasion, he walked into the
district office and saw a rookie constable chatting with four senior men,
apparently monopolizing the conversation. Campbell beckoned the young
man into a corner where he quietly advised: "You talk too much. You see,

when you're talking, you're only telling them something you know. But if you would shut up and listen, you might hear something you didn't know."[1]

When Campbell took charge, he had as officers a group of thirteen well-qualified chief constables, seven of whom had served in the force for over twenty years. Some had been with the RNWMP, others had been members of the Irish or South African constabularies before joining the Provincials. In 1911, the chief constables were Walter Owen at Atlin, C.T. Bunbury at Boundary District (his office was in Greenwood), James Maitland-Dougall at Hazelton, William Fernie at Kamloops, W.J. Devitt at West Kootenay (Nelson), Colin Cameron, Northeast Kootenay District (Golden), Arthur Sampson at Southeast Kootenay (Fernie), David Stephenson at Vancouver–Westminster District, E.C. Simmons at Vernon, C.A. Cox in West Coast District, (Alberni) and Joseph Burr in Yale District (Ashcroft). The Vancouver Island District was run by Inspector McMullin from the Victoria headquarters office.

The Provincials numbered 186 men and officers, a small force for a population that had doubled in the previous decade to 392,000. However, the larger cities had their own municipal police forces and Provincials policed there only when the attorney general called on them in special circumstances. Although the BCPP had jurisdiction everywhere in BC, a Provincial apprehending a suspect in a municipality generally turned the captive over to the city force, which laid the charges. The majority of provincial constables continued to patrol independently, keeping peace and enforcing law, recording their daily activities on the three lines allowed in the monthly summary. That made reporting terse: "While apprehending a burglar, a bullet entered my thigh. Burglar taken to lock-up, doctor removed bullet," the constable at Fort George wrote. Then two days later, he reported, "Quiet day, regular duties. Preparing prosecution of burglar."[2]

In the pre-war years, complaints about automobiles grew more numerous. The residents in Goldstream, a few miles outside of Victoria, were typical. Year after year, they filled the Victoria newspapers with letters to the editor, raging against the disruption caused by the automobile trade coming to the local hotels. "They have become resorts for fallen women and men of degraded characters. Carloads of partyers roar up to the resorts from Victoria every weekend and the Constable does nothing!"[3]

However, there was little the police could do. The hotels held liquor licences and there were very few motor vehicle regulations to be broken. Constables could not identify most cars anyway, hidden as they were in swirling clouds of dust. The majority were black Model As and all looked alike; so did their drivers, unrecognizable in dust coats, bulky scarves and goggles. As well, although more regulations were being developed, there were few ways to enforce them.

All anyone had to do to be a legal driver was to pay the local Provincial constable two dollars for a registration number stamped on a leather licence, then hang the licence on the vehicle. As the number of cars increased, so did the number of accidents, complaints and run-ins with horses. The Victoria and Vancouver detachments each had received a Model A in 1910, "to be used for police business only,"[4] but the force did not quickly change to patrolling by car. Most constables continued to use horses or bicycles for short trips.

Superintendent Campbell was much more involved in giving day-to-day directions than Hussey had been during his last few years. A typical day saw him writing to the constable in Nanaimo about switches found open on the Esquimalt–Nanaimo Railway and requesting him to ensure it did not occur again. He wrote to Chief Constable Fernie in Kamloops about removing thistle from a nonresident's property, directing him to bill the owner for costs under the Noxious Weed Act, and forwarded a complaint to Chief Constable Bunbury at Greenwood about a cow carcass rotting in the river that people used for drinking water.

Campbell liked to get personally involved in cases. In 1911, when American authorities reported they were sure that the counterfeiting headquarters of Albert Leon, a talented engraver from Russia suspected

*Colin Campbell, BCPP superintendent from 1911 to 1917.*

*Constable Geoffrey Aston died after being shot by a prisoner aboard the SS* Okanagan.

of manufacturing facsimiles of US treasury bills, were located at Nootka on Vancouver Island's west coast, the superintendent joined a squad of Provincials and two American detectives in the chase. Leon must have known his game was up. When the police arrived at the isolated cove, they found only a massive printing plant, obviously deserted in haste. Three months later, Campbell was notified that Leon had been arrested trying to board a Brazilian ship in New York. It turned out that Leon, in his fight against the pogroms in Russia, had been helping to finance fellow Russian revolutionaries by exchanging his bogus dollars for thousands of bona fide American ones. Numerous exhibits from the Nootka plant were used by the prosecution during his trial in New York. Albert Leon was sentenced to ten years.

Not all police actions ended so well. In 1912, the force lost two men, the first to die on duty since John Usher was shot by the McLeans in 1879.

Constable Geoffrey Aston was shot in March 1912 by one of the prisoners he was transferring from Penticton to Kelowna. When he and the Penticton police chief had arrested the cold-eyed Boyd James, an American army deserter, for an armed robbery in Kelowna, the chief removed James's .44 revolver but missed a .22 derringer. James and his accomplice, Frank Wilson, were held in the Penticton jail that day, then delivered to Aston. Because the robbery had occurred in Kelowna, the charge had to laid there, so Aston and his prisoners left on the *Okanagan*, a lake steamer. James was roped and handcuffed to the top bunk, but he was able to reach the derringer. In the middle of the night, he began coughing and requesting water. As Aston reached toward the prisoner with a glass, James shot him in the head. Then he managed to get the keys to unlock his shackles, and he and Wilson escaped into the night at Peachland when the steamer stopped for freight.

When the doctor pronounced the popular Provincial's head wound inoperable, shock waves reverberated through the province. The forty-year-old Aston was a veteran of the force, having served in Midway, Hosmer and various Kootenay locations before being transferred to the Okanagan. As his life ebbed away in the Kelowna hospital, hundreds of volunteers, militia men and police officers combed the shores of Okanagan Lake and searched the orchards and barns in the hills. Residents were enraged at such violence occurring in their valley. On the third day of the manhunt, two ranchers captured James and Wilson on a wagon road above Wilson's Landing. They tied them securely together and marched them to the nearest steamer landing, where the prisoners again went aboard the *Okanagan* to complete their trip to Kelowna, except this time they were roped to the mast. When the half-frozen pair were unlashed in Kelowna, the crowd on the wharf cheered at their misery. The prisoners were quickly hustled off to jail and charged with attempted murder and robbery later that day.

Ten days later, Aston died. Kelowna businesses closed for two hours so all could attend his funeral. After the service, a long procession wound up to the graveyard, located high on a hill above Okanagan Lake. Aston's horse, with spurred boots reversed in the stirrups, was led behind the hearse.

The charge against Boyd James was changed to murder and he was transferred to Kamloops jail until the spring assizes. The charge against Wilson was dismissed when it was learned that he was actually an innocent bystander whom James had sat with in the Penticton beer parlour moments before he had been arrested. James was found guilty and sentenced to hang. During his last months, he kept trying to escape. Although he was held in leg irons and searched daily, once he managed to conceal a tube of pepper, which he blew into a guard's eyes, and almost broke free. On another occasion, guards found that he had concealed a tiny piece of sharp metal in his shoe and was close to sawing through his shackles. James was hanged on the Kamloops scaffold on August 9, 1912.

Meanwhile, the Provincial Police had lost another member. Just outside of Clinton, Constable Alex Kindness was shot from his saddle as he led a posse in pursuit of two murder suspects, Paul Spitlum and Moses Paul. Almost a year earlier, twenty-five-year-old Moses Paul had been arrested for the murder of William Whyte, a teamster, with whom he had been drinking and arguing at Ah Chew Wye's place the night before. Paul was locked up in the Provincial Police jail in Clinton, but his buddy, Paul Spitlum, gathered up a supply of ammunition and food and helped the accused murderer to escape.

After the jail break, the men proceeded to the old Chinaman's where they eliminated the prosecution's main witness by splitting Ah Chew Wye's head open with an axe. Provincials organized an intensive search, but Paul and Spitlum, both Shuswaps from the Dog Creek area, both expert horsemen and woodsmen, knew the wilderness around Clinton well. Ten months passed without results. At this point, young Constable Kindness replaced McMillan at the Clinton detachment, pleased that he would be patrolling the massive rangelands, a new experience for him. A recent immigrant from Scotland, he had been with the force for only a year, and that in the Vancouver area.

When a ranch hand came rushing into the village on May 3, 1912, to report that he had just encountered Paul and Spitlum on Pollard's ranch, Constable Kindness and Constable Forest Loring, a longtime Provincial who was raised in the Cariboo and happened to be in Clinton on a court case, organized a posse. As the mounted men approached the spot where the fugitives had been seen, the crack of a rifle echoed and Kindness slumped in his saddle. Two more shots rang out, one breaking Loring's wrist. As the riders frantically dismounted, one of them grabbed Kindness and discovered he was dead.

Crouching behind their horses, the posse fired a fusillade at the pile of fallen deadwood from which the shots had come, but none were returned. Moses and Spitlum had vanished again. Provincials converged on Clinton, among them Superintendent Campbell and Chief Constable Fernie who brought a team of expert Indian trackers from Kamloops, including the famous Alphonse Ignace. But the intensified search, which lasted through the autumn months, did not turn up the fugitives.

However, in the meantime, Chief Constable Joseph Burr and Indian Agent T. Cummiskey had been meeting with five Indian chiefs in the region, and in December these conversations resulted in a secret agreement. Shortly after, the tribal leaders produced the two thin, worn-out fugitives. After two trials — there was a hung jury in the first one — Spitlum was sent to the gallows in Kamloops and Paul was sentenced to life in prison. He died eighteen months later of tuberculosis.

The government offered reward money to the Indian Chiefs for the capture of Moses Paul and Paul Spitlum, but they refused it as "blood money." They also declined silver medals of merit, an official thank-you gesture from the BC Legislature. In an official ceremony, each of the five dignified chiefs was formally presented with, then equally formally rejected, the thank-you token.

Losing two Provincials to violence emphasized how rapidly law enforcement needs were changing. Superintendent Campbell and Attorney General William Bowser worried that many areas soon would not be adequately patrolled by one constable as BC's crime rate continued to climb. From 1910 to the start of World War I, policing grew in complexity, particularly labour policing and crowd control.

As inflation ate up workers' wages, the miners in the Vancouver Island and Kootenay regions, most of whom had family responsibilities, were as discontented as the "blanket stiffs," the migratory labourers who travelled throughout western Canada to short-term jobs, carrying most of their worldly possessions in blanket rolls on their backs. Constables regularly reported complaints about low and uncertain payment of wages, dangerous working conditions and usurious prices for food, clothing and hospitalization. Yet although workers were needed, no man individually had much value to an employer; during that period, pressured by the powerful owners of BC mines and railways, the Canadian government continually provided more cheap labour. Thousands of new immigrants continued to arrive in British Columbia, and employers often tried to replace one ethnic group with another willing to work for less money.

Superintendent Campbell directed that labour disputes continue to be policed as they had been under Hussey, using force as a last resort. Adamant that a few policemen could often maintain an uneasy peace, while too large a show of strength might provoke confrontations, he pointed out to constables that only a small percentage of the work force were likely to incite violence, and that many people attending rallies or protests were uncommitted spectators. Small conflicts were usually handled by one or two constables. When a large demonstration occurred, Campbell usually took charge himself, assisted by mature constables and specials he could rely on to stay calm. During the wait for the employer and strikers to find a resolution, Provincials were expected to supervise, to do nothing unless circumstances became dire, to avoid discussion and avoid issuing orders.

When employers imported strikebreakers and the government directed the superintendent to protect them, constables were then expected to use force only to protect nonstriking workers from harm. One former senior constable recalled:

> We were well aware that we would be out of a job if our definition of dire circumstances was not the same as the superintendent's. Although we were armed, I don't know many constables who ever pointed their pistol, let alone used it. When labour situations became violent, which was not often, we used truncheons or batons, usually as we tried to avoid being hit by a swinging two-by-four. The batons were effective from horseback but less so in a brawl. Sometimes the specials under us were difficult to control. But conflicts were the exception, physical confrontation not part of every strike. Men were not very committed to strikes, especially the "blanket stiffs," so it was common to be able to arrest the suspected leaders without encountering much resistance. Whereas now we talk about legal strikes and illegal walkouts, I don't remember any of that then. Such a different world then—communication was slow, there were few labour rules and lots of disorganized confusion.[5]

Although the majority of workers did not belong to any union, rivalry between unions for members became intense as paid organizers competed with each other to sign up workers. A constable's report often identified three or four different unions working an area, trying to increase their membership by criticizing other unions in the area. In addition, as international political unrest grew in the pre-war years, the federal government perceived some work stoppages as a danger to national security and a federal matter. As fear of subversion grew, the RNWMP became involved, particularly in mining areas along the Alberta–BC border, where governments and administrators feared dissidents would create disturbances.

In 1911, two major strikes occurred. A strike by coal miners at Crowsnest Pass in the Rockies dragged on for months, throwing several thousand people out of work and affecting thousands more who were laid off when coke ovens and smelters closed for lack of fuel. There were few strike fund benefits and no unemployment insurance. Provincials reported many workers and their families going hungry. Although constables could in some cases requisition government funds for temporary relief of destitution, starvation because of labour conflicts did not qualify. Some mines closed by strikes shut down permanently, and poverty in the Kootenays increased.

Then the men working on the terminus of the Grand Trunk Railway near Prince Rupert went out, and the dispute grew to involve more than 1,000 men. Additional Provincial police were transported to Prince Rupert on the HMCS *Rainbow* to control rioting; they arrested fifty-six individuals, confining them in a newly built stockade as the local jail only had six cells.

When masses of workers laid off for the winter months gathered as usual in Vancouver, labour organizers became more active in urging workers to join the fight for higher wages and better working conditions. Faction fights within the workers' rallies grew increasingly unruly and at the end of January 1912, the mayor ordered city police to disperse a large gathering. The confrontation ended with twenty-five arrests and some injuries.

Tension grew over potential work stoppages, and as the construction season began again in February 1912, the government ordered close supervision in problem areas. A BCPP constable and an undercover agent kept the superintendent and attorney general informed about work conditions in each major labour region, and about the arrival and activities of any known labour organizers. "Conditions are worsening here, workers getting poor meals and no medical help," the constable patrolling the Canadian Northern rail construction outside of Hope reported, "though a dollar a day is deducted from wages for food, and a dollar a month for doctor's services. No facilities for sanitation, foremen fire workers immediately when they complain about anything. Weather has been unseasonably wet and cold, the very young men generally look gaunt and unwell. Rumours abound that the big-wig Wobblies are coming soon."[6]

When organizers for the Industrial Workers of the World, or Wobblies, began arriving in the Fraser Canyon, the desperate Canadian Northern workers supported the IWW's strategies and agreed to strike. In late March 1912, a walkout began, and it spread quickly throughout the 300-mile construction area between Hope and Kamloops. Records of worker populations in the area vary, but over 4,000 men supported the strike; the Oriental and native workers in the region also stopped working (though, as usual, they remained separate).

Superintendent Campbell arrived to take charge along with chief constables Joseph Burr from Ashcroft, William Fernie from Kamloops and David Stephenson from New Westminster–Vancouver, and to supervise the fifty regular constables and specials brought in. Initially, the Provincials watched as the IWW organizers and strikers built camps in all the villages along the line, quickly becoming organized despite having to communicate in over a dozen different languages. They voluntarily policed themselves and, at their request, Superintendent Campbell closed all saloons for the duration. During the first two weeks, he reported to Attorney General Bowser that the workers remained peaceful in the camps, though there were more complaints about the food each day. He also reported inadequate and rapidly deteriorating sanitation facilities.

By mid-April, the powerful CNR contractors' and sub-contractors' lobby for government intervention succeeded. The attorney general directed Campbell to "prosecute and imprison [the IWW] on every possible occasion."[7] Bowser directed that if men would not return to work, they were to be treated as vagrants and moved out of the area. The Public Health Act was to be used to remove the IWW camps. The superintendent imported an additional 100 specials, and in the third week of April, police began tearing down the camps. They ordered the men to go to work; those who declined were made to board trains and moved out of the area. The police action met little resistance. Thousands of men willingly returned to work, restless after three weeks of doing nothing and increasingly discontented about being kept under much stricter supervision as strikers than they were used to as workers. Known IWW organizers and adherents were arrested: "strikers were sentenced to terms ranging from three to twelve months on such charges as vagrancy, unlawful assembly, intimidation and conspiracy. By June there were 250 Wobblies in BC jails."[8]

Labour unrest continued. The Grand Trunk Pacific Railway construction workers went out again in the Prince Rupert area and additional Provincials and specials were shipped into the area. Workers' support was sporadic and the strike ended quickly and without violence, but a number of additional constables were assigned to the Prince Rupert area until the rail terminus was completed.

In the financial uncertainty and unstable labour climate of the pre-war period, the provincial economy began to suffer. Once again reductions were ordered for all government services, including policing. Superintendent Campbell had to order his chief constables to make radical cuts in expenses, even as the need for law enforcement increased.

In the fall of 1912 one of the largest and bitterest strikes in BC history began in the coal mining towns outside Nanaimo. Miners went out on strike to support Oscar Mottishaw, a member of the gas safety committee at the Extension mine, who had made a report about unsafe gas levels in the mine in June. The owners had dismissed him and apparently black-listed him at every mine on the island. In September, over half of the miners at Cumberland, Extension and Ladysmith became members of District 28 of the United Mine Workers of America and voted to go out on a "holiday" until Mottishaw was rehired. The company, in turn, locked out the miners, then ordered them to sign two-year contracts if they wanted to keep their jobs. Owners threatened to evict miners from company housing if they did not sign. But the miners in the Cumberland region resolved to keep the mines closed by whatever means necessary, and with the hefty UMWA strike fund supporting them, they were in a strong position to fight the owners.

Chief Constable David Stephenson, who was now in charge of the BCPP Nanaimo district, feared the situation would explode into mass violence. When approximately one-third of the white miners signed contracts to return to work two weeks later, along with all of the Chinese miners, who remained fearful of deportation, Stephenson judged conflict would be inevitable. Additional Provincials, including the twelve-member mounted patrol, were sent in. Meanwhile, Superintendent Campbell heard rumours of another factor that might prolong the strike. Not long before,

*The BCPP mounted troop patrolled during the 1913 coal miners' strike on Vancouver Island.*

the Dunsmuir family had sold its island coal mines to Canadian Collieries Ltd., a company owned by the notorious railway builders, MacKenzie and Mann. Some claimed that the new owners considered the strike a convenience. The stock they had issued when the mines changed hands was drastically watered and labour difficulties gave the new owners an excuse to pay poor dividends. Motivation for settlement appeared weak on both sides.

During the initial weeks of the strike, Constable Stephenson reported fewer incidents than he had projected, "an uneasy calm." He dismissed some specials, emphasizing to Campbell that he needed only mature, competent men. Canadian Collieries reopened the mines at Cumberland, first operating with the workers who had signed their contracts, then importing miners by hiring through private British and American employment agencies. Most of the new miners arrived unaware that they had signed on to be strikebreakers.

The striking miners quietly vacated company housing, some bunking in with friends and relatives, others building cabins from old lumber. They helped each other willingly and a new sense of community developed. Men who had laboured six days a week suddenly had time for other activities. As one miner's daughter recalled, "We lived on beans, rice, venison and our big gardens—and lots of humour. Funny, I remember that time clearly, I was ten then, because we were a happy family for a while. All the neighbours were friendly with each other, we had sing-songs, Mom and Dad probably went to more dances—hard-times ones, only cost a nickel—than they ever did. The next year, things got bad. Then we moved Washington and two years later, Mom left Dad and brought us back to Vancouver."[9]

Undercover agents posing as striking miners reported to Superintendent Campbell that the regular strike pay, small as it was, gave men lots of free time and a little money. Strikers met regularly to plan strategy over glasses of beer, enjoying camaraderie as they took their turns harassing the strikebreakers going back and forth to work. Very few were judged to be radicals by the undercover agents who reported on them: "Most are men with little hope of finding work above ground themselves, but with strong hopes that their children will not have to be miners."[10]

However, as the UMWA organizers grew concerned about how the strikebreakers' production was increasing at the Cumberland mines, demonstrations increased. Chief Constable Stephenson summarized the situation at Cumberland on November 20:

> Since early November the striking miners have begun to gather in large groups of up to 500 with wives and families to escort the working miners to and from work. . . the afternoon mobs are especially dangerous as certain of

the strikers spend their time in Cumberland bars and their courage is
enhanced by alcohol. The mob hoots and screams at the non-strikers and
sings the Marseillaise and waves red flags. The women are especially vocal.
They have formed a section of their own and are headed by a band composed
of a fiddle, accordionists and a trombone player."[11]

All that winter, Stephenson's constables accompanied working miners
to and from work. When the most aggressive strikers began attacking
individual strikebreakers on dark back streets, harassing families and
threatening to burn homes, the government posted twenty additional
Provincials and specials in Cumberland. Then, when the mayor appealed
for more, additional specials were hired and sent in, some creating more
problems than they solved. Recruited from the unemployed in Vancouver
and Victoria, they were untrained and inexperienced. Stephenson immediately dismissed twenty-nine of them, but decided to keep seventy-eight
under his close personal supervision. In early December, he also received
seventeen more horses and extended his mounted patrols to all eight of
the scattered Cumberland mines, and to the docks at Union Bay twelve
miles south of town.

By spring, the amount of coal the strikebreakers were taking out had
increased almost to pre-strike levels, as Canadian Collieries brought in
more experienced miners. Stephenson reported each month that more of
the non-striking miners were being beaten and threatened. Then in May
1913, as the UMWA claimed 95% support from members and affiliates,
the strike spread to all the mines in the Nanaimo coal fields, including the
large ones at South Wellington and Nanaimo. "In the summer of 1913 on
Vancouver Island, 3500 men were idle."[12] The Provincial Police and
government administrators prepared for open warfare. The attorney
general informed Superintendent Campbell that martial law would be
declared at his request, but the government preferred that the Provincials
handle the conflict if possible. More specials were sent in as tensions
increased.

Then, in mid-August 1913, as more mines reopened with imported
strikebreakers and with men who had been accepting strike pay the
previous week, the area exploded. Gunshots, dynamite and shouting
echoed first through Ladysmith, Extension and South Wellington, spreading on subsequent nights to Nanaimo, then Cumberland. Newspaper
reports estimated 1,000 men were involved in the riots, blowing up
buildings, stoning strikebreakers and police, chasing families into the
woods before burning their homes.

According to Provincial Police records, as the strikers rampaged,
Chief Constable Stephenson ordered miners at work to stay in the mines
when their shifts were over and ordered all available manpower out to

guard the off-shift miners and to protect their families. Provincials throughout the island and lower mainland were ordered to Nanaimo, and seventeen regular members of the force arrived from Victoria and Vancouver along with additional specials. But the law enforcers continued to be overwhelmed and the police sustained many injuries in the violence. Six reinforcements coming in from Victoria were beaten, and their car was burned. When more specials, nicknamed "Bowser's Bulldogs" by UMWA organizers after Attorney General William Bowser, arrived by ferry, strikers swarmed onto the Nanaimo wharf to greet them. A bloody battle seriously injured three more constables and Nanaimo's police chief, then the mob forced the specials back onto the vessel. After this incident, Superintendent Campbell notified the government that the police could no longer control the situation, and Attorney General Bowser ordered out the militia "in aid of the civil power."

Police officials and the military strategists decided that troops had to be moved in under a tight cloak of secrecy. Police agents reported that miners had been stockpiling dynamite and certainly knew how to use it. Officials, fearing that the whole area would become a massive battleground if strikers had any warning or time to prepare, used an elaborate subterfuge. A private train was booked and the information leaked to the press, including the Nanaimo paper. Then a Canadian Pacific ferry, which had appeared to depart for its normal Vancouver sailing, went instead to Esquimalt where it was transformed into a troop ship. When she sailed, Provincial policemen severed telephone and telegraph lines into the Nanaimo region. The troops landed in complete secrecy.

By August 16, 1913, approximately 1,000 troops were in the area, from the Seventy-second Regiment Seaforth Highlands, the Sixth Regiment Duke of Connaught's Own Rifles, the Eighty-eight Regiment Victoria Fusiliers, the Fifth British Columbia Regiment, the Signal Corps, Canadian Field Engineers and a squad of the Royal Canadian Artillery.[13] The main force, 450 men, landed at the Brechin mine wharf in the middle of the night, along with two mounted guns. Forming into two units, they marched off with bayonets fixed. One unit entered Extension, where the men took control of the devastated town and put out the fires still burning. They also started a rescue operation to collect and aid the terrified, cold, hungry people, many of them children, who were still hiding in the woods. From the Extension area alone, eighty adults and forty-two children were taken by Provincials to Victoria to be housed and fed.

The second unit occupied South Wellington, Ladysmith and Nanaimo. Those troops disembarked at Union Bay and took control of Cumberland. Order quickly returned to the area with their presence. Once military guards were posted on all mine property, strikers kept their distance. Unauthorized meetings were prohibited, as were gatherings in the streets. Colonel A.J. Hall, commander of the militia, consulted with Chief Constable Stephenson and Nanaimo's chief of police and decided that civil authority could only be re-established by making massive arrests. Authorities gave permission to the strikers to hold a meeting at the Athletic Hall in Nanaimo. Once the men were inside, troops surrounded the building and protected the police, who arrested everyone wanted in connection with the recent riots. City police, assisted by Provincials and troops with fixed bayonets, marched the prisoners to Nanaimo's small jail, then onto a ferry to New Westminster for trial.

By the end of August, authorities judged that the danger of large-scale violence was over, and most of the troops left. To supervise the continuing strike, 165 militiamen remained on guard in Cumberland, Ladysmith, South Wellington, Extension and Nanaimo. The Provincial police also retained many special constables on staff and continued to use the mounted troop for patrols.

A number of strikers decided to leave the area but most stayed, assured by the UMWA that they would be supported until the fight was won. Attorney General Bowser directed Superintendent Campbell to continue to employ Pinkerton agents, both to help judge the mood and to seek out the organizers. Pinkerton Agent 29-s infiltrated the ranks of the strikers' most radical wing and his lengthy detailed reports recorded the extremists' mood. "Dec 6, 1913 – a wave of exultation among strikers, which has been caused by the reported acquittal of Crowler, et al. at Westminster," he wrote, after the New Westminster trials of the strikers arrested at the Athletic Hall. "The strikers figure that in none of the subsequent trials will a jury believe the word of a policeman as against that of a civilian. . . One can readily see by the tone and character of the talk that most all testimony for the defense is plain perjury. . . Non union men seemed to have taken warning and have not shown themselves on the streets today."[14]

The special agent reported on the hardcore strikers' activities and feelings from September until January. He was one of the boys, part of the group who met over beers to consider what could be blown up next, but who blew up nothing. He reported that most strikers and their families were surviving on strike pay. Constable Stephenson reported the same thing, forwarding details such as the Nanaimo butcher saying that many strikers had bought Christmas turkeys. The UMWA was reportedly paying out $16,000 weekly to subsidize the Vancouver Island strikers, and though their families made do with little, it was clear that they could survive indefinitely at their current financial level.

When the Pinkerton agent's contract ended on January 28, 1914, he described the most active strikers to Superintendent Campbell by saying: "Law and order are nothing to these men and their doctrine is one of overthrow for every form of law and government now in existence and the establishment of a form which promises the working man complete control of everything and everybody... The local situation is not discussed to extent, principally because there is nothing for the strikers to talk upon unless they at once reach the conclusion that the strike is lost to them."[15]

Finally, fifteen months after the start of the general strike of Nanaimo coal mines, the UMWA announced in July 1914 that after supplying almost $1,000,000, they were going to have to stop payments due to increasing demands elsewhere. Within a month, the largest, most intense labour action policed by the Provincials had ended. But demand for Vancouver Island coal had dropped because of unsettled world markets and because Seattle-area mines had increased their coal production to supply the west coast market. Chief Constable Stephenson reported that many former strikers were working only a few shifts weekly and were finding it economically difficult.

Provincials throughout BC reported deteriorating conditions in work camps. One unemployed man, a European immigrant, arrived at the Prince Rupert detachment with a teenage translator and reported he had been beaten at his camp. After being given a plate of uncooked pancakes for the third morning in a row, he had rushed over to the manager's shack with his plate, screaming in Russian. The foreman and two assistants beat him, then he was fired. The Prince Rupert constable knew the camp, a collection of cold, mildewed buildings infested with lice, but informed the injured man that no charges would hold up in court, as he had started the fight.

Other incidents reflected BC's economic hard times. The muddy little railway town of New Hazelton, for example, was wakened from its small-town slumber one April morning in 1914 by the sound of blazing gunfire. The New Hazelton bank was being robbed in broad daylight for the second time. Reverend Donald McLean rushed home for his .303 Lee Enfield, then ran down the street toward the bank, shouting. Other armed residents appeared from the restaurant, the barber shop and the grocery store and opened fire. But it was mainly the Reverend's sharp shooting that brought down six of the robbers. A seventh masked man disappeared into dense bush at the edge of the village. Suddenly the shooting stopped and a loud silence descended on the town. Then, one by one, the residents of New Hazelton came out of their hiding places, amazed and relieved to find that none of their side had even been wounded.

The injured and dead robbers were suspected to be the same ones — a group of Russian immigrants — who had scooped up $17,000 and wounded a teller at the bank just six months before. When the Provincial constable arrived from Hazelton, he organized a hunt for Bekuzaroff, the man who had escaped with the money. They found blood spots on the trail but no missing bank robber, and a Russian interpreter could get no information from the prisoners. Many people thought the fugitive had perished in the Omineca wilderness; others knew Bekuzaroff was a tough nut. Banished by the Czar from Siberia to rock quarries on an island north of Japan, he had been released, then worked on rail construction in Mexico before travelling north to British Columbia. The constable at Hazelton was convinced that Bekuzaroff had survived, and he kept a close watch on all Russians in the area. But Bekuzaroff never was found, despite a hefty reward being offered for his capture.

The case of the bank-robbing Russians highlighted the problems facing the Provincial Police in the "new" British Columbia. The province was not a happy melting pot. Immigrants were flooding in from around the world, even as the number of jobs available decreased steadily. In larger centres, they chose to live in ethnic neighbourhoods, which made keeping the peace more difficult. It was an era when British Columbians uninhibitedly referred to Slavs as Bohunks, Italians as Dagos and Chinese as Chinks. As one Provincial recalled: "It sometimes seemed that the more a group could fight with those who were different from themselves, the better they liked it."[16] Immigrants were blamed for rising unemployment, and many of British Columbia's long-term residents lobbied politicians to keep all non-English speaking immigrants out, particularly those from the Orient and South Asia.

Asian immigration to BC had been drastically reduced after the 1908 federal orders-in-council required all immigrants from Asia to have $200 cash and to travel to BC via a continuous passage from their native land. Canadian immigration officials claimed that the legislation took precedence over the right of all citizens of the British Empire to migrate to each other's countries, and based entry decisions on it. Then they also tightened screening procedures when it was learned that some East Indian immigrants had earlier been active in Indian politics and had advocated violent means. Because of these measures, Sikh and Hindu immigration had almost dried up.

When the *Komagata Maru*, a tramp steamer, steamed into Vancouver Harbour on May 23, 1914, with 376 East Indian men on board, Canadian officials declared the passengers did not qualify as immigrants and refused to let them land. The passengers' spokesman demanded that they be allowed to disembark as landed immigrants, stressing their rights as British citizens and members of the British empire. Tensions rose quickly, both on shore and off, and Superintendent Campbell was instructed to send extra Provincials to the Vancouver district.

Newspaper editors and the public demanded that the East Indians on board the *Komagata Maru* be barred from landing. They lobbied their

*Police and soldiers escorting prisoners after the August riots during the coal miners' strike.*

*Scene of the shootout outside the Union Bank in New Hazelton.*

federal representatives about the "Hindu problem" and attended public demonstrations against Asian immigration. East Indian residents demanded that the would-be immigrants be allowed to land, and they arranged for the matter to be put before the court. Meanwhile, immigration guards made sure that no one left the ship, which had become a prison with rationed water and supplies.

The suspicious atmosphere was official as well as public. Even as East Indian leaders lectured their communities that the issue must be fought only in the courts, the attorney general ordered Superintendent Campbell to guard against possible insurrection, particularly to stop Sikhs from coming in from the United States. A Provincial constable did arrest one Sikh leader who tried to enter Canada carrying two automatic revolvers and 300 rounds of ammunition, but it was an isolated incident. Months before the *Komagata Maru* arrived, provincial and municipal police forces had been directed to watch for any law breaking by East Indians. At that time, Superintendent Campbell reminded his chief constables that suspected dissidents could be charged with any minor offence – from vagrancy to substandard health conditions – to get them into court, where there was then a good chance they would be deported. But there had been few offences or arrests of East Indians, despite the close supervision.

After more than eight weeks of negotiations and court hearings, the people aboard the *Komagata Maru* were ordered deported. More specials were brought in immediately by the Provincial Police and the Immigration Department, who expected a confrontation. It occurred on July 18 when deportation orders were issued. Tons of food were taken out to the ship, but it was refused in a last-resort ploy to delay the forced sailing. When the tug *Sea Lion* returned to the wharf, 170 Provincials, city police and Immigration Department specials crowded aboard with orders to deliver the food to the ship by force if necessary.

A well-thrown grappling hook bound the tug to the steamer, but the *Sea Lion* sat fifteen feet lower than the *Komagata Maru*, whose passengers began to rain pieces of scrap metal, chunks of coal and fire bricks down on the police, who were packed shoulder-to-shoulder without shelter on the *Sea Lion*'s deck. They were sitting ducks; some were seriously injured. Some Provincials were armed, but they obeyed orders not to draw their revolvers. Four shots were fired from the *Komagata Maru*, striking no one.[17] The barrage continued until a Provincial used a fire axe to sever the sturdy bowline that bound the two vessels together. The tug limped back to shore, where the injured were taken to hospital.

Informed of the latest developments, Prime Minister Borden called out the militia and ordered the HMCS *Rainbow* to sail from Nanaimo. At the same time, he instructed the federal agriculture minister, Martin

Burrell, to notify the East Indian passengers of the navy's orders to supervise the *Komagata Maru*'s sailing. On July 21, the *Rainbow* came through the narrows and anchored a few hundred yards southwest of the *Komagata Maru*, then her heavy-calibre guns were uncovered and aimed.

Vancouver residents speculated whether the would-be immigrants would try to fight the Canadian navy, and they crowded the waterfront for a good view of the confrontation. But the *Komagata Maru* sailed from the harbour without further incident, escorted by the HMCS *Rainbow*, the *Sea Lion* and two Immigration Department launches.

Such dramatic policing episodes were the exception, rather than the rule. Most police work continued to be repetitive, routine tasks. But as war approached, Superintendent Campbell and Attorney General Bowser worried about who was going to be available to perform those tasks, aware that as soon as war was declared, many senior Provincials would join up: staffing and training the force was going to be a problem.

On August 4, 1914, Britain declared war against Germany and, four days later, landed troops in France. Far distant British Columbia reverberated with patriotism, fear and uncertainty. Would coastal cities be attacked by German ships? What was being done to capture German spies living in BC? Would the Japanese invade Canada if they became German allies? What defence system did BC have? Where did one go to join up?

In the weeks after the war began, the BC Provincial Police received hundreds of queries and warnings about suspicious aliens, strange boats, men loitering around railway switches, lights flashing offshore. Constables checked every incident, but as one pointed out, "as we were unsure of what constituted a security risk and what didn't, it was difficult to decide what to do next."[18] Chief constables were instructed to forward all genuine concerns about their area's security to headquarters for Superintendent Campbell to sort out with the military authorities. Guarding bridges and railway lines was given top priority and all BCPP districts were instructed to take charge until alternate arrangements could be made. "In our immediate region, there are thirty-seven vulnerable bridges and two available constables per shift. Can Specials be hired?"[19]

One of the most surprising developments in the war's early days was the unofficial addition of two submarines to the BCPP marine patrol. As Premier Richard McBride organized defences for the west coast, he decided to obtain two submarines being completed by a Seattle shipbuilder for the Chilean government. Ottawa and London delayed making a decision on the purchase, and McBride worried that application of American neutrality law would follow immediately on the declaration of war, which would make the purchase impossible.[20] Despite the fact that all defence was a federal matter, the BC premier purchased the vessels and on August 5, the first day of the war, the submarines arrived in Esquimalt.

111

They were already sailing up the coast when the telegram authorizing McBride to proceed finally arrived from Ottawa: "Prepared to purchase submarines. Telegraph price." He wired back: "Have already purchased submarines." What involvement the Provincial Police had in negotiations and transfer is not certain. A series of police couriers went to Seattle, and two experienced marine BCPP constables journeyed there "on assignment" during the period. Also, Superintendent Campbell requested a Seattle undercover agency to "please supply me with a Spanish interpreter immediately."[21] (All operating directions for the subs were in Spanish.)

For three days, British Columbia had its own navy. It was a tightly guarded secret, so much so that when the submarines arrived off Esquimalt, the shore batteries almost fired on them. Then the federal authorities took them over and the subs initially joined the elderly *Rainbow* and the much newer HMS *Newcastle* as the main marine defence for the West Coast. All Provincial Police craft were also considered to be part of the defence system, even though the current vessels had been assessed years earlier as inadequate for policing purposes, let alone for defence. New purchases had been scheduled for 1912, but upgrading of marine equipment had been one of the police expenditures delayed when the provincial economy had deteriorated.

Provincial police responsibilities multiplied with the outbreak of war, particularly in the lower mainland and on the island. Chief Constable Colin Smith of the BCPP Vancouver district was directed to take responsibility for guarding the wharfs and railways and watching for sabotage, Germans, Austrians or anyone suspected of carrying firearms. His constables posted close to the US border were to search for firearms and watch for aliens.

As expected, manpower was an acute problem. Not only was the force losing men steadily, the municipal police forces of Vancouver, New Westminster and Victoria were also receiving resignations. Yet wartime duties assigned to the Provincial Police force grew weekly. By October 1914, the Canadian War Measures Act was law. All subjects of the German Empire, Turkish Empire or Austro-Hungary Monarchy resident in Canada had to register with the police. In British Columbia, that meant the Provincials. One former member recalled:

> It was quite a task. Not only did the aliens lose their right to communicate with families back in the old country, they were now so limited here. As well, many of them were young men who had been brought to British Columbia as babies, who had no ties with another country. They were bewildered, hurt, as they suddenly were scorned by many who had known them for years, angry that they suddenly were considered second-class citizens in their own country. They weren't supposed to travel to the next

town without my permission. They could no longer buy or use dynamite to blow stumps. They weren't supposed to hunt because they couldn't carry firearms, which would have caused severe hardships for some of them and their families – hunting then was for food! I gambled in many instances, despite the edict, and let them continue to carry rifles. After all, they had to eat.[22]

Internment camps opened across Canada to confine aliens considered to be security risks. British Columbia had camps at Vernon, Nanaimo and Morrissey. Provincial police assisted in deciding who in a district was a possible risk, then arresting and transporting them. Not all internees were locked up because they jeopardized national security. As the war progressed, some became destitute as many employers refused to hire "foreigners." Patriotism grew to fervent extremes in some places and often the constable was the only person to whom the desperate men could turn as they tried to keep their families from starving. In the camps there were regular meals, at least, and their families qualified for public assistance if the "alien" husband and father did not live at home.

Resignations were taking a toll on the BCPP. Many men left to join the Canadian Expeditionary Force or to rejoin military units they had belonged to in England, Scotland or Ireland before coming to Canada. Qualified constables were in short supply, and the ratio of experienced constables to rookies declined annually. Superintendent Campbell authorized his chief constables to hire suitable men within their own districts, a radical policy change that created some problems. The force was again more open to political influence, and some men hired under these circumstances later refused to accept transfers, believing they had been hired to work in a specific place.

Troop and supply movements increased, which meant that guarding railway bridges from sabotage became more important. Chief Constable Robert Sutherland reported from Golden on February 20, 1915: "As there is a number of Austrian and German subjects around Blaeberry, and three troop trains were going East on the night of the 15th, I placed two constables to guard this bridge, until the last trainload of troops passed through."[23] He went on to explain that he had to use regular constables, as the choice of specials available was dismal. Two whom he had hoped would be reliable had recently been found inebriated, asleep in the snow, unaware that the train they were supposed to guard had passed.

There were more family-related problems during the war years as well. In small towns and rural areas, Provincials were asked for many kinds of help, mainly by women or older people who could not control a disobedient adolescent whose father was overseas, or who did not know how to intervene when a drunk was battering his wife and children, or whose grocers refused credit when army dependents' cheques did not arrive. One new recruit found there were few choices for him in offering assistance; he wrote to his district headquarters to report on personal funds he had loaned to three different women "to keep them going until the problem was solved."[24] The chief constable acridly replied that as he could not deliver the mail himself, one had to be realistic. He agreed to request reimbursement, but could not guarantee it would be refunded, and he advised the constable that he had best act accordingly.

Superintendent Campbell resigned from the BCPP at the end of 1916. In September, a provincial election had resulted in a stunning upset when the Conservative government, led by William Bowser, was soundly defeated after sixteen years in power by Harlan Brewster's Liberals. Bowser finally relinquished office to Brewster on November 23, 1914, having delayed transfer on the excuse of counting the soldiers' vote on two referenda. Campbell was considered very much a "Bowser man": the deposed premier was the attorney general who had recommended Campbell's appointment, and the two men had worked together closely during the Nanaimo labour crisis and the early war years. As well, Brewster initially appointed M.A. Macdonald, who had topped the poll in Vancouver, attorney general, and Campbell had reportedly disagreed with Macdonald in his earlier years as chief constable in the Vancouver district. However, after Campbell left, Macdonald resigned because of allegations raised during an investigation into improper campaign contributions. J.W. de B. Farris was appointed attorney general, but the confusion and the delayed appointment of a new BCPP superintendent left most members of the force unsure what to expect from the change of government.

CHAPTER SIX

# "Co-operate fully with the Mounted Police" 1917–1921

B C'S 1916 ELECTION changed more than political parties: voters gave
women the right to a vote and authorized prohibition. The temperance
movement celebrated, the Provincials pondered the difficulties inherent
in enforcing the new liquor ordinances. Confusion prevailed in the early
months because of difficulties in the attorney general's administration and
ongoing revisions to prohibition enforcement procedures. An official
prohibition commissioner, W.C. Findlay, was appointed and liquor inspectors hired; initially they worked primarily in Victoria and Vancouver.
The BCPP, directed to assist the prohibition commissioner, supervised
disposal of stock at most licensed establishments in the rest of the
province.

Prohibition increased the amount of policing required in another way
as well. Outlawing the sale of alcohol did not stop most residents who
used it from seeking a supply. The demand for bootleg liquor attracted an
influx of criminals. "The rich will drink smugglers' imported brandies and
the poor will drink bootleggers' rotgut. But they will not stop drinking,"
senior officials agreed. "Pursuing bootleggers is going to be a massive
task."[1]

During the transition, licensed premises disposed of their stock,
then claimed compensation. A provincial constable or liquor inspector
certified how many hundreds of gallons were poured down drains or
into the snow. Some presumably looked the other way. A former
Provincial explained:

Although we were theoretically barred from having an opinion about Prohibition or any political issue, we of course did, and I didn't know anybody, teetotaller — and there was quite a few of us who took pride in not drinking — or drinker who thought the Prohibition legislation was beneficial or enforceable. Most were sympathetic to the small hotel owners who were being forced out of business and some supervision of how the liquor was disposed of was cursory, particularly since the government was so slow about making payments to the poor blokes. Quantities of wines and liquors were listed as "given away" on the licensee claim forms but most of that was probably used to stock private cellars at cost.[2]

"Prohibition beer" had to contain less than 2 percent alcohol, which satisfied beer drinkers not at all. Charges laid for drunkenness declined as rapidly as the pursuit of bootleggers, smugglers and distillers grew. Hidden stills dripped out home-brew throughout the province, and men who had never broken a law now began to do so. Many respected citizens who would have been horrified to be brought before the court on any other charge were fined for breaking Prohibition laws. The concept of obeying the law changed: men who were normally law-abiding thought nothing of selling a few gallons of homemade brew to each other. Some doctors got rich giving out "drinking" prescriptions for a fee. Bootleggers thrived.

Previously, the penalties for contravening the Liquor Act had been light, considered by many a cost of doing business. With Prohibition, the law's teeth became sharper, imposing automatic prison terms for some second offences. Consequently, bootleggers became cagier and more

*During Prohibition, liquor smugglers became increasingly innovative. At Tête Jaune, police found bottles of whisky stashed inside these butchered carcasses.*

ruthless. Illegal sales were big business, despite the increasing penalties. As another Provincial explained:

> I think Prohibition caused more problems than it cured. Alcohol was manufactured in numerous backwoods stills and sold in the second-class joints in towns. Some of it was pretty dangerous stuff. Owners of such joints would pretend that they made enough to stay open through near-beer sales but we'd know it was not very likely. I recall finding a large supply of liquors behind a removable panel on a soft drink bar. The senior constable with me poured it all out and told the owner that if he tried to replace it, he'd have to charge him the next time. Guess he should have charged him then but it would have meant six months in jail and a $1,000 fine for the fellow. I think that owner closed the hotel shortly after and moved his family to the Okanagan.[3]

The BCPP did most of the policing related to illegal manufacturing, even though distilling alcohol was actually a federal crime. When the Provincials received a tip, they usually followed it up, brought in the suspect, then had a federal inspector make the complaint. Although all costs incurred for enforcing federal statutes were billed to the Dominion, the new superintendent, William G. McMynn, questioned whether it was logical for the Provincial force to be stretched thin enforcing federal statutes, a point that received much discussion in the next few years.

William G. McMynn had been officially appointed superintendent of the BCPP early in 1917. A tall, lean Scot who had joined the Provincials before the turn of the century, he was respected by those who knew him for his legal knowledge. But some BCPP members considered him a questionable choice as he had not policed in the lower mainland or on Vancouver Island. As a constable, McMynn served in Revelstoke and at detachments throughout the Kootenays. He opened the first police station at Midway, between Osoyoos and Grand Forks, then served as chief constable of the South East Kootenay District for seven years. In 1914, he became warden of the new Oakalla Prison Farm in New Westminster, where he remained until he was ordered to exchange positions with Colin Campbell, and he became acting BCPP superintendent in late 1916.

As the new superintendent, McMynn inherited a number of problems caused by the manpower shortage and by recent political interference. Since policemen were exempt under the Military Service Act, and as game wardens at that time were sworn in as ex officio British Columbia Provincial constables, game wardens were exempt from conscription. Between the time the new government assumed office and McMynn received his appointment to replace Campbell, a dentist, Joseph Brown, was appointed head of the Game Department. This new government official began using game warden appointments as a thank-you, both to protect the recipients from conscription, expected to become law within months, and to put dollars in supporters' — or their sons' — pockets. McMynn was enraged by the appointments and apparently reclaimed most of the game warden badges the dentist had distributed.

By 1917, the BC Provincial Police had a strength of 227 men and officers. The officers were mainly men who had risen up through the ranks and included Superintendent McMynn, Inspector T.G. Wynn, Assistant Inspector Walter Owen, Chief Detective J.E. Green at Headquarters, Chief Constables Colin Smith at Vancouver–New Westminster, J.D. Simpson at Boundary, W.R. Dunwoody at Fort George, Thomas Parsons at Fort St. John, A.C. Minty at Hazelton, William Fernie at Kamloops, R.J. Sutherland at Kootenay (North-East), G.H. Welsby at Kootenay (South-East), J.T. Black at Kootenay (West), J.E. Aiken at Lillooet Police District, David Stephenson at Nanaimo–West Coast, Ernie Gammon at Skeena–Atlin, H.A. Taylor at Tête Jaune Cache, J.A. Fraser at Vernon Police District, W. Kier at Victoria Police District and C.S. Cameron at Yale Police District. Those sixteen chief constables represented every populated area of the province. Their reports were used by various government departments and often shaped future development.

Prohibition continued to be a major challenge for the force, especially the importation of alcohol. Along with a growing number of professionals, many amateurs began smuggling. Booze was brought in under a load of potatoes or chickens, in ammunition boxes, in molasses cans or under ladies' skirts. Along the construction of the Canadian Northern Railway, which had its railhead at the top of the North Thompson valley, liquor was brought in to the supposedly dry railway zone in kegs of nails, in jam or lard cans and even in carcasses; two or three bottles easily fit into a gutted hog and quite a supply could be carried in a matron's padded corset. Provincials who made the security checks in railway stations or on paddlewheelers became adept at finding hidden caches, increasingly astute at deciding which butchered hogs to inspect and whose corsets were suspicious.

Corsets and skirts created a whole new problem for the Provincials, as they had little experience policing women. But as women filled in for husbands, sons and brothers off fighting the war, as they rolled up their sleeves, shortened their skirts and went out to work, the situation changed. Growing labour shortages meant that women were operating tugboats, streetcars and fishing boats, as well as working in banks, stores and munitions plants. Although many had previously done similar work, it had been under the guise of assisting a husband or father, whereas now they openly took charge. Some now smoked in public, drove motor cars recklessly — and smuggled alcohol.

"Women are going to require more policing than in the past and that means that we have to develop more adequate policies and instructions of how to police them," Superintendent McMynn noted.[4] Recently, one of his constables had stopped a woman who was driving dangerously and too fast. She was a respectable lady, the wife of a well-established shopkeeper, so the constable was embarrassed to discover that she had been drinking whisky. Then, more to his chagrin than hers, he found four one-gallon cans of whisky in the back seat of the car. The constable conducted the woman and her auto to the station, apparently much to her amusement. But when he arrived, the senior constable instructed him to take her home. No charge was laid, and the woman was placed under a doctor's care, the usual treatment if the wife or mother of a prominent citizen ran awry.

Provincials were much more used to dealing with women of ill repute. For years they followed an unwritten policy: prostitutes were tolerated as long as there were no complaints, and as long as they complied with the town's directives, which were indirectly legislated by local wives and enforced by the Provincials. Some municipalities were more concerned than others about the visibility of "whores," so the freedom of movement allowed to the women varied a great deal. There were almost no complaints in Victoria, where madams and "girls" rode about in open carriages, dressed in the latest finery and shaded by elaborate parasols, but smaller towns were much more strict. Citizens of Cranbrook insisted that the women be allowed to use the streets and stores only at a designated time of day. But the enforced curfews did not always suffice. One young constable was baffled by a complaint that prostitutes were allowed to purchase the same new spring material that respectable ladies would be wearing. The constable's answer was to request them to shop in the next town from now on. But that outraged the storekeeper, also a councilman, who threatened to complain to the constable's superior.

British Columbia had many small towns like Cranbrook. Ethics and morals were debated as families dined together, and many residents considered themselves firm believers in law and order, churchgoers who prayed together for a victorious end to the devastating war, responsible parents with well-disciplined children, concerned voters—some who expected Prohibition "to resolve much poverty and misfortune," others who believed it infringed on individual rights. They expected their constables to embody and enforce these values, and felt free to complain to a constable's superior, or the local newspaper, if they did not approve of how he conducted himself. They were basically kind to each other, around their ingrained social standards. They chatted with each other on the street, shared concerns about bad news from the front, and mourned with those receiving official telegrams about missing or dead relatives. Most Provincials were similar to them, active participants in their communities, family men as well as policemen, as proud and concerned about the world they were building for their children as their neighbours and friends were.

As the war continued, there was a growing restlessness in the work force and the Provincials were soon policing work stoppages and strikes again. The labour movement gained adherents as workers tried to protect themselves against a postwar depression. They protested war profiteering, comparing their own diminishing buying power to the profits enjoyed by their employers. Experts were predicting that when the war ended, chaos would sweep the western countries as workers rejected capitalism. Meanwhile, Superintendent McMynn had been directed to reduce police costs, which he did by not replacing men who resigned to join the armed forces. During McMynn's first year of administration, the force was reduced by 15 percent.

As a result, when miners in the Rocky Mountain mines of BC and Alberta were forced back to work by a federal order-in-council in late 1917, McMynn declared that he could not effectively supervise the area. There had been months of work stoppages and lock-outs, and animosity ran high. The BCPP superintendent agreed that the Royal North-West Mounted Police should take responsibility for policing BC's Rocky Mountain coal-mining area. Although the RNWMP was also short of staff, some of its supporters were adamant that it should become the police force for all of Canada. They were convinced that the federal government had to expand its policing mandate at every opportunity, and questioned the policy of subsidizing provincial police forces with federal funds. In 1916, Alberta had formed a provincial force and some federalists worried about what territory would be left for a federal force by the end of the war. They were relieved, therefore, when McMynn made his concession and the Mounties began patrolling in the mining areas of eastern British Columbia, something that had not been allowed since Sam Steele had established Fort Steele thirty years earlier. The Provincials continued to police the rest of the Kootenays.

A federal order-in-council passed on May 25, 1918 added more categories of men eligible for conscription. Although policemen were still exempt, many felt that they could not stand by while others had to join the fight. Military police started zealously checking out everyone who appeared eligible for the draft. Since the BCPP was not a uniformed force, it was common for members to be ordered into a conscription line-up. One Provincial recalled celebrating a third wedding anniversary in a hotel dining room, when he was abruptly ordered to line up by rude MPs:

> That did it. I told my wife we were going to be destroyed internally if this thing didn't end soon. It was a bad time. The Zeppelins were bombing England and the Allied troops in French trenches were suffocating on

mustard gas and intensified conscription was the law. Men reacted in two ways. Either they joined up or they swore they'd never go. My wife understood—I put in my resignation the next day, even though the chief argued I was letting our area down. Things were past simmering, rather on a low boil. Many were enraged by the Compulsory Military Act, particularly many of the hourly work force.[5]

Albert "Ginger" Goodwin, a miner and radical unionist, was one of the men classified eligible under the new regulations despite ongong health problems. He had received orders to report to a depot in Victoria in June 1918, but he failed to appear. He reportedly had fled to the mountains above Cumberland with friends, also union activists who were considered by government officials to be involved in organizing workers and strikes. Various police forces continually kept track of such individuals; though their activities were usually legal, their appearance in mining areas was considered by government officials as a harbinger of labour disturbances. Goodwin had been tracked for years because he had been part of the Nanaimo coal fields strike in 1914, and had once been vice-president of the Trades and Labour Council as well as secretary of the Metalliferous Workers. In July, the Military Police delivered a warrant for his arrest to Dominion Police Inspector William Devitt, who had formerly been a member of the BCPP, and he began a search for Goodwin.

When reports arrived that he was living in an isolated cabin in the mountains behind Cumberland, Devitt requested that Provincial Constable Robert Rushford of the Cumberland Detachment accompany him, Lance-Corporal George Rowe of the Military Police and Dominion Police Special Constable Daniel Campbell up the treacherous trails. Rushford knew the geography and could guide the trio up through the dense forest to Goodwin's suspected hideout. It would be useful to have a fourth man along; nobody knew how many fugitives were at the cabin. On the second day up the mountain, Constable Campbell became separated from the others. He made his way along a path blocked by dense underbrush and suddenly came face to face with Ginger Goodwin. As Goodwin raised his rifle, so did Campbell, and a single shot rang out. Goodwin fell to the ground, fatally wounded. Later examination showed Campbell's bullet had ricocheted from Goodwin's wrist, parallel to the rifle he was aiming, and into his upper spine. When Dominion Inspector Devitt hurried up, a shaken Campbell handed over his rifle. "I surrender to you, Inspector," he said. "It was either him or me."

In the aftermath of the shooting, the provincial government asked the court to investigate Goodwin's death thoroughly, aware of its possible consequences within the labour movement. BCPP Inspector F.R. Murray was directed to charge Campbell with manslaughter. Further investigation of the mountain established that only Goodwin had been living there at the time of the shooting. Some radical publications were found, but were judged relatively immaterial to the case. At the fall assize in Victoria, a grand jury – which included some Cumberland miners – found there were no grounds to send the matter to trial. The jury ruled that Campbell had fired in self-defence, and he was released. Since then, that verdict has been questioned repeatedly and many attempts have been made to determine what actually happened, and why Goodwin was killed only a few days before amnesty was granted to the numerous men across Canada who were also avoiding conscription.

Even before the assize court was held Ginger Goodwin had become a martyr. On August 2, 1918, a one-day strike was called to protest his death. This province-wide action, the first such strike to be organized in Canada, effectively paralyzed activity in the lower mainland and Vancouver Island in memory of Goodwin, though the Provincial constable in Cumberland reported that miners there – men whom Goodwin had worked with and helped organize – worked their regular shifts. But in other areas, particularly Vancouver, support was broad. Streetcar operators abandoned their cars all along the line, workers downed their tools and longshoremen left the docks to join the massive parade winding through the streets. The people involved were generally orderly, as Superintendent McMynn had predicted.

However, veterans in the Shaughnessy Military Hospital were outraged at the martyrdom of a draft evader and organized an attack against the Vancouver Labour Temple. The bandage-wrapped veterans attacked strikers outside the temple with their crutches and their fists. They were joined by hundreds of other veterans who took possession of the temple. Rioters threw masses of records out the windows and forced union officials to kneel and kiss the Union Jack.

During that demonstration, and at workers' gatherings throughout Vancouver, Provincial and Vancouver police watched the activities without choosing sides, as instructed. Except to prevent serious injury or loss of life, they had been ordered not to interfere with either strikers or protestors. One Provincial recalled standing on the steps of the temple and counting over forty fist fights. His only action throughout was to request veterans to please not use the point of a crutch on their opponents.

On November 11, 1918, the Great War officially ended. In Vancouver, despite a virulent influenza epidemic that kept many people indoors and away from each other, 25,000 people gathered downtown, laughing, kissing each other and dancing in the streets. Throughout the province, whistles blew, bells chimed, bands played and people celebrated. Finally, those who were still alive would be coming home.

The BCPP had gone through many changes during the war years. One major change was the 1918 Game Act, which created a Game Conservation Board and transferred administration of the British Columbia Game Department to Superintendent McMynn as ex officio provincial game warden. Most wardens were retained, though a few considered by McMynn as unsuitable patronage appointments or lazy workers, were not. Some game wardens were transferred into the BCPP, now the agency responsible for enforcing game laws and issuing resident firearms licences, while others became employees of the Conservation Board, concerned mainly with developing controls and wildlife preserves and enforcing the Migratory Birds Convention Act. All BCPP members were directed to enforce game legislation.

Meanwhile, McMynn was studying two other areas. First, from information requested from a number of countries, he was attempting to develop a better system to control automobile drivers and traffic problems. Second, he sought expert opinion about whether to put the force into uniform. Opinion was divided strongly; some felt that one of the Provincials' greatest strengths was that they were not identified by a uniform but were known as individuals paid to enforce the law. They argued that uniforms created barriers. Others felt that because the population had grown too large for personal contacts, and because policing crowds of people was increasingly common, the respect to be gained from a uniform would be a benefit.

In January 1919, the Provincial Police had a strength of 145 men. As well, numerous specials were employed on a daily basis. Superintendent McMynn explained in his report how broad the duties of the Provincial Police had become.

> In addition to policing the Province, they were Sanitary Inspectors for the Health Department, Weed and Brand Inspectors for the Agriculture Department which frequently necessitated special trips in all seasons and hours to avoid delaying shipment of cattle, investigators for the Prohibition Commissioner and Fire Department and tax collectors responsible for collecting about half a million dollars in revenue for the Finance Department during the year under the Game Act, the Motor-traffic Regulation Act, the Amusements Tax Act, the Sheep Protection Act, the Trade Licences Act, the Pool-rooms Act and the Poll-tax Act.[6]

Adding to police duties during the winter of 1918–19 was the devastating Spanish influenza. The epidemic killed an estimated 50,000 people across Canada. Smells of camphor, garlic, whisky, disinfectant and formaldehyde lingered in the air as people tried to ward off the flu. It began with a headache and killed within days. A victim's face flushed deep red as the fever soared. Pneumonia set in and as the patient passed into delirium, severe nosebleeds occurred. If help was not available, many died at that stage.

The Provincials worked alongside nurses, doctors and clergy in the ongoing battle. Many caught the bug themselves as their resistance weakened. But although some Provincials were reportedly quite ill and off work for weeks recuperating, none died. Churches and schools closed, public gatherings and festivities were postponed and funerals, often for two or three people at a time, took place outdoors. Newspapers had difficulty publishing, milk went undelivered and hospital staffs staggered under impossible work loads as the wintery weeks passed and the epidemic continued.

Provincials, especially those in isolated rural detachments, were overwhelmed by the number of people in desperate need of help, food and wood. The illness spread like a prairie fire, quickly incapacitating its victims. One constable recalled those months, which he spent in the Kootenays:

> I remember my partner telling me about going down to check on an old couple who lived about ten miles out of town. I was his backup because the roads were treacherous. If he didn't show up again in five hours, I would have started a search—I wasn't going with him because I was swinging a pick, trying to help dig graves in frozen ground. Anyway, he made it to a mile from their place. As he waded in through the drifts, he realized their chimney wasn't smoking and knew that if they had been without heat long, they would both be dead.
>
> But only the old man was. The old woman, delirious, with damp red bandages wound round her face, still lay in bed beside him. Will bundled her up and lugged her back through the drifts. She survived the icy trip to town and eventually was well enough to move back to the farm.[7]

Another incident the constable remembered was a cold trip he made to check on a family living on an isolated ranch. He arrived to find the mother comatose and the father, normally a teetotaller, drunk. (Conventional wisdom claimed that alcohol prevented the flu.) A five-year-old girl was minding her two-year-old brother and trying to keep a potbellied wood stove going. The constable loaded them all in his Model T and took them to town. The hospital took the woman, though the doctor commented that she probably would not last the night. But the constable was unable to find shelter for the rest of the family, especially as it appeared that the father was coming down with the flu. So he took them home to his bachelor quarters. Luckily, a woman in the neighbourhood who had recovered from the flu agreed to come in, nurse the man and look after the little ones. The constable bunked into a jail cell so the patient could use his bed.

By spring, the epidemic was over, though there were still isolated cases. Superintendent McMynn reported that natives in isolated areas were still experiencing outbreaks as were families of recently returned soldiers who perhaps brought back a different variety of infection.

Most Provincials who returned uninjured from the war rejoined the force. However, quite a number of them quit soon after. Others were fired—usually for drinking, though two were dismissed for taking bribes, previously a rare problem. Police administrators across the continent were experiencing similar frustrations. Why? In Superintendent McMynn's opinion, there were many reasons. Some veterans, tired of commands and discipline, found taking orders intolerable. Others said they found the BCPP changed since before the war. A few explained that the people they were policing had become too different and difficult, and they simply did not like being constables any more.

Policing conditions certainly were worse than they had been before the war. There were more people, many with a growing indifference to obeying laws, and there were more laws, yet the force had fewer regular members. As well, its administration continued to be disorganized as the government tried to keep its promises to revise all civil administration practices. One man, who rejoined and stayed for twenty-one years, explained:

> No hours of work were set down. Even if you worked all night, you were still expected to be there in the morning. No shift schedules—it was come when you were called, do what you were told, seven days a week. You could be fired with a minute's notice. There were no boards of enquiry, just an inspector or the superintendent saying, "I don't think we're going to need you after today." You were gone, one of the unemployed. It was hard, too, because of the number of discontented men, with big chips on their shoulders, who sometimes badgered us for something to do.[8]

The Provincials were not alone in experiencing a high turnover of staff. It was a sign of the times, a period when both the veteran and the working man questioned what he was doing and why. There were many more discontented, restless men who did not fit easily into society. Some came home to find the jobs they used to do were being done by someone else and that they would not be rehired. Others came home angry and defiant because of the administrative ineptness they had encountered during the war and repatriation. Many suffered long-term effects from shell shock and mustard gas. One returned soldier warned the federal Royal Commission on Industrial Relations that whereas five years ago, he had waited patiently for work in Vancouver, existing on 5 cents a day, now he would not think twice about putting his foot through a store window and taking what he wanted.

Policing such men was difficult, and Provincial constables felt they were much more on the defensive. As well, postwar demonstrations, where radical speakers talked of following the Bolshevik example and overthrowing the government, along with a larger radical wing in the labour movement, made law enforcement demanding, often frustrating. Especially so when many Provincials were waiting for improved conditions for themselves.

The federal government had been legislating changes that made planning for the development of the BCPP difficult. When the Armistice was signed, the Royal North-West Mounted Police were at a crossroads. The federal force had only 303 men throughout Canada, partly because many members had gone to fight and were still overseas, but also because during the war years, both Alberta and Saskatchewan had organized their own provincial police forces and a number of RNWMP members had resigned to join them. The RNWMP responsibilities had been seriously reduced. Rumours abounded that the federal force would be disbanded.

However, in January 1919, the Canadian government announced that the RNWMP would be increased immediately to a strength of 1,200 men and would take over the enforcement of all federal laws in the four western provinces as well as continuing to police the North. They would enforce the Customs–Excise, Indian Affairs and Immigration acts, as well as "all Orders-in-Council passed under the War Measures Act for the protection of public safety and to generally aid and assist civil powers in the preservation of law and order whenever the Government of Canada may direct."[9] They would replace the Dominion Police, initially in western Canada, and assume its responsibilities. The Dominion Police force had less than 150 members across Canada, who guarded federal establishments such as the Esquimalt dry dock, policed aliens and worked closely with Customs and Immigration officials. During the war, the force had hired many special constables to pursue aliens and draft evaders. When it was disbanded a decade later, a few men became Mounties but most transferred to the Customs and Excise Department or took early retirement.

The Provincial Police and BC politicians pondered the consequences of the Mounties' broad mandate. The federal government had the right, of course, to enforce its statutes. They wondered why, in view of the relatively small number of infractions annually, were the RNWMP planning to set up regional detachments? Was it because political unrest and potential revolution were growing threats? Was the provincial government planning to use the RNWMP for all policing, as Prime Minister Robert Borden wanted? Some BC legislators thought it would be cheaper to contract with the RNWMP to do all policing; others argued that a strong provincial police force was a necessity, that transferring all policing to a

The man-sized target for shooting practice was invented in 1917 by T.W.S. Parsons, later commissioner of the BCPP, when he was chief constable of the Fort St. John district.

Communications changed for the Provincials with the advent of shortwave radio.

federal force negated some of the provincial independence built into Confederation.

The matter came to a head in the mining area of the southern Rockies, where the Mounties were already policing at the province's request. The RNWMP superintendent of the Rocky Mountain Division recommended that his men take over most duties in Fernie, Natal, Michel and Corbin. He argued:

> To obtain the greatest efficiency, we should assume General Jurisdiction, with the exception of the enforcement of the liquor laws and Municipal matters. By doing so our prestige and authority amongst the foreign element and general public would be greater, and we would be in closer touch with everything that went on. It would also do away with any danger of overlapping in work, or clash in authority with any other Force stationed in the [Crowsnest] Pass.[10]

The superintendent went on to recommend that the RNWMP become responsible for all registration of alien enemies as a means of keeping track of the volatile labour situation. Premier John Oliver objected. The provincial government was responsible for maintaining law and order in most labour disputes and, he explained, since many labour radicals did not hold Canadian citizenship, the BCPP used alien registration as a way to keep track of them. Premier Oliver also declined the RNWMP offer to do the general policing in the east Kootenays. Nevertheless, RNWMP Commissioner A. Bowen Perry increased the number of men and the number of detachments in BC. Provincial officials remained unaware of how many RNWMP men were being transferred in until they actually arrived.

Shortly after the transfer, Newton Rowell, president of the Privy Council and the federal minister responsible for the RNWMP, asked Commissioner Perry why so many RNWMP were transferred to British Columbia. Rowell believed that the force was distributing itself too widely and "ought to be more concentrated in central points."[11] The commissioner's reply outlined the amount of work required to enforce the Inland Revenue Act, Indian Affairs and Immigration regulations, as well as to patrol the international boundary. Perry said:

> I had in mind, if the Government of Canada expects to be kept fully informed of the conditions existing in every portion of western Canada, it is necessary to have men stationed pretty widely, as for instance, my distribution in BC provides for. You will notice that detachments are at practically all mining and industrial centres, and in the more important centres, a number of detectives have been assigned to duty.[12]

The commissioner pointed out that he could best aid the civil power by having strong reserves stationed at central points; for instance, the squadron at Vancouver could be moved quickly into other trouble spots as required.

Train cars full of horses and gear marked the RNWMP arrival in British Columbia. Headquarters were established at six locations: the main headquarters of Division E (British Columbia) was in Vancouver, under the command of Superintendent F.J. Horrigan. Sub-district headquarters were opened at Grand Forks, Kamloops, Prince Rupert, New Westminster and Victoria, much to the amazement of the residents and the local Provincials, who had no previous notice of their arrival. Commissioner Perry decided that additional small detachments would be established as required and that for geographical convenience, Kootenay East and Peace River would be in the Alberta Division. The RNWMP took over all Dominion Police functions, as well as all federal statutes previously enforced by the BCPP.

By March 1919, the number of RNWMP stationed in BC had increased from fewer than 20 men to over 250. The Vancouver squad alone had 154 NCOs and men, 6 officers and 160 horses. The new arrivals took over the Dominion Police buildings and equipment whenever possible, such as at the Esquimalt dry dock, but in most areas, new quarters and stables were built. This was achieved quickly and efficiently, without financial delays; quite a contrast to the usual budgetary constraints on the BCPP.

There were many other differences between the federal and provincial forces. Whereas the BCPP opened detachments with one or two men, and expected constables to decide how best to enforce law and maintain order in that area, the RNWMP was shaped by military tradition and procedures. Its constables trained and paraded as part of a troop of men directed by NCOs, who in turn were directed by officers. Though Mounties often patrolled in pairs, or individually on occasion, the general organization and discipline in the federal force was based on the military model: individual Mounties had much less autonomy than Provincials had. The benefits also differed. The Mounties were provided with barracks-style room and board, whereas Provincials had to find and finance their own accommodation. Some were assigned the spartan living quarters attached to most BCPP offices and jails in exchange for guarding prisoners if necessary, but each man was responsible for his own keep and health needs. As well, Provincials paid part of their horse expenses, whereas the Mounties were supplied with excellent horses, fully subsidized. And the Provincials received no clothing allowance, whereas the Mounted Police received a full uniform.

The Mounties' uniformed image attracted attention. Some British

Columbians were delighted by the brilliant scarlet dress uniforms and RNWMP representatives were invited to grace many functions. Other residents, unhappy at having policemen so noticeable and at having so many of them, asked their elected representatives why so many federal policemen had been moved into British Columbia. They queried related costs and constitutional rights. Superintendent McMynn's opinion is unrecorded, except for a brief memo instructing all Provincial constables to co-operate fully with the Mounted Police.

Because the federal force was unfamiliar with most of BC, its members were supplied with information and maps from provincial detachments and sometimes travelled with a Provincial constable. On such joint patrols, it must have fascinated a BCPP constable to watch his federal counterpart try to record all details for his report. Each Provincial's monthly report still had to fit on one double legal-sized page, three lines for each day — wordiness in Provincial Police reports was frowned on. If charges were laid, details were included in the accompanying information form. Or, if necessary, a constable elaborated in a letter to his chief constable. The Mounties, on the other hand, reported in complete detail on all their observations of an area.

As well as developing an overview of federal policing needs, the RNWMP surveyed BC's work force and its ethnic mix. Concern about the labour situation in the four western provinces increased in the early spring of 1919, particularly as workers advocated worker control of industry and the use of general strikes to achieve political change at three major conventions: the British Columbia Federation of Labour, the Alberta Federation of Labour and District 18 of the United Mine Workers.[13] They also voted for One Big Union at the Western Labour Conference in March. The powerful OBU was organized to facilitate political change and organize general strikes as required; the first one was tentatively scheduled for June 1. BCPP undercover agents reported that both workers and growing numbers of unemployed people were increasingly nervous about the slow economy, yet unsure who to support. Many people, worried about the growing number of Bolsheviks reported in Canada, wanted nothing to do with "those revolutionary Red radicals, those advocates of force and violent revolution."[14] But many were impatient with what they earned from their labours compared with the owners' benefits: many did not have the right to vote, their wages bought much less than they wanted and their expectations of a better future decreased as unemployment grew. Unions gained members throughout postwar Canada, from 15% of the work force in 1918 to 22% in 1919 (union membership dropped back down to about 10% of the work force in 1920 and remained there through 1939).[15]

British Columbia was considered volatile, suspected of having the most passionate union adherents and the greatest number of revolutionary radicals in Canada. Both provincial and federal governments prepared for the confrontations that appeared inevitable. "Undesirable" immigrants were deported on any excuse. BC had many to choose from, as her ethnic mix was so varied. For instance, according to RNWMP records, Prince Rupert had approximately 5,000 residents, a population composed of Chinese, Japanese, Norwegian, Swedish, Italian, British, American, Ukrainian, South Asian, native Indian, Montenegran, Greek, German, Austrian, Danish and Finnish people. As police forces considered non-English-speaking workers more vulnerable to radical agitators, officials agreed that the province, particularly Vancouver because of its large population, was like a volcano threatening to erupt. Undercover agents in the OBU reported a general strike was almost a certainty. But much to the dismay of RNWMP Superintendent Horrigan, policing co-ordination details had not been settled. Although Vancouver's municipal police force was in charge of policing the city, the attorney general had the right to transfer that control to Superintendent McMynn and his Provincial Police, or to ask for federal assistance. Horrigan assumed that he and his squad in Vancouver would be on the front line and was concerned about who would be in charge. However, when he asked, Attorney General de B. Farris replied that he would wait to decide that until he knew what the crisis was.

Horrigan, worried that the provincial authorities did not recognize how serious the situation was, and that his men might be put in an impossible situation by the expected strike, wrote at length to his commissioner on May 6, 1919, to summarize current speculation and rumours and his own concerns.

> As you are aware, about half the men here are only recruits. In fact the majority of both horses and men have had very little training, and still in the face of that the people of Vancouver expect us to protect their lives and property against a mob of ten to twenty thousand. To me this is most serious.
>
> It seems to me that between Vancouver and Victoria we should have two thousand Infantry and Artillery... It is really too bad that we have not two or three ships sailing up and down the harbor at the present time. The moral effect I am sure would be wonderful.[16]

When the RNWMP commissioner passed Horrigan's letter on to Rowell, the president of the Privy Council wrote a conciliatory letter to the BC attorney general on May 16, 1919:

> We, of course, fully recognize that the initiative and responsibility in connection with the maintenance of law and order in each Province rests with

the Provincial Government, and with the Municipal Authorities, and that any action we might take should be in co-operation with, at the request of, the Provincial Authorities . . . anything the Federal Government can do to assist in maintaining law and order in your Province will be most cheerfully done . . . If, in order to secure co-operation in effort and a thorough understanding, you thought it desirable to have a small committee, of which you will be chairman, to consider matters which might arise affecting the public safety . . . This letter is to assure you of the whole-hearted co-operation of the Federal Government.[17]

Premier Oliver responded on May 28, 1919:

This Government is only too willing to co-operate with the Military Authorities and the R.N.W.M.P. for the purposes set forth. I may intimate however, that one of our difficulties with this whole matter has been that the Mounted Police and Military Police do nothing unless they refer to Ottawa for definite instructions.

This was instanced strikingly in the recent Princeton riot when Inspector Newson and 2 men were sent to deal with the matter, and finding 75 aliens in insurrection at Princeton . . . [some had left] he did absolutely nothing with the remainder.[18]

The Princeton strike was a work stoppage by railway construction workers that started in early April and grew as 600 workers in the area went out on strike. When rioting began, the two Provincials stationed at Princeton expected assistance from the six Mounties in the area, particularly as those rioters considered the most radical were aliens. But the Mounties did not become involved, even when the RNWMP inspector arrived from Vancouver to review the situation. Superintendent McMynn pointed out to Attorney General de B. Farris that his two men could not be expected to handle a mob of several hundred men. If the Provincial Police did not receive support in labour disputes from the RNWMP, McMynn would have to give his men authority to hire specials, as they had done in the past. Debate over the policing issue continued much longer than the strike.

"As the Mounted Police are not constituted for the purpose of relieving the province or municipalities of responsibility in the preservation of law and order," the president of the Privy Council replied to Premier Oliver on June 5, 1919, "but solely for the purpose of protecting federal property and enforcing certain particular federal laws or regulations, we do not think they should act or interfere in local matters in any province, except upon the request of the government of the province." He then discussed the Princeton situation and assured Premier Oliver that he had requested the RNWMP commissioner to give Superintendent Horrigan, his commanding officer in BC, "authority to act in such cases without reference to Ottawa."[19]

Provincial officials, still concerned about the number of RNWMP who had arrived in BC less than three months earlier, angry that the Mounties had not assisted with the Princeton strike when requested and hesitant about the RNWMP superintendent's projections, did not set up the committee Horrigan wanted.

Meanwhile, a massive general strike began in Winnipeg in mid-May. Though authorities expected the strike to spread across the country, the government of British Columbia did not agree with Horrigan that a show of strength was necessary or beneficial. Perhaps because of experience gained during the massive Cumberland strike in 1912 and 1913, the provincial administrators, de B. Farris and McMynn decided that it would be more effective to establish the lines of authority only if the need arose. The taciturn McMynn, who did not believe in reacting to speculations about what might happen and who believed, like Campbell and Hussey before him, that too many policemen and too much show could create difficulties, met with Horrigan to discuss the situation. He assured his federal colleague that action would be taken promptly when necessary. He also assured Horrigan that the BCPP had heard the reports of radicals stockpiling bombs too, but in his experience such rumours often were blown out of proportion.

Attorney General de B. Farris decided that in a dire emergency, Brigadier General Clark, commander of military forces in Vancouver, would decide when the RNWMP should be called out "in aid of the Civil powers." However, much to the frustration of provincial authorities, that did not satisfy the RNWMP. Commissioner Perry formally objected that his force was not a military body and that such an order placed them "in the hands of the Military Authorities to the extent that it would be embarrassing to the Officer Commanding to refuse although in his judgment the proposed action might be inadvisable."[20]

As the debate continued, the crisis passed. The predicted riots on the west coast did not occur. Even as the general strike in Winnipeg built to a bloody climax on June 21, and many BC workers walked off their jobs in support, incidents of violence and property damage were few. Provincial Police undercover agents reported that most workers listened eagerly to radical speakers, but many disagreed with them.

Meanwhile, the federal police force, now called the Royal Canadian Mounted Police, continued to expand its presence in British Columbia. Some people in the province objected. Were not many small communities being over-policed? Why were so many RCMP detachments needed? What about the massive costs involved? What was the long-term federal government plan? It was suspected that the Dominion government wanted eventually to do all policing.

Individual members of the provincial force carried on as usual, except that they no longer enforced any federal statutes. A constable would call a Mountie, and the two forces co-operated easily in most instances. But not always. Differences in how they policed did create some difficulties.

When the RCMP sergeant for the Port Alberni detachment made his first patrol of the reserves on the west coast of Vancouver Island, he concluded that the Indians there needed close and constant supervision. Constable Will Williams, the Provincial stationed at Clayoquot, who previously was responsible for the area, disagreed and tried to explain why to the sergeant, who then reported him for having "a marked antipathy to the RNWMP."[21] The matter was forwarded to Superintendent Mc-Mynn, who ordered it thoroughly investigated.

Williams had joined the Provincials in 1911 and had been stationed at Kaslo before going overseas during the war. After he returned to the BCPP in 1918, he had been assigned to reopen the Clayoquot detachment. When Williams and his new bride arrived at the tiny fishing village, population 10, where it rained twenty days out of every thirty, they had to make habitable the ancient police station with its attached living quarters. They cleaned out sand, which had been blowing into the unoccupied building for three years, and rebuilt the damaged roof. They painted and scrubbed and Constable Williams began making patrols in a rented boat. The only contact with the outside world was the CPR steamer, which called at Clayoquot every ten days.

During his year and a half there, Constable Williams regularly toured the numerous tribal and fishing camps in the district, often accompanied by one of the missionaries. He reported few problems and was impressed by the natives' well-being. He got to know most elders and received their co-operation when needed, as did the Indian agent. Many natives made return visits to Clayoquot, stopping in for a cup of coffee with the constable, or with his wife if he was away on patrol. Other than two missionaries, there were usually no white men in the area. Williams was apparently respected by the natives who invited him and his wife to many of their social functions.

Investigation of the RCMP complaint revealed that the sergeant perceived the natives somewhat differently than Williams: he believed the Nootka were being treated too leniently. Among other things, he reported that a fourteen-year-old girl was cohabiting with an Indian man, apparently quite customary; game laws were being broken; a New Year's potlatch had taken place with the Provincial constable's permission, and gifts in the amount of $200 had been given away. The sergeant reported: "I am also informed that the Indians consider it a great crime to beget twins, and that one of these unfortunate offspring invariably 'die'. With proper Police supervision no doubt it could be found that these deaths were not always due to natural causes."[22] He was also concerned that neither the missionary at Ahousat nor the one at Clayoquot appeared to have much control over the Indians, and though there were nearly twenty children of school age at Clayoquot, only three attended the Mission school "and the parents simply refuse to send their children to school, saying that the Father poisons them, and they only die. I reported this matter to the Indian Agent who is asking for instructions regarding getting the children to school."[23] One thing that apparently surprised the sergeant was the number of Indians who owned their own power launches and made good wages fishing or working at canneries. "There is no reason they should receive any more lenient treatment than other class of people," he wrote.[24]

Superintendent McMynn transferred Williams to Campbell River and closed the Provincial detachment at Clayoquot. Before the Williamses left, the Indians gathered from many villages and gave them a send-off feast, the children giving Mrs. Williams bouquets of flowers, the adults presenting the family with a carving. According to the 1884 Indian Act outlawing the potlatch, the feasting and gift giving were illegal. But Provincials had for decades interpreted the laws with discretion. A few followed the law to the letter, barring and interrupting all feasting, while most considered the circumstances and often decided the occasion was a celebration, not a potlatch. Traditionally, when they were the enforcement officers on reserves, they dumped any alcohol they found and charged drunks, but they laid few charges under the potlatch legislation.

Policing on reserves was usually accomplished co-operatively by the Provincials and the elders. Although native people grew increasingly concerned about the infringement of settlers and industry onto their lands and waters, individual BCPP constables were normally welcomed when they visited and given help when they needed it. The force continued to employ many natives as guides and assistants. At the same time, the BC government's concern about natives diminished. An increasing non-native population, the growing mission system and number of residential schools had increased white dominance. And Indian agents controlled many facets of natives' lives, particularly if they were geographically easily accessible. However, in the Chilcotin, the Fraser Canyon, the Cariboo, the North and many coastal areas, most Provincials policed the Indians in their areas much as Constable Williams had. That created some difficulties when the RCMP took over the policing of Indians; they were used to following written law and detailed instructions from superior officers and assumed the Provincials' system was the same.

Despite the transfer of some responsibilities to RCMP, there was no shortage of duties for the Provincials. There was a massive population boom in BC after the war, and policing needs were increasingly diversified. As the number of cities with municipal police forces grew, the BCPP became the co-ordinating law enforcers as well as the rural force. Criminals were much more mobile than in the past, so keeping track of suspects or searching for wanted men became more necessary, and the BCPP developed a system of tracing known offenders. How an individual committed a crime was often as telling as his fingerprints, so when it could be established that a suspect who used a certain method was in the area, it often shortened the pursuit dramatically. If it was established that he was geographically too distant to have been involved, his name was crossed off the suspect list.

The known-offender system worked well because communication had become much faster. Telephone and telegraph lines went down much less frequently and were repaired faster. Constables could send warnings out about suspicious men moving from one area to the next, confer with each other more easily and request instructions or additional support as required. Superintendent McMynn reported to the attorney general at the end of 1920: "the men are conscientious, with good integrity, and only one dismissal was made this year, and that for drinking. Much less restlessness than last year...We are in immediate need of patrol boats but have obtained adequate vehicles for the present."[25]

*Roughing it in the bush, a constable on patrol uses the frayed end of a pack rope to lather up for shaving.*

By 1920, there were about 25,000 licensed motor vehicles in the province. The Provincials were becoming quite innovative in their methods of patrol. In March 1920, the first motorcycle highway patrolman in North America went into action:

> Inspector Frank Murray, a huge man about six foot five with a mop of white hair, told me to take the motorcycle and patrol the Island Highway. "I want you to pay particular attention to the buses, we are getting an awful amount of complaints." At the end of the week during which I had trailed the buses through clouds of dust, I reported that the bus drivers were the best drivers on the road. They hugged the correct side all the time, went up every hill in low gear, never exceeded the speed limit. The thing that caused the complaints was that the public was appalled at the size of buses. They had never seen anything so big on the highway before![26]

As most BCPP detachments obtained Model Ts, distances shrank. A constable could be summoned by telephone, get into his auto and be ten miles out of town in less than half an hour! Distances that had once taken days were now travelled in hours. The Provincials' marine fleet had also grown and having additional boats helped keep track of the many new logging and fishing settlements along the coast. But the expanding number of people there necessitated more patrols and rescue missions, and more searches for suspects taking refuge in coastal hideouts. Despite McMynn's continued lobbying for more vessels, the BCPP's marine fleet was not large enough to perform adequately all the duties expected of it.

Since its enactment, Prohibition legislation had become a confusing mishmash of amendments that were difficult to interpret and to police. Abuse of the permit system and bootlegging were rampant, and enforcement was almost nonexistent. "Over 300,000 prescriptions were issued from the date of the prohibition law to April, 1919, during which time only nine doctors were prosecuted for flouting the law. Equally abused was the permit system which allowed directors of corporations or industrial establishments to keep liquor on hand for emergency purposes."[27] When Premier Brewster had died in March 1918, a compromise candidate, John Oliver, assumed leadership and BC's administrative policies underwent a series of conciliatory changes. Since liquor use was the hottest issue, Oliver held another referendum. On October 20, 1920, voters chose controlled government sale of liquor over complete Prohibition. Then, on the wave of the referendum's success, a general provincial election was called for December 1, 1920, delaying formation of the Liquor Control Board. Meanwhile, the Provincials were unsure of what the provincial law actually was about liquor, but the federal law about manufacturing was clear, and they continued unofficially to assist both the RCMP and Customs and Excise in enforcing it.

Even as Liquor Control Board alcohol became available in the spring of 1921, many isolated stills continued to drip away as bootleggers made a fortune supplying moonshine to natives, who were still prohibited from buying intoxicants. Legally, supplying alcohol to natives could be either a provincial or federal infringement: selling liquor to natives was a provincial offence; manufacturing it and selling it was a federal one. But in the 1920s, both activities dropped off quite quickly, for two reasons. Friends of natives obtained quality alcohol at reasonable prices at government liquor outlets, and some bootleggers switched to being rum-runners when the Volstead Act (1919) imposed Prohibition in the United States. Transporting illicit alcohol south of the border became a much more lucrative business than bootlegging within the province.

As long as the Canadian Customs and Excise taxes had been paid on the alcohol, transporting booze to the US broke no Canadian laws, so neither the BCPP nor the RCMP was involved — until the competitive trade started attracting hijackers into British Columbian waters. Then there were gun battles out at sea, and some derelict wrecks and corpses washed up on Vancouver Island beaches.

In the same period, another battle intensified along waterfronts in Vancouver, Victoria and New Westminster. The federal Department of Health requested that the RCMP mount an anti-narcotics campaign, and a war against drugs and opium began. As distributors became cagier and their methods became more elaborate, Provincials, Mounties and Municipal policemen sometimes co-operated in trying to untangle confusing webs of evidence.

One such joint effort resulted in thousands of dollars worth of narcotics being washed away, probably among rocks and driftwood on a lonely beach. A ring of drug smugglers planned to steal the Powell River Company's executive boat, but because the engineer of the *Iphis* always transposed ignition wires, the thieves could not get the big cruiser started. Someone heard them frantically trying and called the Vancouver Cordova Street police headquarters. They notified the Provincials and sent two municipal constables down to the Royal Vancouver Yacht Club in Coal Harbor. Those first two constables, guns in hand, crept cautiously aboard the cruiser and soon discovered a broken skylight. Just as they were about to apprehend the lawbreakers, they found out hostages had been taken. Two Provincials arrived; one of the policemen yelled, "Get some gas!" to make the three suspects nervous. It worked. Everyone knew veterans who had been permanently damaged by wartime gassing, and all types of gas were equally feared. By the time reinforcements came pounding down the wharf, the would-be pirates had announced they were throwing out their pistols and releasing the two hostages.

As he came out, one man tried to dump a suitcase overboard, but a policeman managed to grab it in time. It held a chart of Juan de Fuca Strait, a short-wave radio transmitter and a receiver. The chart was marked off Cape Flattery with a bold cross and a plot line was pencilled in from the First Narrows to the cross. Shortly after, a fishing vessel with a Provincial and an RCMP officer aboard, both dressed in fishermen's clothes, chugged from Victoria to Cape Flattery and waited. The next day, the *Empress of Russia* passed almost exactly over the spot that had been marked. But vision was limited because of drizzle and there was a chop of eight-foot waves, so it was impossible to know whether anything had been thrown overboard. The gigantic passenger ship was searched in Vancouver the next day, as were all ocean liners, from stem to stern. Customs and Excise men examined all disembarking passengers even more thoroughly than usual but found nothing.

Then one of the suspects under arrest decided to talk. He explained that a "colonel" had approached them in Vancouver, apparently because of their reputations as quality organizers, and had offered them a good price to pick up an oilskin package off Cape Flattery. Detailed planning had gone into the manoeuvre, and he was sure that package had gone overboard, even if they had not made radio contact. The Provincials who patrolled those waters searched thoroughly for information on an oilskin package, reportedly held afloat by three small red buoys, but nothing was ever discovered.

Superintendent McMynn continued to work toward reorganization but as he pointed out to the attorney general, it was somewhat confusing to project what duties the BCPP would be performing in the next decade. Federal and provincial lawmakers had not designated clearly the areas of responsibility; many municipalities had organized their own police forces but expected immediate Provincial assistance in emergency situations. And some knowledgeable individuals projected that all policing would soon be federal. Before McMynn could reorganize anything, he had to know what he was to reorganize. Only then, to use one of his own expressions, could he "get on with it."

# CHAPTER SEVEN

"Maintain proud standards"

1921–1932

THE WAR AGAINST NARCOTICS went public in 1921. Vancouver newspapers carried numerous stories about the increasing use of opium and other drugs by whites as well as by Chinese. They also initiated a citizens' campaign to assist with the fight, arguing that drug use was everyone's concern. The number of papers sold skyrocketed as drugs became a popular topic with readers, and reporters became as investigative as the police. RCMP undercover detectives and the various drug reporters exchanged details as they delved for information. Newspapers in all lower mainland cities joined in the massive publicity campaign; almost every edition included a story about drugs.

The *Vancouver Sun* began running a series of "first-person experience" articles by J.B. Wilson, a reformed addict. "PROVINCIAL POLICE LAX IN CURBING DRUG SALES," blared the headline on May 9, 1921. "Dope Peddlers Found On Busy Streets as Well as Back Lanes, Says Wilson; Foreigner Found Selling Drug Over Table. The Provincial Police are evidently willing to let the drug business flourish, but surely the Provincial Government is not unaware of the menace of this noxious traffic in our city . . ."[1] Three days later, Wilson wrote:

DRUG EXPOSURE CAUSES MASS MEETING TO BE CALLED TO FIGHT EVIL – Vancouver Citizens interested in the fight to stamp out the drug traffic in this city will meet tonight at the City Hall . . . It is planned to launch at the meeting an organization to be known as the White Cross Society, under whose direction the anti-drug crusade will be continued . . . I am going to make an appeal at that meeting on behalf of the fallen and broken men who are addicts – slaves to the pipe and the needle . . . I am in touch with the Royal Canadian Mounted Police, that splendid body of officers who are bending their energies to rid our Canadian soil of the Oriental filth of the drug traffic . . ."[2]

Almost every supplier and user lived in a city with a police force, and it was municipal police who laid the majority of drug charges. Attorney General Alex Manson ordered Superintendent McMynn to investigate charges of police laxity as the BCPP had authority to enforce laws anywhere within the province and, at the discretion of the government, to assume policing from a municipal force. McMynn directed Provincial Inspector Frank Murray to examine drug enforcement, though both McMynn and Manson doubted that the local drug trade was as large as newspapers were implying. In fact, Provincials experienced with opium users questioned whether its use was increasing; they agreed there was definitely more opium smoked in the Vancouver area as users moved there from other places. But new users of opium became quite ill, which discouraged them, as did the amount of paraphernalia required to smoke it. They worried more about cocaine: its new users, more each year, were usually youths.

The Customs Department seized a variety of drugs aboard the ocean-going liners that regularly docked at Vancouver but reported some of those shipments were in transit to the United States. When the RCMP began assisting Customs officials with searches of vessels, the amount of contraband goods seized increased rapidly. On February 2, 1921, the joint federal forces confiscated 146 cans of opium, some cocaine, a large quantity of Scotch whisky and many cigarettes and cigars from the *Empress of Asia*, but laid no charges against crew members suspected of smuggling.

Since opium use had been ruled illegal in 1907, the Provincials and municipal forces had been fighting its distribution, taking users before the court and methodically pursuing suppliers. They were usually lenient with aging, unmarried Chinese men who smoked small quantities regularly, but less forgiving of suppliers. Some of BC's administrators were also concerned that the anti-drug campaign was being used by some to inflame public opinion against the Chinese, such as Wilson's statement about "the Oriental filth of the drug traffic."

Anti-Orientalism was strong in British Columbia. After the war, as competition for jobs grew, Oriental labourers were frequently replaced by veterans, especially on railways and in the pulp and paper mills. Many employers, powerful men who were no longer desperate for labourers, felt that the province had more than its share of Orientals. The general opinion was that the war against opium users would serve just fine as a pretext to get rid of as many "celestials" as possible. Newspaper articles filled with unsubstantiated "facts" strengthened their position. "DRUG SQUAD OF THE RCMP—Many Convictions, Seizure and Fines Registered in Four Months," proclaimed the Vancouver *Province*.

> The campaign against the drug traffic started some months ago . . . developed from the determination of the authorities to check the spread of the drug plague. Late in December, the RCMP was instructed to assist, acting as agents of public health and not as officers enforcing the criminal statutes . . . Members of the silent squad of the force went to work. They co-operated with city and the municipal forces in every way and this co-operation has engendered the good feeling already existing . . . The investigations of the squad have uncovered matters almost as interesting as drug finds. Caches of ammunition and arms were discovered in parts of the Chinese quarters and in one case, a hoard of $10,000 in gold was found . . . There is a large element of law-abiding Chinese that is also anxious to have the traffic eliminated, but there are others who are active in it.[3]

Groups of white English-speaking residents continued to lobby Ottawa to prevent further immigration of Orientals, claiming that it would be the first step in halting the drug trade. Provincial police reported a growing nervousness within various Chinese communities as they were cast as villains. Most opium charges were pressed against Chinese men who had a pipe of opium now and then, as they had for years, so municipalities questioned the point of keeping them prisoners. They also questioned the expense: who paid for a prisoner's keep depended on the seriousness of the crime, and the statute being broken. Under the Drug & Opium Act, the penalty for smoking opium was usually $400 or two months' imprisonment, and increasing numbers of offenders chose to serve time, which created a dilemma for municipalities who were billed by Oakalla for their residents' imprisonment.

In June 1921, the city clerk for North Vancouver wrote to the RCMP commanding officer in Vancouver:

> I am instructed by the Board of Police Commission of this City to respectfully point out, with respect to the raids which are being made by your Department, that the estimates of the Police Department are being "shot all to pieces" by reason of so many being sent to Oakalla, and in so far as we have ascertained, the raids . . . have not resulted in catching the parties supplying opium or other drugs, at least in any quantities. The City Police department has been gathering the most of these same men in, periodically . . . [4]

The RCMP assistant commissioner, responsible for the force in

EIGHTY-FIVE PER CENT OF ALL THE CRIMINALS SENTENCED IN VANCOUVER COURTS ARE DRUG ADDICTS

The Vancouver Sun, after a thorough investigation of the situation in Vancouver, is convinced that the illicit drug traffic is the biggest menace to health and happiness that this community is facing.

It used to be feared that our young men—occasionally some of our young women—might become addicted to booze.

The menace to the youth of Vancouver today is not whiskey. It is DOPE.

To eradicate this menace The Vancouver Sun feels would be the kind of public service a great newspaper should give a great city.

Dope must go in Vancouver. The dope peddler must place this on the list of forbidden cities.

Beginning tomorrow, The Vancouver Sun will print details of the dope traffic in Vancouver. The Vancouver Sun will give the actual names of traffickers and addresses of places where dope may be obtained. It will deal in specific cases. When The Vancouver Sun has done the organized dope traffic of this city will be broken up.

The Vancouver Sun has employed trained investigators to expose to the light of day the dark secrets of the pernicious traffic.

This paper will co-operate with Chief of Police Anderson and the Vancouver Police Department in the fighting of the drug evil.

Important announcement of the anti-dope campaign will be published by The Vancouver Sun Tuesday morning.

*In 1921 the* Vancouver Sun *newspaper waged a war on drugs with feature articles exposing the illicit traffic.*

British Columbia, reported the complaint to Commissioner Cortlandt Starnes:

> The demeanour of the officials of North Vancouver has not been very cordial, as far as we are concerned, and although we have no absolute proof, I strongly suspect that there is some kind of understanding, which our activities have somewhat upset. The N. Vancouver City Police have been trying these cases heretofore under the Code, and not under the Opium & Narcotic Drugs Act. This enables them to give a very much lighter sentence, and these fines have been, I believe, paid readily heretofore. The heavier fines imposed under the Opium & Narcotic Drugs Act rather upset their calculations.
>
> I think that if it is made clear to the Attorney General's Department that in all cases under the Opium & Narcotic Drugs Act, the fines must be paid to the Federal Government; and that in the event of a prisoner going to gaol at Oakalla, the expenses (which amount, I think, to 50¢ a day) would be defrayed also by the Federal Government, the difficulty might be in a large measure solved. In any event, this is a matter that should be adjusted, otherwise I fear we shall have a good deal of trouble.[5]

BCPP Inspector Frank Murray continued to study the issues and report to Superintendent McMynn. He described the municipal forces and the federal force as "tripping over each other in their zeal."[6] Municipal policemen who had previously enforced Prohibition or pursued bootleggers switched to seeking drug abusers. In early 1922, public meetings to discuss drug issues also began discussing Chinese immigration. Attorney General Manson met with representatives of the Vancouver Branch of the Asiatic Exclusion League and attempted to explain the facts behind the much-publicized statistic of 801 drug convictions in 1921, mostly Chinese people. However, the situation remained unchanged and there were continuing demands for "no more Oriental immigrants."

Though the number of RCMP members and detachments in BC worried some residents and caused others to question their Members of Parliament about the cost of having so many policemen, neither Superintendent McMynn or Attorney General Manson wanted the BCPP to resume enforcing federal statutes. It was too costly and time-consuming. As they planned for the next decade of policing, they anticipated that the RCMP would continue to handle all federal matters.

By the end of 1922, the Provincial Police force had 153 officers and men, a reduction of 13 from the previous year. A larger number of specials had been hired for temporary duty during that period. Constables were still waiting for the better salaries, benefits and reorganized promotions system promised to them after the war; many wondered whether they should change careers. Then, early in 1923, the legislature passed a new

Police and Prisons Regulation Act. Finally the legislation was in place to expand the Provincial Police force. The Act provided for improved equipment and facilities and the hiring of additional Provincials. It changed the BCPP chain of command, creating more senior positions to allow for faster promotion and varying pay ranks. Constables were paid by years of service, creating a seniority system. New members were probationers during their first year. Chief constables became inspectors or sub-inspectors, senior constables became staff-sergeants, sergeants or corporals, depending on responsibilities and qualifications. The previous title of inspector was changed to assistant superintendent. Reporting procedures changed so that more details about each incident were recorded, and copies were kept at the detachment, district office and headquarters. As he introduced the new Act, the attorney general also announced that, at Superintendent McMynn's request, a new superintendent was being sought to oversee the reorganization.

Shortly after, when Attorney General Manson asked Lieutenant Colonel John H. McMullin to become the next superintendent of Provincial Police, the highly regarded McMullin accepted the appointment on two conditions: a guarantee that he would encounter no political interference, and the government's assurance that reorganization of the force, as outlined in the new Act, would progress immediately. Once the government agreed to those conditions, McMullin was sworn in as superintendent in March 1923. Provincials throughout BC expected that long overdue changes were about to be made.

As Superintendent McMullin started to implement the new Police and Prisons Regulations Act, BCPP members realized that a new style of administration had also arrived. According to a number of Provincials who worked under McMullin, he was an impressive organizer. Naturally reticent, saying no more than was absolutely required, he assessed the world through the smoke of his ever-present pipe. McMullin had patrolled many of the fourteen districts in BC. He exuded calm and was known as a perceptive listener and a man who did not tolerate fools or laziness gladly. "If we choose to tolerate those who perform less well than they are able," he once told a young constable, "we are creating a poor standard. What standards do you want for the force you are now part of?"[7]

During McMullin's first few months on the job, he visited most district headquarters, stopping at all detachments en route to meet and talk with the men. McMullin was proud of the comradeship within the force, and of the BCPP's good reputation with the public, and he let his men know it. To the Provincials, he quickly became the "Old Man," respected and liked. McMullin was well respected in Ottawa as well. He had earned a history degree in England, then served with the Third Hussars in India, moved to Canada in 1893, and was awarded medals for his service in the

*Easter, 1932, Provincials parade in strength down the main street of Ashcroft. The police were in the area on strike patrol.*

*The BCPP mounted squad performed for the public regularly. Their human arch was a popular manoeuvre with spectators.*

South African war and World War One. Manson hoped that McMullin's spotless reputation, excellent contacts and tactful style would enable him to sort out the province's policing dilemmas, which were increasingly becoming front-page news.

Previously, policing in British Columbia was not very newsworthy. Members of the BCPP were used to receiving little publicity, except for the usual crime reports, the occasional commemorative story about the force and announcements of new superintendents or changes in policing policy. Provincials were not easily identifiable to the public; they did not wear uniforms and they seldom gathered as a group. Each region had its constables who were well known in that area, but the constable was more often a topic of neighbourly gossip than a newspaper story.

Depending on which residents were asked, a constable would have been judged as doing too little or too much. People held strong opinions about how government spent or wasted money, and often informed the constable about them. However, Provincials were taught to have no opinions in such discussions. Law and order was still maintained by visiting with people, by knowing what was ordinary and what was not, and by talking a lawbreaker into correcting his or her ways. In both rural areas and towns, residents and constables knew each other, often by name. A farmer in his field, a waitress in a coffee shop or a young boy fishing from a bridge were all sources of information, and although much patrolling was now done by vehicle rather than on foot or horseback, a constable still stopped to chat. As well, he was expected to prevent law breaking. He would drop in on the offending party and explain why he might have to lay a charge, adding, as he set a time limit on solving the problem, "wouldn't it be best for both of us if I don't have to?"

Effective as it was, such policing did not make interesting newspaper copy, and the BCPP received little publicity compared with the RCMP. With the arrival of the Mounted Police, newspaper stories about law enforcement began generating reader attention. Stories about the drug traffic from an "insider" perspective, for instance, attracted the most readers and were given top billing. According to some Provincials, accuracy in these stories was often less important than continued public interest.

In February 1923, concerned citizens in Vancouver, including some powerful businessmen, organized an Anti-Narcotic Drug Association and invited Attorney General Manson to attend their second meeting. They wanted to know what Manson was going to do about the drug problem and the police situation. Since the RCMP's arrival in 1919, Vancouver had almost twice as many policemen as previously. Some of those attending complained about that as "inefficient and unnecessarily expensive," while others queried why drugs had been allowed to grow into such a problem. Some suggested that the Provincial Police take full responsibility for policing the city, replacing the municipal force, particularly in light of growing suspicions about police honesty. Manson was told at the meeting that some municipal policemen were unreliable and that two of the RCMP engaged in pursuing drug traffickers were apparently open to bribes.

Back in Victoria, Manson wrote to Sir Lomer Gouin, the federal justice minister. He explained the accusations circulating about the RCMP and other drug enforcement officials, and suggested putting a couple of special investigators on the case. Manson offered to share the costs of the investigation and requested that the men be supervised by his department. The justice minister agreed, and he passed the problem on to RCMP Commissioner Starnes. During the same period, McMullin became superintendent. So it evolved that Starnes and McMullin were appointed to supervise an undercover investigation, to be made by RCMP detectives Frederick Syms and C. Cox.

At the same time, speculative drug stories continued to be daily front-page news, with RCMP investigators often quoted as sources. At Manson's direction, McMullin questioned the RCMP about the wisdom of its drug squad co-operating with reporters as much as they were. Perhaps it jeopardized investigation and indirectly increased drug use? They were also concerned that an increasing number of Orientals who had never smoked anything were being harassed by both police forces and the public.

Co-operation between the RCMP and Vancouver's municipal force was almost nonexistent: in the matter of policing drug activities, each force apparently spent a good bit of time investigating the other's undercover agents. BCPP Chief Constable Forbes Cruickshank reported that despite the large number of arrests the RCMP continued to make, few dealers had been apprehended and the arrests of users created little change to the overall drug scene. But Manson and McMullin knew their limitations; they could only question the RCMP. Though the BCPP could replace municipal police forces if the attorney general so ordered, the provincial government had no such power over the federal force.

Vancouver's drug world became crowded with secret agents. The BCPP investigations of the municipal force continued as the RCMP investigations of the RCMP drug squad and Customs officials began. When the two RCMP agents, Syms and Cox, arrived from the east, they had two brief meetings with the attorney general, then one with Superintendent McMullin and Inspector Cruickshank before going undercover on the streets of Vancouver. In mid-March, as they began establishing contacts, Syms reported that the drug traffickers were well-protected and "it will take some time and scheming to get on the inside."[8] They visited the drug traffickers currently serving time in the penitentiary, including one reputed to be the drug king of Vancouver. But they gained little through that source and found penetrating the underworld in Vancouver more complex than they had expected.

At a meeting with Manson in late April, Syms recommended that two or three special agents be engaged by the provincial government, "preferably from the East, one to be placed in the Customs Dept., the other two, for the purpose of working their way into the confidence of the Drug Traffickers, with a view to checking up on the activities of the respective Police Officers, and also as a means to work back to the heads of the Drug Traffic."[9] McMullin concurred. However, the attorney general questioned whether there was any hope of getting evidence: would he end up only with rumours, like those Syms and Cox had learned, but no evidence that would stand up in court? Syms suspected the motives of RCMP Special Agent #23, having discovered that #23 and a man who had bribed a Customs official had boarded the *Empress of Russia* before she cleared Customs, but his suspicions meant little without evidence of what they did aboard ship. The same special and an RCMP constable were also suspected by the BCPP of having taken drugs and money from a house they went to search, but no charges had been laid.

Summarizing the meeting and Attorney General Manson's concerns in a report to Commissioner Starnes, Syms explained that he had not been able to interview either the special or the RCMP constable, as both had recently been discharged from the federal force and had disappeared. He also reported that "very bad feeling" existed between an RCMP staff sergeant and a senior Customs officer who suspected him of wrongdoing, even though the Customs man "admits that he has no grounds to prove that this Non. Com. Officer is not carrying out his duty honestly." Syms reported irregularities but no evidence "against the Vancouver Detachment of the R.C.M.Police, especially in regard to Staff Sergeant Munday and S.A. #23."[10] He explained that the staff sergeant's motives were also suspected by the BCPP, as he had twice allowed the Crown's main witness in narcotic cases to leave Vancouver after the witness had been subpoenaed. In the first case, the assizes had been delayed until the witness could be brought back. In the second case, charges against a sea captain had to be dismissed after the staff sergeant allowed the prosecution's main witness to write a report and depart for South America. The Provincial constable involved swore that the staff sergeant was aware the subpoena had been served when he took the witness's written deposition of evidence and allowed him to leave, but there was no concrete evidence.

Those incidents weakened Attorney General Manson's confidence in the investigation, particularly when he learned that Syms questioned the complaints made about the staff sergeant, believing they showed "the conditions that exist between Provincial Police Officials and our Office."[11] Manson decided against hiring additional men. "I have advised the Attorney General that so far as the actual enquiry is concerned, nothing further can be done," RCMP Detective Sergeant Syms reported. "It now remains for him to decide whether or not any action shall be taken between the Departments concerned, as to verification of these different inferences . . ."[12]

In May, the RCMP commissioner agreed that Syms and Cox should end their investigation. Meanwhile, on reviewing the events with Superintendent McMullin, Attorney General Manson decided that Syms' investigation was inadequate and he requested that the Dominion government make further inquiries. While that request was under consideration, the RCMP continued to arrest numerous small users. Then in August, Customs officials at Victoria arrested two RCMP agents for illegal possession of opium and pipes, apparently with BCPP assistance. The men were later convicted.

As tensions between the drug enforcement agents increased, the Privy Council of Canada appointed J.P. Smith, a prominent lawyer from Toronto, to hold a Royal Commission to delve further into the situation. During November and December, he held hearings in Vancouver and Victoria, the evidence accumulating to over 3,000 transcribed pages. When Commissioner Smith refused to take judicial notice of the convictions in the Victoria case, Manson's representative, E.P. Davis, a Vancouver lawyer, made the charges against the RCMP narcotics squad in general, and specifically charged Colonel Wroughton, head of the RCMP in British Columbia, with inefficiency.[13] Then on December 6, after a dispute over the province's right to re-examine a federal prisoner, BC withdrew from the Royal Commission. Smith announced that the Commission would continue without a provincial representative. On January 28, 1924, after six weeks' consideration, he ruled that the evidence failed to substantiate charges of RCMP members trafficking in drugs.

When the findings of the Royal Commission were reported, the Vancouver *Daily Province* reported Manson's comments to the legislature: "in government circles here, the exoneration of the mounted police came as no surprise . . . a new commissioner should be appointed to carry on the investigation as the government is not satisfied with the conduct of the commission by Commissioner Smith."[14]

During 1923, drugs were not the only source of provincial–federal conflict over policing. Alan Neill, the MP for Upper Vancouver Island, had continually attempted to reduce the number of policemen in BC: on March 16, 1923 he had written to the minister of justice:

I may be mistaken, but I am under the impression that I was informed by the Government [of Canada] last year that they had asked the Government of BC if they desired the RCMP to remain longer in the province, and that the reply was in the negative. May I trouble you to enquire if this is true? As an illustration of the overlapping I may mention that the Valley where I live, which is some 15 miles long by say 10 wide, and sparsely populated, perhaps one thousand inhabitants in all, we had recently two North West Mounted Police, one Provincial policeman, two Municipal Policeman, one Indian Policeman (White man), a Game Warden, a Fishery Overseer, and a Fire Warden. Since then, one of the RCMP has been removed, and I had the Indian policeman transferred but even at that you can see what the situation is.[15]

Shortly after, the justice minister announced that twenty-four RCMP divisional posts and detachments in BC would close. However, he did not announce which ones, when or where. Superintendent McMullin queried who would enforce Dominion statutes, but the issue was undecided. In May 1923, shortly after the joint drug investigation ceased, RCMP detachments at Kamloops, Nelson, Stewart, Midway, Trail and Port Alberni all closed. Within days, the men, their horses and much of their equipment were gone and the buildings boarded up. Provincial Police in those locations temporarily resumed enforcing specified Dominion statutes.

During the remainder of 1923, the members of parliament from BC had continued to question the number of RCMP in the province. Then, as the Royal Commission hearings ended, Neill demanded most detachments be withdrawn, as had been agreed earlier, even though RCMP Commissioner Starnes had recently defended the RCMP coverage in BC, particularly for policing natives. Neill replied:

As to the Indian Dept. needing such services, the Indian Department has been running since confederation without the aid of the Mounted Police, from the time when the Indians were uneducated savages. If the Indian Dept. were able to have justice enforced in those days with the help of the Provincial Police, why cannot it do so today with the aid of the same Provincial Police, when the Indians are educated and more lawabiding than the same number of whites?

Have the Indians got worse since 1918 or 1919? To the extent of requiring these Mounted police be scattered all over the Province? An answer to these questions will either condemn or support my claim that the maintenance of these small stations in country points already fully covered by Provincial Police are a source of irritation to the public, of very unnecessary expense and a reproach to any Govt. claiming to exercise due economy . . .
There might be a detachment at Vancouver and another in the interior . . . but

I question the necessity... There are two stations in my district where they [RCMP] are particularly uncalled for, Alert Bay and Cumberland.[16]

Neill had received a variety of complaints from members of the native community around Alert Bay on an RCMP sergeant's methods of policing.

Almost all Mounted Policemen were withdrawn from British Columbia in early 1924 and Provincial Police again began enforcing all Dominion statutes in areas without federal agents. Superintendent McMullin proceeded with reorganizing the BCPP, taking into account that most detachments' duties had again broadened to pre-1920 responsibilities. The force was now divided into A, B, C and D Divisions, A having two subdivisions, Victoria and Vancouver, complete with fingerprint experts and detectives. Thus there were six divisional headquarters, sixteen district offices and eighty-three detachments. Each member was assigned a regimental number and measured for a uniform. All police motor launches were painted an identifiable light grey and two new vessels were ordered, increasing the Marine Department's equipment to seven launches and six powerboats.

McMullin finished writing the *BCPP Constable's Manual*, initially begun by Hussey and updated by McMynn. Designed to fit in a shirt pocket, the leather-covered booklet contained fifty pages of concise instructions covering the basics of Provincial policing. It instructed a constable as to his duties, limitations and general deportment as well as carefully outlining court procedure. There were directions to cover most situations a constable would encounter, under the subheadings General Duties, Suspected Persons, Vagrancy, Disorderly Conduct, Murder, Fires, Public Meetings, Arrival of Boats and Trains, Streets and Highways, etc. Another section informed a constable how to conduct a criminal prosecution before a justice of the peace or police magistrate, giving step-by-step directions and outlining the relevant provisions in the Canada Evidence Act, which a constable needed to understand before presenting a prosecution. Then court procedure was dealt with, including how a constable was to behave: "Details are disclosed in cross-examination which oft-times are unknown to the prosecutor, and the constable should make a note of them when they occur, so that he will have them for future reference." Courtroom etiquette was summarized:

Fairness in the manner of examination by the constable is advisable... In case of dispute the Constable must take the ruling of the Court, even though he may think it a wrong direction. He may argue strenuously before the decision is given, but he must not argue at all after it is once given, as it can do no good, and perhaps will do considerable harm to his case... In any

*Each new decade brought technical advances that made it easier to identify suspects. Here, Sergeant Bailey classifies a set of fingerprints.*

*A mounted BCPP, in full uniform.*

153

argument such as this before an inferior Court, the constable is urged not to unburden the whole statutory and case law on the Court. Common sense argument, along with references to Statutes of the Province and Dominion, giving section and page is far better than a lengthy address.[17]

For the first time, new BCPP members had concise written instructions of what was expected and how they were to proceed. Still, as comprehensive as the manual was, it did not cover everything. A young constable who had been on the force for only a few months before the manual was distributed recalled welcoming the small blue book enthusiastically, grateful to finally have written directives. When he was ordered out to an isolated detachment that had been without a constable for months, he felt well-prepared. Shortly after his arrival, he had to take a case to court.

> I methodically read the new manual and followed it step-by-step to prepare my case, checking by telephone with an experienced constable about sixty miles away on any details which were unclear to me. But then I found out that I had to open court, too, and realized that I did not know how. And when I tried to phone to find out, the wire was down again. The manual did not say how to do it nor did any of the untidy jumble of papers left by the previous man. Nothing! Finally I approached the magistrate with my dilemma, just as he started into the courtroom. He looked at me blankly, then said, "just say something, laddie. Start with Hear Yea — when you stop, I'll start."[18]

By mid-1924, most Provincial Police were smartly attired in khaki and dark green. The uniform consisted of a long, tailored khaki jacket with dark green epaulets, brass badges and buttons, a khaki shirt, a dark green tie and riding-style khaki whipcord breeches. The breeches had a dark green stripe down the outer leg and leather inner-thigh patches. Strathcona boots, buffed to a high-gloss brown, were doubled-laced to mid-calf over the breeches. Spurs were added for dress occasions. A Stetson-style hat, a Sam Browne belt with a handcuff pouch and revolver holster along with a green lanyard, which clipped to the pistol butt, completed the uniform. For motorcycle and marine patrol or whenever a Stetson was inconvenient, a khaki military-style cap was used. When more convenient for duty, plain khaki trousers and brown shoes could be worn instead of breeches and boots. In winter, a black peajacket with brass buttons and shoulder insignia was supplied, along with a helmet-style leather hat and a set of oilskins for wet weather. From sub-inspector to commissioner, the custom-tailored uniforms had gold-threaded chevrons and sleeve markings, and detailed gold-braid decorated the caps. "It was an incredibly comfortable uniform made of high quality wools — you could sleep in it in the bush, brush it off the next day and feel well-dressed," one man recalled. "And in the winter, I sometimes actually felt warm."[19]

Most Provincials welcomed the switch to uniforms, mainly for the automatic identity the uniform gave but also because they now were finally supplied with work clothes. Policing was hard on clothes, and until now the men had received no subsidy. But some voiced hesitations, saying: "perhaps the uniforms will build barriers, make us too much apart." While most Provincials agreed that uniforms would certainly be effective in policing crowds, supervising traffic or patrolling labour disputes, they also knew that some people would feel less comfortable with the local policeman. Didn't the uniform make the man wearing it appear less accessible, too authoritarian?

The Provincial force had always prided itself on its approachability. Over the years, in little communities and out in rural areas, some constables had been regularly sought out by individuals with a need to talk to someone, the constable being the only one he or she could think of who might be able to help solve a problem. "What should I do about an elderly neighbour who needs care?" might be the question. Or it might be about a wife who was suspected of being suicidal, or a husband who was drinking up all the food money, or a son who was turning wild. Or it might be just the need to talk, to sit and explain one's frustrations about the government or a neighbour and to have someone to listen and suggest solutions over a cup of coffee. If people could not discuss something with family or friends, they turned to a minister, priest or constable. "Will those people feel as comfortable if the guy is wearing a uniform?" some of the old-timers asked.

However, the uniforms arrived and were mandatory attire for most Provincials. A few of the older members, who had never been much interested in what they were wearing anyway, compromised by wearing some of the issue: one day, the Stetson and shirt; another day, the peajacket and maybe the tie with a blue shirt. One famous character, whose policing record and integrity were held up as an example to young constables, was remembered as never having worn the whole uniform at once. But although that drollery was tolerated from a few, the other 99 percent were expected to be in full uniform, pressed and polished.

While the BCPP reorganized and became a uniformed force, the governments sorted out who was policing where, and individual Provincials investigated a growing variety of crimes. Two have become well-known incidents. In July 1924, a young nursemaid named Janet Smith was murdered, and her body was found in the home of her employer, F.L.

Baker, a wealthy Vancouver businessman. Initial investigation by the Point Grey municipal police was inadequate, as was the first inquest. Manson authorized McMullin to investigate the matter discreetly; McMullin recruited Inspector Forbes Cruickshank, chief of the Vancouver division of the BCPP and a highly respected senior member of the force; Cruickshank in turn authorized a private "commission man" to abduct the Bakers' Chinese houseboy and try to extract information from him. Public opinion was on Cruickshank's side: many people assumed immediately that because he was Chinese, Wong Foon Sing was the murderer and that drugs were involved in the crime. In any case, kidnapping an Oriental man to "closely question" him was not considered unfair or unethical by most Vancouverites in the 1920s.

The Janet Smith murder was a difficult case for the BCPP. Forensic science was in an embryonic stage, and the Point Grey municipal force had made serious errors in gathering the initial evidence. Public opinion was inflamed for months, and there was subtle and perhaps direct pressure on the force not to embarrass one of BC's most influential families. As the case dragged on with no charges being laid, there was increasing evidence of corruption and coverup at all levels, from the local police to members of the legislature.

By the mid-1920s, smuggling liquor into the United States had become big business, attracting big-time criminals. Rum-running became increasingly violent. During the first years of Prohibition in the US, most west coast rum-runners purchased shipments of bonded alcohol in international waters just off BC, then smuggled the cases of booze past the US Coast Guard and Customs to lucrative markets. But some raised profits by turning pirate, and hijackings became frequent. The slow-moving former fish boats used for transferring booze were sitting ducks. They carried hundreds of cases from freighters outside the three-mile limit to hidden inlets with quiet waters, where the valuable cargo was then transferred to a fleet of high-speed powerboats.

In September 1924, the lighthouse keeper at Turn Point, Washington discovered a big fish packer washed up on the shoreline. He found no one aboard but he noticed numerous bullet holes in the cabin door and wall and what appeared to be blood on the cookstove, settee, cabin floor, forward hatch and starboard bulwark. As the *Beryl G.* was out of Vancouver, the American authorities immediately contacted the BCPP, who agreed that the crime had most likely occurred in Canadian waters. Superintendent McMullin directed Provincial Sub-Inspector Cruickshank to take charge of the case.

The investigators learned that Bill Gillis, the owner of the *Beryl G.*, and his seventeen-year-old son regularly transferred liquor in the forty-five-foot fishing boat, which could easily carry 600 cases at a time. There

156

were few leads until an American racketeer whose rum-runners had been supplied by the *Beryl G.* offered to assist Cruickshank as much as he could. Through his sources, he identified Harry Sowash and Owen Baker as the hijackers and murderers, and said that a third man had been an accomplice and that a Victoria boat had been involved. Apparently Baker had planned to pull his usual "Customs man trick" where he dressed in a uniform and confiscated cargo. However, even though officials now had an idea of what had occurred, they had no evidence. Cruickshank and his men kept chasing leads along Seattle's and Tacoma's waterfronts.

One of them led eventually to a commercial fisherman/beer runner, Joe Stromkins, the owner of a fish boat, the *Avalon*. When additional evidence confirmed that the Victoria man was acquainted with Baker and Sowash, Sergeant Bob Owens brought him in for questioning. After a lengthy interview with Inspectors Parson and Cruickshank, Stromkins explained how he had become involved in the hijacking. He had agreed to take the threesome out for a fishing trip, and they had forced him to set course for Sidney Island, where they located the *Beryl G.* in an inlet at dusk. Leaving Stromkins guarded by Charles Morris, the third accomplice, Sowash and Baker rowed over to it, dressed in blazers with gold buttons and captain hats. Shortly after, there were sounds of a gun battle. Baker returned, furious that Gillis had started shooting at him and that he had had to kill him. He climbed aboard and ordered the fish boat over to the packer. As they approached, they saw Sowash strike down Gillis's son. They then lashed the packer in a port-to-starboard tow and ordered Stromkins to head out into the strait. During the trip, Sowash and Baker tied the bodies of Gillis and his son together, attached them to a loose anchor and pushed them overboard. Later, in calm water under a rising moon, they transferred the *Beryl G.*'s 600 cases, then abandoned the old packer. Baker decided to cache the booze at various island hideouts and then to go to Anacortes. When they got there, Baker threaten the terrified Stromkins, swearing he would say he was an accomplice if he talked, then let him go.

When Stromkins agreed to be a Crown witness, the Provincials finally had evidence. The hunt for Sowash, Morris and Baker intensified, various American forces assisting. Eventually Sowash was arrested in New Orleans and Baker in New York. Sowash and Baker hanged, and Morris was imprisoned for life.

Drunkenness, brawling and bootlegging charges continued to be laid frequently by the BCPP. Though the Liquor Control Board now sold bonded liquor on behalf of the BC government, the number and locations of the outlets as well as the short opening hours discouraged many individuals from purchasing from them. People bought liquor for each other, to supply friends or to supply anyone for a small profit. As well, blind pigs and private clubs continued to flourish as men sought companionship as well as booze. Provincial constables frequently watched such small-time operations through a blind eye, according to some former members. "We were well aware of what was going on," one explained. "But we didn't get any brownie points for laying charges, so most of us used our own discretion. Most people up island could not easily get to an LCB so them paying a couple of extra bucks for someone else to supply them with a bottle was not considered a big thing. However, if there was any disturbance or complaints, we stopped it fast."[20]

After the Royal Commission on Drugs ended, public interest in the subject apparently waned. Opium smokers appeared regularly before judges and had to choose between fines and brief jail terms. Most distributors and kingpins in the drug trade managed to elude the police, but not all did. The Provincials and the Customs and Excise men became convinced that many small-time users were being supplied indirectly by one wholesaler, an experienced importer who distributed a wide range of commodities. They developed profiles on likely candidates, compiling information on all importers who supplied corner stores. It was a slow process.

A Chinese peanut oil wholesaler, whose warehouses were in Nanaimo and who supplied oil to small grocers throughout BC, became the main suspect. For two years, Customs men sample-checked numerous cases of each shipment to him and found only peanut oil. Yet the investigators remained convinced that somehow Lum Chow was importing and distributing opium. When Inspector Norris from the Customs & Excise Department notified Provincial Sergeant J. Russell that another forty-five cases had just arrived from Hong Kong, they decided to check each case personally. As they started opening crates, Russell noticed that a few cases on the bottom of the stack had an inconspicuous black 8 crayoned beside the shipper's stencil. They ripped open one of those cases and finally had their evidence. One can of oil was missing and the space was filled with stacks of small round opium tins—1440 cans of opium in the marked cases. Chin Ming King, alias Lum Chow, was charged, then sentenced to six years, even as he continued to protest that the shipment was not actually for him.

As the Provincials' duties broadened and changed, the force increased in size, improved offices and jails, and purchased additional vehicles and vessels. There was better co-operation with other forces, particularly Alberta's provincial police and state and municipal forces along the American seaboard. More municipalities requested that the BCPP take over policing their towns under contract, an option made available to them by the 1923 Police Act; civic governments were having a hard time financially because of the fast population growth. As the BCPP began policing municipal statutes as well as provincial and federal ones, Mc-

Mullin emphasized to his men that they had to learn new skills to police larger towns effectively, particularly skills related to crowd control and enforcing traffic regulations. He also directed that members of municipal police forces being disbanded, whose qualifications and reputation for integrity were of BCPP standards, be invited to join the Provincials. Many a community ended up with the same policeman in a new uniform.

In rare instances, the attorney general ordered a change in policing. Such a case occurred in 1928 when two councilmen in Port Alberni contacted Premier John D. McLean with concerns about the honesty of their police and some elected officials. After a brief investigation, the Provincials were ordered to take over Port Alberni's police station, "without warning being served." A Provincial sergeant and two constables arrived at the station at midnight and took charge. Subsequently, charges were laid against the municipal police chief.

The Provincials developed a growing sense of fraternity as more members became stationed together. Also, the public developed a new image of the force as they became more involved in town activities and uniformed constables began to fulfill ceremonial functions: marching at the front of a parade or presenting awards to lodges and clubs. A few members, those older men who had been opposed to uniforming the force, questioned using police for ceremonies, arguing that it made it too military, something a civil law force should not be.

Though the southern half of the province grew rapidly, other areas had changed little after fifty years. Provincials continued to be the first non-natives to penetrate remote parts of the province. In June 1926, relatives of two missing trappers requested that the BCPP try to locate them, explaining that the missing men had gone trapping in the area

*Constables C.G. Barber, right, and E. Forfar leave Fort St. John on their lengthy journey to Fort Nelson.*

between Pouce Coupe and Fort Nelson, and had not been heard from. Since much of the far northeast corner of the province was still unknown wilderness, the government decided that the Provincial Police could do some exploring while they searched for the missing trappers. Provincial constables C.G. Barber and E. Forfar were instructed to contact Indians, make a visual survey of the country, estimate timber stands, watch for surface minerals and survey the area's agricultural potential.

The trip was incredibly difficult. The constables pushed through the first 200 miles of treacherous muskeg on horseback. It took them twenty days, twenty days of pulling their horses out of slimy bogs and fighting off the hordes of blackflies and no-see-ums. Near the Sikanni River, about 200 miles from Pouce Coupe, the constables met up with a small party of Indians. The Indians had seen the trappers the previous fall and said that they had lost most of their supplies. The natives had given them some food but they doubted that the men had survived the severe winter.

Barber and Forfar bought a flimsy spruce-bark canoe and headed downstream to Fort Nelson. They travelled the 150 miles in just under four days, whizzing through numerous rocky rapids and around treacherous whirlpools. The Fort Nelson trader was most surprised to see them. He didn't think any other white men had travelled that stretch of river. He hadn't seen the trappers, so after two days of rest, the Provincials started the harrowing trip back upstream. Now they were going against the current, and the 150 miles took them two weeks of back-breaking paddling. When the exhausted constables reached their guide and horses, they rested for two days before starting back through the bush and muskeg again. By the time they reached Pouce Coupe, they had been gone for forty-nine days, forty-five of which they had spent travelling. They must have chuckled wryly when told that an MLA in Victoria had suggested the BCPP should be making two such patrols a month. The missing trappers were eventually presumed dead.

In a slightly less remote spot, but still way up north to the majority of BC's population, a shack town developed on Goat Island in Quesnel Lake to supply illegal alcohol, wild women and continuing card games to the province's latest influx of gold miners. Goat Island attracted a particularly rough element, according to the undercover man sent in to assess the situation. "Bootlegging, swindling, hijacking and prostitution are in full swing," he reported, warning that it would take quite a few Provincials to clean up Goat Island.[21] Late one Saturday night, twelve Provincials under Sergeant G. Greenwood travelled down the lake under cover of darkness and staged a raid. Before it was over, eighty-two men and women were manacled to trees. At daybreak, the Provincials secured their prisoners together in threes for the long trip out to Quesnel by barge, horse-drawn wagon and eventually ancient bus.

However, despite the lack of change in isolated areas, the pace of life had speeded up for most BC residents. Steamships, trains and motor vehicles travelled faster and farther. People flew through the air with barnstorming pilots, danced the Charleston, bought autos, watched Charlie Chaplin's antics in silent movies, listened to the radio and surreptitiously sipped from hip flasks at dances or in the back seats of roadsters. Every year brought more new laws to be obeyed and every year more laws were broken, particularly those restricting drinking, hunting and driving. Though convictions were obtained in about 85 per cent of all charges the BCPP put before the courts, the public did not consider those infractions "real crimes" and penalties were no longer the deterrents they had been in earlier days. Superintendent McMullin and Attorney General Mason, worried about the increasing amount of policing required to enforce the Liquor, Motor Vehicle and Game acts, searched for solutions even as the infractions continued to increase at a rapid rate.

To summarize Provincial policing, McMullin began presenting a comprehensive annual report to the legislature. In it were detailed administrative statistics: operation and equipment, number and results of prosecutions and summaries of major cases. The reports recorded how the force expanded and what new departments were organized and why. For instance, when preparing for assize court cases began to require too much of regular constables' time, McMullin appointed a plainclothesman, Carl Ledoux, to help the Crown counsels gather evidence. Ledoux developed quite a reputation for exposing con men and unearthing real estate and investment frauds. When the demand for his services became more than one man could handle, the BCPP formed a separate criminal investigation bureau under his direction.

In 1928, the BCPP began using shortwave radio. When enthusiastic members spent hours of their off-duty time putting together bits and pieces of wire and experimenting with shortwave, it changed policing as much as the telegraph had sixty years earlier. To cut costs and control quality, the radio buffs initially built all their own sets, but later the BCPP set up a Radio Operators division, the first Canadian police force to develop and operate a shortwave network. Within a couple of years after the initial experiments, the short wave system connected Victoria, Vancouver, Prince Rupert, Nelson and Kamloops. Later, as the innovators developed portable sets able to transmit Morse code messages, private communication with BCPP headquarters became possible from isolated northern detachments and from police motor launches (PMLs) far out at sea.

When the government changed in 1928, the newly appointed Attorney General, R.H. Pooley requested McMullin to continue as superintendent. Pooley assured him that the BCPP would be free from political pressures or influence and that it would continue to receive adequate funding. He also authorized McMullin to proceed with plans for Douglas House, a BCPP training school to be located in Victoria. By April 1930, the academy for Provincial Police probationers had students learning about first aid, general police work, marksmanship and squad drill. As well, they learned from BC's most respected lawyers about the laws they would be responsible for enforcing, and sometimes prosecuting. The new government also authorized the superintendent to continue upgrading the marine fleet and the various BCPP buildings.

McMullin asked Pooley for permission to re-create a small mounted squad, and the attorney general authorized a ten-horse troop. The constables and their horses boarded at Oakalla Prison Farm and travelled by truck or train to ceremonies or trouble spots. One recruit recalled joining the troop:

> The sergeant took me on a trial ride and we moved pretty fast through some rough terrain. My riding ability was obviously not what I'd said it was. I had ridden every day one summer nine years before on a farm, but the horse had been a gentle mare of twenty. I didn't think I had a hope of being accepted after that trial. Then a couple of days later, he called me in and said, "you're part of the squad but, man, you're the worst rider of the bunch and you better not be a month from now." I wasn't. But how my body ached in the interval. For the first couple of weeks, it was a pleasure to have the riding day over and be allowed to shovel manure.[22]

BC's Game Department was separated from the Provincial Police in 1929, a move Superintendent McMullin had been recommending for five years. The Provincial force could not hope to achieve maximum efficiency, he argued, when its men were being used to do everything from licensing motor vehicles to checking out Workmen's Compensation inquiries to selling fisheries licences to catching poachers and counting deer. Forty-nine Provincials became game officers under Commissioner A.B. Williams. They became responsible for the bulk of game-law enforcement, although all Provincial policemen remained officers under the Game Act and all game officers were ex officio members of the BCPP.

One area of policing remained unresolved. Since McMullin had been superintendent, the Sons of Freedom, a sect of Doukhobors in the Kootenays, had been an enigma for him as they had been for McMynn earlier. Theoretically pacifists, they were nevertheless believed responsible for numerous burning and bombing incidents. Other Kootenay residents, some frightened, others enraged, frantically demanded the government put a stop to the depredations. McMullin tried, as the BCPP had been given full support initially by Attorney General Manson, then by Attorney General Pooley. As well, RCMP experts and CPR detectives investigated and analyzed the situation regularly, all forces co-operating fully with each other. But the incidents continued.

Almost 8,000 Doukhobors had fled from Russia to Canada in 1899 and settled on homesteads in Saskatchewan, seeking to build a community where their religious beliefs and agrarian pacifist lifestyle would encounter no interference. However, their leaders and the Canadian government, who, desperate for immigrants, had offered asylum to the sect, did not finalize the terms whereby they could be land-holding Canadians without conforming to the conditions of Canadian citizenship. The three sects of Doukhobors—the Community, the Independents and the Sons of Freedom—built fifty-seven communal villages and turned the raw prairie into productive farm lands through their intense labours. In 1905, when the Canadian government sent in Homestead inspectors, all Doukhobors were horrified, believing that they had come to Canada on the promise of no government interference. They wanted no schooling, no census taking, no oaths of allegiance. When they were pressured to conform to Canadian law to finalize ownership of their homesteads, a few zealots from the Sons of Freedom sect began protesting by parading nude and going on hunger strikes when arrested by the RNWMP.

In 1908, the leaders decided if they owned massive private land rather than homestead land, their people would be free of government regulation. They purchased land in the Kootenays for a new settlement for the majority of the Doukhobor community, planning to abandon thousands of prairie acres. The Independent sect, fewer than 1,000 individuals, claimed their Saskatchewan homesteads. The Community and Sons of Freedom Doukhobors, welcomed by BC's government, moved to the Kootenays. By 1913, over 5,000 lived in the Kootenays with more members arriving each year. Their organization and collective labour quickly turned the semi-arid land into lush fields. They also worked for Kootenay lumbermen and farmers as contract workers. A hard-working people, they cherished their children and their religion with its rich oral history and music, and venerated their leaders. They carefully taught their children that the good of the community was of the utmost importance, and they discouraged individualism.

During the Doukhobors' first ten years in BC, the government had occasionally ordered the BCPP to enforce the Schools and Statistics acts, but without any consistency. Those attempts had achieved few results, except to intensify Doukhobor determination to live without interference. The elders eventually agreed to educate their own youngsters and a few schools were built, though attendance at them was not enforced. The zealots, mainly Sons of Freedom, protested the community's co-operation with the government dictates. A few schools burned and the Doukhobors began parading nude in nearby villages, interrupting weddings and funeral processions. In 1922, Premier John Oliver and his government decided that all Doukhobor children deserved schooling. Despite Doukhobor protests, the Schools Act, which guaranteed every BC child the right to six years of education, would be enforced. As well, they decreed that all Doukhobors must henceforth register births, deaths and marriages. By then, the numerous Doukhobor villages, mainly located between Trail, Castlegar and Nelson, had over 8,000 residents. Shortly after he became superintendent, McMullin ordered the Provincials in the Kootenay area to meet with each village's elders, discuss the situation and try to determine how best to enforce schooling and registration.

Those meetings had few results, though schools were built and the children attended sometimes. Provincials visited communes regularly and were welcomed cordially, though most questions were answered only by smiles, shrugs and nods.

> We would meet in the communal dining room, usually just me, occasionally my sergeant, too, and three or four elders — each Doukhobor village had less than a hundred people. We would visit about the crops and weather for a bit, then I eventually would mention the teacher had informed me that none of their children had gone to school last week. We would mull it over, no one saying much except all did agree the children had not gone to school last week. Eventually, I would decide that perhaps I had persuaded them as much

*Sons of Freedom Doukhobors disrobe in front of the BCPP office in Nelson.*

164

as I could and that the children might show up next week. So I would say goodbye and drive away, wondering if their children's school would be the next one burned.[23]

Whenever Doukhobor children were forced to attend a school, that schoolhouse soon burned to the ground. Then twenty or thirty Doukhobor men and women would go into a nearby town and stage a protest march, which often turned into a nude parade. The Sons of Freedom parades were an annoyance to communities and the public nudity scandalized residents of British descent: it had been less than ten years since their women had raised their hemlines off the ground and obtained the right to vote. The west Kootenay area was home to many British immigrants, who wanted quiet, dignified neighbourhoods, similar to those they had left in England. Non-Doukhobor residents throughout the region became increasingly offended by the disturbances, and some threatened to take the law into their own hands if the provincial and municipal forces did not control the "Douks" better. People formed into protest groups to try and force the government to make the "foreigners" move on. Even those who regularly bought produce from Doukhobors, or employed them as carpenters or household help, grew more nervous of offending a radical sect member, always unsure which of the Doukhobors were "radicals."

Police uneasiness also increased, particularly about the vulnerability of the railway. Superintendent McMullin agreed with his district officers that it was impossible to patrol a railway adequately, especially one that wound up and down mountains on a narrow ridge above river canyons. On October 29, 1924, Peter "Lordly" Verigin, the Doukhobors' religious and business leader and "divine" ruler, was killed along with nine others when a dynamite bomb exploded on CPR Kettle Valley train, inward bound to Grand Forks. From then on, constables throughout the Kootenays checked each departing passenger train for suspicious-looking persons or parcels. Since most people usually carried bags, picnic lunches, blankets and suitcases for the trip, the security precaution did little to relieve passengers' fears or reduce the risk. One constable recalled:

> My boots would echo on the train floor as I marched down the aisle, looking official and, initially, embarrassed. I'd check a few big bags for appearances but I was always mystified as to what I was accomplishing. Almost everything carried on looked suspicious. As well, many Doukhobor women were large, wore full skirts that could have concealed quite a bit, but thank goodness there was no instructions to arrange for matrons to check those. Chances of finding anything was more than remote but I fulfilled my orders.[24]

The explosion was thoroughly investigated. For two years, BCPP

Staff Sergeant Ernest Gammon and his team, along with a CPR detective and his staff, searched for leads. Strong circumstantial evidence pointed to disputes within the Doukhobor communities, but nothing could be proven and no one was charged. As Provincial policemen who worked in the area pointed out, it was impossible to get much information from Doukhobor individuals. In that close-knit community, the threat of banishment was terrifying, a potent method of control. A leader's commands had to be obeyed, without question, without comment and in complete secrecy.

In 1925, the school inspector for British Columbia and BCPP Inspector William Dunwoody were instructed to impose fines on the whole community for the massive amount of government property recently burned. Fines totalled $3,500, and when payment was not made, Doukhobor property was seized and sold. For a few months, it looked as though this policy had had the desired effect. Sons of Freedom helped rebuild the schools, then sent their children to them in unexpected numbers. That year, McMullin reported to the legislature in his annual report that he was optimistic. But shortly thereafter, the schools that had been rebuilt were again burned.

The Sons of Freedom parades and gatherings grew in frequency and size in the Kootenay villages, jeopardizing other residents who formed resistance movements to drive the "invaders" out of town. A dozen or so people would appear with horsewhips as the Sons of Freedom disrobed and paraded, shouting loudly that the "Douks" better get out of town or be thrashed. But the nude Sons of Freedom would pack tightly together and chant louder as residents flailed at them. The community's mayor would phone the nearest Provincial Police office and demand help. However, as two different Provincials who spent years policing in the Brilliant area pointed out, what was described by some as "radicals rioting" was described by others as "a gathering of people who refused to disperse." Though Doukhobors shed their clothes and sang religious dirges, the daytime demonstrators were passive and nonthreatening, destroyed no property and caused no injuries. They broke no statutes or laws, so no charges could be laid.

Another Provincial recalled how frustrating it was to break up demonstrations week after week, month after month. Provincials got to know the leaders well, and while they sometimes arrested them, usually the police just got the parade moving out of town. "After all," he explained, "when we arrested a leader, it just meant that a larger group of Doukhobors were going to gather in protest." He described how one municipal official reacted:

> There was a story going round about the mayor of Greenwood. He felt he had a riot on his hands again – he did regularly – so he phoned Grand Forks

and asked that the Provincial Police be sent. Well, we were a scattered police force — if we ever had ten Provincial policemen at one point, you wondered how many rioters they were about to tackle. So when the next train came into Greenwood, one policeman got off.

The mayor said, "What! There's only one of you?"

"Yes," said the constable, "you've only got one riot, haven't you?"[25]

Additional Provincials were stationed in Division B and more specials hired after two Brilliant area schools burned in July 1928, then the Grand Forks school and Doukhobor flour mill and warehouse, and schools at Champion Creek and Krestova burned in August 1929. McMullin directed Provincial Sergeant H. King to make arrests, to find some charge for bringing in the suspects. King searched through the Criminal Code, then finally arrested two Doukhobors at Grand Forks on the thin charge "of having one's face masked or blackened or otherwise disguised by night without lawful excuse."[26] When the accused appeared for remand, one prisoner was released but the other, Paul Vlasoff, was transferred to the gaol in Nelson to await trial.

A short time before Vlasoff's arrest, the Community Doukhobors had turned out a group of Sons of Freedom for their refusal to pay the communal taxes. The leaders of those 150 banished individuals, unsure where to take their followers, decided the group should go to Nelson to protest Vlasoff's arrest. Nelson's mayor warned the Provincials that residents would riot if the Sons were allowed into the town. Police stopped the marchers a few miles out and the leaders met with officials at the Nelson Provincial Police office. They informed authorities that if Vlasoff was not immediately released from jail, 500 Sons of Freedom would come to parade. But Inspector Cruickshank was firm. Vlasoff would continue to be held in jail until his trial, and parades would not be allowed into the city.

A parade of 100 Sons started toward Nelson but Cruickshank, Staff Sergeant Ernest Gannon and five constables stopped it a mile out of town, where they set up camp. Over the next two days, their numbers swelled to over 300. Most of the newcomers were from the Sons of Freedom sect, but Provincials recognized some as Community Doukhobors. Peter Petrovich Verigin, son and heir of the Peter Verigin killed in the 1924 train bombing, arrived to negotiate. He offered the evicted Sons of Freedom shelter at Porto Rico, an abandoned logging camp owned by the joint Doukhobor communities. Scorning that offer, they began to strip. The inspector went for reinforcements and trucks, read the Riot Act on his return, then ordered his constables and specials to start making arrests.

"It was a beautiful summer day, blue sky, slight breeze," recalled one constable.

# British Columbia Provincial Police Annual

### 1931

### Colourful Stories of Romance and Adventure of the Provincial Police in British Columbia

Price 50c

*The first and only* BCPP Annual *was followed seven years later by the* Shoulder Strap, *a biannual magazine published by the force until 1950.*

I was young and nervous and wished I was somewhere else. I had many illusions about the nude form. Although not all the Doukhobors stripped, many did. Some of the women were old, with pendulous breasts down to their knees, while others were lovely shaped women. Many of the men had stringy legs and potbellies but there were fewer of them as quite a few more women stripped than men. They squished in around us. At first when the arrests started, it was hard to know where to put one's hands as we had to literally pick them up and load them into the trucks. But soon it didn't matter and I stopped feeling terribly embarrassed. There were so many, all passively unco-operative, heavy. It was just hard work, lifting and carrying.[27]

Police arrested about a third of the Doukhobors and took them to the Nelson gaol. One hundred and four were convicted of indecent exposure and sentenced to six months at Oakalla Prison Farm, where they refused to work and went on hunger strikes. Provincials moved the other 200 to Porto Rico, having first to lift them all into trucks, then to lift them out on arrival. Supplied with food and clothes by the Independent Doukhobor Brethren in Saskatchewan, they passed the winter in the dilapidated sawmill.

"There are signs of lessening enthusiasm and it's possible that in time the refractory movement may gradually disappear," Superintendent McMullin reported to the legislature in January 1930. He also acknowledged official suspicion about the possibility of unknown motives and organizations, behind the highly organized disturbances, motives unrelated to the Sons of Freedom abhorrence of schooling and statistics laws.[28]

# CHAPTER EIGHT

# "May I see your I.D. please?"
# 1930–1938

"THE ABNORMAL LABOUR CONDITIONS have produced a situation that requires constant watching on our part," McMullin reported to the BC legislature in his 1930 annual report. "It is fortunate that the great bulk of those who are unemployed have shown a great deal of forbearance in their trouble. However, the activities of professional agitators have been causing constant trouble and several situations have arisen that have required tactful handling."[1]

That spring, he had sent the BCPP mounted troop in to help control angry strikers at the Fraser and Barnett mills in Vancouver, the first time it was used for duties other than ceremonial ones.

BC's economy had crashed along with the stock market in 1929. Employers laid off workers, cut wages and closed up shop. Confrontations became common when a mill or mine cut wages or work hours. Its workers often disagreed; one group would go on a protest strike while the other group fought with the strikers, determined to cross picket lines, sure the company would close if they did not accept the cuts and keep working. Though many businesses struggled to survive, others used the poor economy as an excuse to increase profits at the expense of employees. Workers disagreed about their employers: the strikers were sure they were being robbed, the others were often sympathetic to the employer. When they clashed, the Provincials were sent in to prevent violence and property damage.

As policing needs increased, provincial revenues plummeted and the administration ordered policing costs cut. In August, McMullin closed

Douglas House, the BCPP school, both to cut costs and to use its instructors and probationers to form two emergency mobile squads. He eliminated the position of assistant superintendent and transferred Walter Owen to Oakalla as warden, he amalgamated the detective bureau into the Vancouver and Victoria districts, eliminating one BCPP department administratively, he froze annual salaries and he cancelled orders for patrol cars and a new ship. When announcing the changes and cutbacks to his officers, he also notified them that he had changed his title to commissioner, as it gave a more accurate description of his duties.

During that period, unemployment increased weekly and destitute men demanded the government do something more to help them. The first demonstrations occurred in December 1929, when about 200 unemployed men, angry about the ineffective aid system, raided the Vancouver relief office. The next day, they paraded through the downtown streets. The day after that, Vancouver city police prevented the marchers from parading and, without assistance from the Provincials, arrested two men on the grounds that they were Communist agitators. Though there were large numbers of men involved, the police followed the usual Vancouver law enforcement pattern: the BCPP detachment was prepared to assist when the chief of the Vancouver Municipal Police requested help.

Those incidents marked the beginning of widespread unrest, and the government began planning how to control angry unemployed men. Like many politicians across Canada, the BC government decided agitators were magnifying the unemployment problem, "stirring up" the people for hidden political reasons. Law enforcement had to be tighter, they decided, and they ordered increased surveillance on all suspected subversives. As spring came and men began moving about BC looking for work, Provincials began questioning transients on the street, demanding to see identification, asking them where they came from and where they were headed. As fear of subversion grew, Provincials arrested people faster than before. The men were instructed to bring in any suspicious person and check him out, even when prosecutable evidence was scanty. Though most were released a few days later for lack of evidence, the Provincials' list of suspicious persons grew lengthy.

Commissioner McMullin faced another dilemma as he tried to keep up with demands for additional policing. In 1929, the BCPP policed twenty-two municipalities under contract, all having made the transition from a municipal force with little difficulty. McMullin knew that had been achieved because experienced Provincials had been carefully matched to the town they were to begin supervising. But when Attorney General R.H. Pooley notified him that the BCPP should expect to take over a number of others in the next few months, as some municipalities were almost bankrupt, McMullin knew that he did not have enough experienced men available. He made a new policy: when the BCPP took over a municipality, any municipal men who qualified to join up were immediately transferred out. "I ended up in Barkerville, quite a surprise for a city policeman. But when North Vancouver could not meet its municipal payroll for the second month, the BC government took over all administration. I was hesitant about agreeing to go north but other jobs were few and far between. Besides, I liked being a policeman."[2]

The Depression deepened and authorities across Canada grew more alarmed about communism. As people searched for reasons for their collapsed economy, it became easy to kindle their hopes and anger, to get them to consider new ideas. The Canadian Communist Party gained supporters and grew increasingly active. Individuals who had never been involved in politics before, some who had never even bothered to vote, started attending communist rallies. Undercover agents judged that the majority of the new adherents were desperate people who hated the long empty hours of poverty unemployment had brought them. They craved something to believe in, and someone to tell them what to do with their time.

Aware that communism advocated violence when necessary, governments and police forces grew increasingly nervous, unsure who the enemy was. The BCPP, Military Police, and RCMP started investigating immediately when posters promoting revolution went up on telephone poles close to the armories in Victoria: "All Soldiers and Sailors – Organize with the rest of your class who are going to end capitalism and establish workers' rule. . . Remember that when the workers rule, your delegates will be members of the Canadian Soviet and will help to make your laws. Forward to the Soviet Revolution."[3]

Some officials, including McMullin, suspected that they were hunting for an individual, perhaps a bit crazed. Others argued that though communist organizations had not previously functioned that blatantly, the matter could not be treated lightly: the posters might be the start of an expanded political campaign.

Within days, authorities traced the posters to Ronald Steward, a British immigrant who had served with the Welsh Regiment and with the Royal Air Force. Because he had been suspected of theft, he had recently been discharged from the Princess Patricia's Light Infantry Regiment in Victoria. When the investigators learned Steward had been involved with Communist Party activities in South Africa, they arrested him for printing and distributing the seditious posters under a charge unique to BC: "Inciting troops to mutiny." He served a two-year sentence; then, as he was released, immigration authorities met him at the penitentiary gate and immediately deported him as an undesirable. Despite the authorities' continuing investigation, which included a stool pigeon planted in prison, they did not discover any ties to the Communist Party or any other

Canadian political group. No similar posters appeared elsewhere in Canada. However, some continued to believe Steward had not acted alone and was symbolic of the times. To preserve order, each suspected dissident movement had to be nipped in the bud.

In Hope, Princeton, Kamloops, Vernon, Penticton, Grand Forks, Cranbrook, in all the towns along British Columbia's railway tracks, hobo jungles grew as the Depression deepened. By the end of 1931, almost 25 percent of the Canadian work force was unemployed. Many of them, particularly men from the drought-stricken prairies, decided opportunities would be better in British Columbia – at least the climate was warmer – so they hopped on freight trains and came west, hungry, restless and flat broke. British Columbia's unemployment rate soon climbed above the national average. Some locals who lost jobs to out-of-province workers willing to accept less pay went with friends to harass the newcomer, often violently forcing him to move on. Such incidents were apparently ignored by most Provincials.

For the BCPP, the Depression was the beginning of a frustrating time. As one constable recalled:

> For years, we kept those poor unemployed men on the move, counted their numbers, over and over again. The freights had many more people riding on them than any passenger trains did then. Men would come into a place like Kamloops and would hop off outside of town, either to disappear into the jungle or drift through town, probably stopping at a couple of houses to see if they could chop wood in exchange for a sandwich. Then on the other side of town, they would catch a freight on the way out. They had insufficient food and skimpy clothes which did not keep them warm. So many people with nowhere to go. Most were patient, stoic, polite.[4]

A senior officer summarized the hopelessness of the unemployed and his own sadness at their plight:

> Sometimes there might be fifty people camped in the underbrush, other times, two hundred and fifty. They lived in shacks made out of old boards, flattened tin cans, cardboard. Hard to tell numbers. They moved about frequently, hoping to get even a day or two of work. Men looked gaunt, unwell from months of living in damp and cold with barely enough food to keep them alive. Many of them were young high school graduates who had grown up during the golden twenties, while others were veterans in their prime who couldn't believe that, after a youth spent in French trenches, this was now happening to them.[5]

In rural areas, and in municipalities policed under contract, the

*Highway patrol vans, placed in service in 1935, could be used as ambulances or paddy wagons.*

*The province's first motorcycle police stand proudly beside their Harleys with sidecars in front of the Old Courthouse in downtown Vancouver.*

destitute made application for relief through the Provincial Police. There were no worker benefits and provincial relief was available only for families in dire need and a few individuals who qualified. Constables recalled how difficult it was to explain why the government could not give financial assistance. An older single man might come into the detachment in great embarrassment and hesitatingly say that he had never asked for help before but he had nothing left and he did not know what to do next. The constable would have to tell him that he was too young to qualify for government assistance.

While the number of restless hungry men wandering BC grew into the thousands, the provincial and federal governments discussed what to do with them. BC's administrators stressed to the Dominion that they could not absorb even half of the financial burden created by the unemployed moving to BC. In October 1931, desperate to do something before winter, the British Columbia legislature established temporary relief camps. A year later, in even greater desperation, they authorized additional volunteer work camps. Aware that provincial funds could not support the camps for long, they also demanded Ottawa take them over.

The camps were established in remote areas of the province that needed road and airport construction. The first men into the camps built bunkhouses, a common room, bunks, tables and benches out of slab lumber. The nearest Provincial policed each camp as requested by its administrator but did not have to patrol the camps regularly. Thousands of unemployed men applied to live in the camps. They laboured with shovels, picks and wheelbarrows for eight hours daily in exchange for ladles of porridge, soup and stew. They soon became the forgotten men, stored in isolation as they waited for the Depression to end, waited without the companionship of women, without movies, ice cream cones or beer.

The residents could not know how long they would have to live in the camps, but each one knew that he could be ordered to leave without recourse, and would be barred from all other camps, so disturbances were few. Provincials were called out occasionally to pick up someone who had become deranged or to expel someone for fighting. By the time the federal government assumed responsibility for the camps in June 1933, BC had 237 camps with over 18,000 residents, one-third of the total number of work-camp inmates in Canada. Even after the army took over all relief camps, formalizing rules and setting up a minute pay scale, the Provincials continued to be called out when a man was expelled. That started to happen more frequently as conditions worsened and men's tempers became frayed.

One former Provincial recalled his nervousness when, as a new constable, he was requested to pick up two agitators being expelled from a camp fourteen miles from Hope. As he drove out to the camp, he worried about what he would do if the men were not co-operative, knowing that 100 men lived there and that the administrator had a reputation for disappearing once he had notified the Provincials of what he wanted done.

> When I arrived, I could not believe how stark it was. The two being expelled sat patiently in their dorm waiting for me. They had got into an argument with an older man who had been telling them they were lucky to have shelter and food. It hadn't been much of an incident—a bit of a fight in the main hall, a broken chair and lamp. I certainly did not judge them to be agitators, they were just angry at the monotony and scared by the hopelessness of the situation.
>
> On the hot dusty ride out, they were so pleased to be in a car again. They talked about missing things—girls, family, hearing kids playing and laughing. One fellow came from the Guelph area, hadn't heard how things were back home for over a year, although he had sent two postcards to them when he'd had enough money for stamps. The other was from Prince George, but he didn't think he could go home because the younger kids were always pretty hungry and he didn't want his mom to have to try and feed him too. I gave them all I had with me, less than $3. They got on a freight to Vancouver. I've always remembered them, they were about my age."[6]

As the BCPP grew in size, it attracted many highly qualified candidates who probably never would have become policemen had it not been for the Depression. A constable's salary, modest as it was, was suddenly desirable again. Like all employees on fixed wages, Provincials found their income went further than before because the cost of housing, clothing, meat, butter and eggs had declined. But only regular members of the force enjoyed such security. For special constables, that large group of men who were hired daily as needed, it was a difficult time. They might get five days' work one month and twenty-nine the next. Still, there were few options and every special hoped someday to make it into the permanent force.

New members were sent to the mobile emergency squad, which moved around the province to wherever additional policing was needed. In May 1934, for instance, two game wardens who had been acting for the Provincial Police supervising municipal relief road workers in Prince George, were attacked and injured by strikers. A troop of fifteen BCPP probationers and regulars was dispatched. One of the probationers reminisced:

> We arrived from Vancouver after an all-night trip, first travelling by train to Ashcroft, then the rest of the way by rickety old bus. The bus filled with dirt each time we hit a pothole in the Cariboo road. We were tired and dirty when

we filed into the Prince George hotel where we were billetted. The labour problem dissipated quickly with our show of strength later that day. Then, a few days later, we were ordered to join in the celebration of the Queen's birthday, suitably spit and polished. All probationers were to march in the annual May Day parade, a big event in Prince George as it was in most of British Columbia's communities.

We formed up behind the band, feeling quite impressive in our khaki and green uniforms. Just the four regular constables marching with us wore Stetsons — the fifteen of us still had to wear the caps because we were probationers — but we made quite a troop. A sergeant with impressive handlebar moustaches and magnificent vocal cords marched us proudly through the streets. Then we arrived at the cul-de-sac in front of City Hall where the dignitaries' grandstand was set up. The sergeant barked, "Right turn!" when he should have said, "Left turn!" We paused, then our whole troop obediently proceeded to march right into the band.

So he bellowed, "Halt!" then tried another "right turn!" But it was too late. We were facing every which way, standing at attention, managing to remain poker-faced. The spectators had never enjoyed a parade more. The sergeant, his face a deep red, mumbled a plea for the troop to carry on and form rank, please. We did so and the ceremonies finally commenced.[7]

Even if things didn't always go quite as planned, little towns and big towns enjoyed their celebrations despite the bad economic times. Provincials marched in parades regularly and the BCPP mounted troop continued to perform around its other duties. Constables also participated in community activities in a variety of ways. They visited schools to impress children about safety and to familiarize them with policemen. They spoke to service clubs about interesting experiences in their careers and they volunteered for youth groups. It was often a constable who was the wrestling coach or the one who flooded the skating rink at six in the morning.

However, policing was changing because of the nature of the times. Every month, confrontations became more Provincials' main beat. Though the number of strikes decreased as the unemployment rate rose, those that did occur were more violent. Constables attempted to stop battles when strikers swung rock-filled socks at workers trying to cross the picket lines, who in turn swung bicycle chains at the strikers as they charged past.

At the same time, family conflicts increased and constables dealt with more battered women and children. And they regularly stopped fights that broke out when the men working for municipal relief were harassed by the men who refused to swing picks and shovels to qualify for it.

Doing relief work was demoralizing and so was policing it, one constable remembered.

Municipalities demanded that men who took dole to feed their families had to work in exchange. Most were made to repair roads. Yet municipal governments had no money available to purchase adequate repair materials so reliefers often had to fill in the same pothole, again and again. A man would shovel in the dirt, pack it down, then have to begin all over again each time a car drove over it. The roads were in terrible condition and there was no way a man with a shovel could do much to improve them. But day after day men who needed public money had to shovel or their families did not qualify for food vouchers. They worked on the main thoroughfares, shovelling for eight hours, while the men who declined to do so, the strikers, stood at the edge of the road and harassed them. Although we knew that agitators were sometimes behind it, the knowledge in no way helped prevent spasmodic outbreaks of violence between the two groups.[8]

During 1932 and 1933, unrest spread throughout BC. Fishermen on the Skeena and Nass rivers and canneries at Rivers Inlet went on strike for a week in June 1932. In September, workers at a large lumber company in New Westminster walked out when the owners tried to cut wages. Intensive picketing resulted and the owners closed the plant. When the government offered them assistance, they reopened it and a large Provincial force guarded the employees who chose to return to work. Then in December, after another wage cut at the Tulameen mine, a strike erupted among the coal miners in Princeton. Though the miners went back to work in January, the unrest spread into mines in the surrounding area during the spring of 1933.

BCPP constables and undercover agents had previously judged the Similkameen region as unstable and kept close track of the ongoing faction fighting among different groups of workers. They identified three main causes for the frequent work stoppages: the area had a high percentage of non-English speaking miners, owners of mines regularly reduced wages and ignored workers' concerns about safety, and communist labour organizers aggravated each situation with propaganda and support. During the December strike when non-strikers attacked picketing workers, 500 men had become involved in the melee and the five BCPP constables needed reinforcements. Commissioner McMullin ordered the mounted patrol and the BCPP emergency squad to help regain order and directed that any suspected agitators be arrested.

Provincial police arrested a labour organizer, A.H. (Slim) Evans, an avowed communist, a passionate defender of working men and, later, a leader of the On-to-Ottawa trek. He was remanded to the spring assizes and denied bail. Shortly after the strike ended, a booklet about Evans' case and the Princeton strike, written and printed anonymously, was distributed widely throughout the province. It became a classic. Undercover agents reported that most readers judged the information to be accurate, including non-English speakers who were read interpreted versions at labour meetings. In the booklet, Evans was the hero battling against the government brutes, the Provincial Police. Actual events were re-told under subheadings such as Police Terror, Frame-up Continues, Kidnapping and Threats, Campaign to Smash Union Exposed and Petty Prosecution. Evans' pamphlet became a symbol to the BCPP constables and administrators of the professionally prepared propaganda they were up against, which referred to "the slimy hand of capitalist justice" and declared that:

> When capitalism tries a case, it is a case of whose ox is being gored and the sniveling magistrate lives up to his role of defender of his class...One can hold Communist views in Canada but they must be kept locked up in one's own bosom and trotted out only in the parlors of the safe and sound philosophers. The workers must not hear about such heretical doctrine. Evans not only told the workers how they could better their immediate condition but also pointed out to them the rottenness and hypocrisy of the whole capitalist system.[9]

BCPP officials worried that fictionalized accounts of this kind created a climate in which violence was acceptable, even necessary, and they knew the booklet continued to sway many people toward Evans' cause even though he was serving time in jail for "advocating force and violence." Provincial officials believed certain European immigrants were particularly vulnerable to this material, coming as they did from countries where police brutality was the norm.

As they tried to anticipate policing requirements during 1933, Commissioner McMullin and Attorney General R.H. Pooley analyzed the deteriorating conditions. Layoffs and wage cuts continued throughout the province. In the crowded relief camps, administrators expelled anyone considered a troublemaker, with the result that hobo jungles had more restless men inclined toward creating disturbances. As well, McMullin reported, he had reliable reports that agitators and organizers from across Canada were moving into British Columbia.

One spot where labour strife was blamed on outside agitators was Anyox, a company town up the coast from Prince Rupert where workers mined copper for the Granby Consolidated Mining, Smelting and Power Company. On February 1, 1933, the constable in Anyox informed Inspector J. Shirras at "D" Division Headquarters in Prince Rupert that some workers were planning a strike and threatening to damage the ore concentrators. Shirras, a staff sergeant and eight men promptly boarded the PML 8 and departed for Anyox. When they arrived, Shirras surveyed the situation and radioed Victoria for reinforcements. Ten more Provincials were flown in.

At dawn on February 350 strikers armed with steel drills, pieces of hose pipe loaded with bolts, and other homemade weapons marched from the mine toward the concentrators on the beach, where the workers were not on strike. To get there, the strikers had to cross a narrow wooden bridge over a ravine where Constable W. Smith set up a police protection post. He informed the leaders that since the group was armed, it constituted an unlawful assembly, and he suggested that a deputation be chosen to go down to talk to the beach workers. As the leaders considered this plan, however, strikers forced past them and attacked Smith. Four other constables immediately came to his aid but during the fight, the outnumbered Provincials were severely beaten. The police outpost fell and strikers swarmed to the beach and took possession of the massive concentrators.

"At this point it was certainly mob rule," Inspector Shirras explained later. "I called the leaders together and tried to impress upon them that it would only be a short time before we could be in a position to enforce law and order."[10] He emphasized the penalties facing them, and the leaders managed to persuade most of the strikers to withdraw, leaving pickets to guard the concentrators.

Two days later, strong reinforcements arrived, including seven members of the BCPP mounted troop with their horses, the emergency squad and numerous specials. Strikers who had been involved in the fight were arrested, and the Granby Company discharged about 400 men. Those men were immediately loaded aboard ship and taken to Prince Rupert, the last port of call for ships bound from Vancouver to Anyox. There the discharged employees resumed their battle, attempting to prevent new labourers from going to the mine. Police guards were posted for passenger protection. On March 21, 300 men attempting to board a Canadian National steamer for Anyox attacked 21 Provincial guards. Passengers rushed off the steamer, armed themselves from a nearby rockpile and helped police repel the attackers, who were then chased for several hundred yards up Prince Rupert's main street. There they were met by another group of Provincials, a baton charge led by Sergeant W. Service. This broke the back of the disturbance and there were no further major confrontations. Two weeks later, the guards were withdrawn from the Prince Rupert wharf. Reviewing the incident, Commissioner McMullin credited radio communication and air transportation with helping the Provincials regain control of Anyox.

After a lengthy investigation, the deputy minister of labour attributed the Anyox strike to poor bunkhouse conditions, wage reductions and agitation by a Serbian society, which was suspected of being affiliated with

# Wanted for Murder

A Reward of One Hundred Dollars ($100) is hereby offered by the Government of the Province of British Columbia for information leading to the whereabouts, either dead or alive, of John Lake, wanted on a charge of murdering Emil Perle at Colleymount on August 26th, 1935.

The following is a description of Lake, whose picture appears on this circular:—

Finlander; age 54, looks younger; 6 ft. 2 in.; 220 lbs.; blue eyes; dark-brown hair, greying at temples; large, red, round face; nose large, fleshy, rather flat, and very noticeably red; clean shaven; wears No. 11 shoes with three or four calks in instep; last seen wearing blue denim shirt, blue overalls, bare head. He was carrying two rifles, calibre 303, one a Lee Enfield and the other a Winchester, and he had about five rounds of ammunition.

Any information should immediately be communicated to the undersigned.

## J. H. McMULLIN,

*Commissioner, B.C. Police.*

*Wanted dead or alive, murder suspect John Lake. Reward posters like this one went up in public buildings around the province.*

the communist movement and which had been active in Anyox for months before the miners went out. Before the strike, one-third of the workers spoke only Serbian and were easily influenced by the leaders' analysis of events. Another group of about 100 men spoke languages other than English or Serbian. The deputy minister emphasized that the company was currently improving bunkhouse conditions, and commended the Provincial Police for preventing a serious clash between beach and mine workers.

Provincials continued to patrol in strength at Anyox for a short period, policing the Granby Company as well as the workers. By mid-April, Staff Sergeant McNeill reported that the sanitary conditions and the food were much improved. He also reported that the camp was almost up to full strength again after the arrival of 350 men. Seventy-one percent of the newcomers were English-speaking, a shift McNeill believed would help "make a more satisfied group." He reported that the company had rehired only 25 of the 400 men discharged and was taking precautions to prevent any agitators from entering. In 1935, as world markets disappeared, the mine closed and all of its workers became unemployed.

For some Provincials, the thirties were demanding years of patrolling transients riding the rails. They cleared men off the train car roofs, warned them about the dangers of riding freights and recorded names. Constables at transfer points like Spences Bridge, located on both the CPR and CNR main lines and the closest connection point to the Pacific Great Eastern line, were particularly busy. Between March 25 and September 2, 1933, the two Provincials there recorded the names of 4,344 transients.

In August, a transient youth from Merritt fell from a freight car and dislocated his shoulder. He claimed the constable had pushed him. His mother wrote letters to the Merritt *Herald* and the *Vancouver Sun*, complaining of police brutality. Constable Ted Fordham's report claimed the youth had slipped. Commissioner McMullin directed T.W.S. Parsons, the newly appointed assistant commissioner, to set up a formal investigation, assuring the press that the Board of Inquiry would include members of the public and that its findings would be made public. Complaints about the BCPP were unusual and were not taken lightly. Constable Fordham told the inquiry:

> On the day the youth hurt his shoulder, I was walking along the top of a box car. At no time was there a transient nearer than one car off. . .I have been on this particular work since April and hundreds of transients have been handled. Some I have had to speak to sharply but for the most part, there has been no trouble and I have never had to fight any of them except once when I arrested Olie Johnson. Even this man was only lifted up and carried to the station, then later he was taken to Ashcroft and given 30 days.[11]

The investigators eventually decided that the complaint was unsubstantiated. Cleared of the charges, Fordham was transferred to another region.

Commissioner McMullin had received permission to appoint an assistant commissioner in May 1933, when he pointed out that demands on him were great, and because he was getting older an assistant would ensure continuity in administering the force. He chose Parsons, quite a contrast to himself. Whereas McMullin appeared a perfect gentleman, even as he was recommending harsh measures or questioning someone's integrity, Parsons was a big, blunt, almost larger-than-life man. As one former member recalled, "Parsons could appear to be giving an order when he actually was asking a question. Capable man, vast experience. But certainly different than McMullin."[12]

In January 1934, Commissioner McMullin presented his annual report to Premier T.D. Pattullo's new government. After his summary of 1933, the details about the force, the labour incidents and the crimes considered the most challenging, he pointed out that prejudice and racial tensions had increased along with the unemployment rate. Constables all over the province reported incidents of immigrants being harassed. English-speaking white people accused other immigrants of taking jobs from "decent people," wrote letters to the editor and asked each other why Chinese and Japanese owned cafes, corner stores and laundries, why recently arrived Finns had jobs in whaling stations, why so many Italians worked on the railway and why Doukhobors controlled so much of the Kootenays. Many employers began to hire "English-speaking whites only," making it even more difficult for anyone else to find a job. Native Indians, the men and women who had been employed in the seasonal logging and fishing industries, found it particularly difficult to find work in the context of such prejudice. Many chose to live on reserves full-time. Though they were less desperate economically than many of the unemployed, the endless hours with nothing to do weighed heavily, particularly on men who had never been unemployed before. Consumption of bootlegged alcohol increased and the elders' traditional control eroded. Dominion Police were responsible for policing reserve lands, though a Provincial was often asked by the local Dominion constable to help out and usually complied. After all, if an inebriated Indian left the reserve, the Provincials became responsible for any law enforcement required. "The vast majority of natives seldom came to town and did not know many white people," one former BCPP member explained. "And we seldom knew much about them. Then there were the few who were drinkers and just as drunken whites did, they often turned into brawlers. We got to know them."[13]

Provincial Percy Carr had patrolled in Merritt for seventeen years and

183

was proud of his town and knowledgeable about its people. "He was a big friendly capable fellow. When I was there, it was amazing to walk down the street with him," a fellow Provincial reminisced. "He called everyone by name, including numerous Indians, and everyone we met expected to stop and chat. He must have introduced me to half the town on our way to his home for lunch."[14] Carr co-operated easily with other officials and had a reputation for helping out. When Frank Gisbourne, a Dominion constable, moved to Merritt, Carr assisted the young man frequently, particularly since he knew Gisbourne was charged with reducing bootlegging, which was a serious problem on the five nearby reserves. Gisbourne and Carr frequently worked together and covered for each other if one man had to go out of town.

On May 23, 1934, Gisbourne was away for the day, so when the call came in about Enas George stabbing his wife, Carr located the doctor and headed out to their reserve. By the time they arrived, George had fled, having told friends he would return that evening. His wife needed immediate hospitalization, so Carr drove doctor and patient to the Merritt hospital, then waited to report to Gisbourne. When he returned, Gisbourne decided to go out to arrest George that night and ask Carr to go with him. He arrived at the Provincial's house just as he was finishing dinner. Carr said, "Sure, I'll come along for the ride." He left the table, his holster and revolver still hanging on the kitchen chair, kissed his wife and followed Gisbourne out, saying to his family, "see you in a while."

Carr and Gisbourne were murdered that evening. According to witnesses who testified at the trials, when the peace officers arrived at the reserve, Carr remained in the car while Gisbourne went to arrest Enas George. Most likely Gisbourne had requested Carr not to accompany him; shows of force on reserves were avoided when no trouble was expected. A few hundred feet from the car, Gisbourne met the four George brothers behind some buildings. A fight broke out and the brothers, who were drunk, started pounding the constable with bottles. When Carr heard a gunshot, he rushed to the scene. By that time, Gisbourne was on the ground, and the brothers turned on Carr. The big constable fought frantically but went down almost immediately. The witnesses, who thought they were just watching a fight, saw the brothers drag the policemen around a corner and out of view. The Enas brothers confessed later that they had loaded the bodies in Gisbourne's car. When they got it going, a slow process as not one of the four had driven a car before, they headed for the Nicola River where they dumped the bodies into the fast water, then pushed the car into a hiding place on the steep bank.

When Gisbourne and Carr did not return, a search began. Carr's wife and the doctor knew that they had gone to the reserve to arrest Enas George, so suspicion centred on him, particularly as he and his brothers

*Even in the modern era, the force relied on some old-fashioned ways of patrolling the back country. Here a constable treks through the snow near Smithers in 1938.*

*The investigation of the Carr and Gisbourne murders was extensive: left to right, Staff Sergeant W.A. MacBrayne of the CIB, interpreter Albert Stirling, witnesses Henry Brown and Joseph Edwards, and Sergeant W.J. Service.*

were missing. Once the investigators found the bloodstained car a few days later, Enas was located and arrested. Everyone on the reserve was questioned. After claiming that they did not know the policemen had been murdered, the witnesses implicated the other three George brothers.

Enas and Richardson George eventually were hanged for the murders. Joseph went free because he was not involved in the actual slayings. The fourth brother, Alex, had his death sentence commuted to live imprisonment as a show of mercy because he suffered from severe tuberculosis.

In the aftermath of the murders, Provincial and Dominion policemen became more wary. McMullin directed all members of the Provincial force to remain armed while on duty. The use of a revolver was an absolute last resort – firing warning shots was not acceptable BCPP practice – but, McMullin told his men, knowing how and when to use a pistol was part of policing.

During the thirties, much policing did become unpleasant work and the rights or wrongs of a situation were often unclear. Large groups of people – strikers, Sons of Freedom, transients and others – viewed the police as adversaries. However, Provincials still often got to perform "regular" policing duties which left them feeling good about their work.

Two men arrived in British Columbia from the United States in the summer of 1934 and assumed the roles of an eye doctor and his assistant. The men offered free eye examinations to elderly people in rural areas, diagnosed cataracts and offered to remove them to prevent blindness. An aged victim would then be told that the necessary eyedrops had not yet been licensed in British Columbia because the government was so slow. The cons, of course, had the right drops with them, but they were expensive. If the victim bit, and offered as much money as he could raise, the eye doctor proceeded with a mock operation and showed the "patient" a bit of cellophane carefully held in forceps when it was over.

At the same time they were working the area near Nanaimo, Sergeant J. Russell was training a young constable and introducing him to local residents. When he asked the usual questions about strangers in the area, three different elderly people told him about the eye doctor. One man added that he was in the process of trying to raise some money to have his cataract removed when the doctor returned next week. The sergeant knew it sounded peculiar. On his return to Nanaimo, he queried all other detachments by radiogram and sent a constable out to check with the company where the two cons had rented a luxury car. The sergeant's suspicions were soon confirmed. A return radiogram from the Fraser Valley reported that a "doctor" recently had swindled $700 from an elderly man, whose regular doctor told him to complain to the police. The sergeant organized a search and the bogus doctor and his assistant were found and arrested. Charged with practising medicine without a licence, they each received a five-year sentence.

Policing also had its funny times. One spring day, a constable who was testing a pretty girl for her driver's licence ended up in a Hudson's Bay store display window. Apparently, just as she turned to smile at him, she accidentally accelerated and lost control, and they crashed through the Bay's corner window. There they were, with glass tinkling all around them, fully displayed for all the interested shoppers and storekeepers. The constable said it was a type of fame that he tried to forget, particularly as he had worked at that Bay store before joining the Provincials.

The thirties continued to be a demanding time for police. As the work camps became crowded, conditions deteriorated and men left, most voluntarily, although an increasing number were expelled. Transients again, most headed to Vancouver, walking and riding freights, staying for a night or two in each town's hobo jungle. Both federal and provincial governments feared rebellion, the option recommended by communist adherents. "On one hand, I think most politicians were aware of how rough it was for those poor blokes who couldn't find work," a Provincial NCO recalled as he tried to explain the Depression years.

> But on the other hand, I don't think any of them had ever had to try and scrounge potatoes for a community stew pot. They didn't know how it felt when they talked and argued about what was good for the unemployed. They worried about seditious literature and tried to make the hard times into a communist plot. Sure, that was a risk, a definite risk—people with no money listen to ideas from guys like Tim Buck...We checked ID all the time, picked up any wanted men. Once a transient's name was put on the list of suspected agitators, it stayed. Rough for those who weren't. An effective way of tracking those who were.[15]

Men suspected of being agitators were often arrested as vagrants. But lack of space in the jails and the cost of feeding prisoners made that an impractical solution, particularly when other transients found with the suspect insisted that they were equally guilty of whatever the charge was, so needed to be arrested as well. Most of the time, Provincials prevented suspected agitators from going to meetings by taking them into custody, then sending them on down the line under guard without any charges being laid.

Government costs skyrocketed and revenues plunged. When Prime Minister Mackenzie King was re-elected in 1935, he emphasized to the provinces that they could not expect any additional funds from the federal treasury except as loans. Provincial governments became desperate to

187

reduce their relief costs. British Columbia still had an estimated one-third of all the unemployed men in Canada, and more people arrived every day. Many were single men who had been unemployed for years; others were part of the increasing stream of married couples who had abandoned prairie farms, packed up their families and headed west. Deliberating how to stem the flow of "economic refugees," Premier Pattullo's government came up with a drastic solution. They decided to partially close the province's borders. No longer would all Canadians be allowed to enter. Commissioner McMullin was directed to organize Provincial Police guards for all the main crossings between Alberta and BC.

Guard the border between Alberta and British Columbia? Provincials must have been incredulous when they heard about their latest duty. The BCPP established checkpoints at Michel and at Crowsnest, the main points of entry for all road traffic from Calgary. All vehicles travelling west were stopped and refused entry if the driver did not have sufficient funds to purchase a provincial driver's licence and vehicle licence plates. Cash on the line or no admittance.

Licensing stations were operated by the Provincials round the clock, seven days a week. Constables had to establish whether people were tourists or future residents. If they claimed to be tourists, a sticker with their departure date was stuck onto their windshield. No checks were made on travellers coming in by bus or train, nor on those who entered through northern routes. One former Provincial recalled:

> The hardest duty I ever had to do as a constable was the Crowsnest border patrol. So many people had been blown out of the prairies. They would come with everything piled in an old haywired truck – children, dogs and chickens. We would stop them at the border and if they didn't have enough money to immediately purchase BC plates for their truck and a driver's licence, we had to turn them back. Sometimes grown men would stand at the counter and cry.[16]

Another former Constable recalled how he hated his months as a border guard:

> But it was the thirties. Some of the things that we had to do were not easily done. I've always remembered one of the NCOs I worked under there as the hardest man I ever met. I was so glad when I finally got transferred out. All those skinny kids and women with big eyes, devastated, sobbing hopelessly, when the man would have to turn the ancient overloaded truck around. I was a lean man but I felt fat compared to most of them. But my dad was ill and I was the only one able to help out. So you did what you had to do or you were one of the unemployed.[17]

Fifty years later, a few former Provincials reflected on the border patrol, wondering who had conceived the idea and deducing that few men other than raw recruits had worked it. They pointed out that information about it remained scanty. One volunteered that, a few years later, he had had the dubious pleasure of working with a man who had been a corporal at the border, explaining that in any group of people, a small percentage seem to be short on compassion and long on authority "for authority's sake."

Another man, who had been a raw recruit assigned to the mountain border, reminisced:

When they phoned and told me to come down because they had an opening, I rushed right over. I had a little shortwave experience, which was probably what got me in. I immediately agreed to go to Crowsnest when asked, even though I had no idea where it was. I was so glad that they wanted to hire me, I would have said yes to wherever they wanted to send me.

I signed on and the clerk took me into a storeroom. He passed a pair of boots to me but they were enormous and turned up at the toes. I said I didn't think I could wear those so he grabbed another pair. "Only big sizes left," he said. So I ended up with an eleven and I take an eight. Then he tossed a tunic, pants and other gear at me and ordered, "Come on, I'll get you a train ticket. Go home, put on the uniform and be at the station in four hours." Those boots! I had a terrible time getting them tied as they laced from the knee down the side, then laced down the middle of the front. My uniform was much too big, the pants only staying up because of the belt. But I got to the station on time, boarded the train and soon retired to my upper berth.

The next morning was quite a struggle. I got all the gear back on but I was not sure if it was quite right. I discovered it wasn't when I had to change trains at Nelson. There was a six-hour wait so I was walking the streets, smoking a cigarette, debating what to do. Luckily, it was a bit early to go for a beer because I did not even know that a constable didn't do that in uniform. A patrol car drove up and the constable inside it said, "Get in, would you please? I'm going to take you to my house for coffee and give you a few pointers. You look awful, bloody awful. We have to put your Sam Browne on right, polish buttons and get those bloody bows off your boots! And didn't anyone tell you not to smoke on the street?" He was a fine chap. He and his wife fed me and fixed me up...I sure felt better leaving his place than I had on arrival. Plus I had some idea of what was expected of me.

Then I arrived at Crowsnest and endured that situation. It was dreadful. I'd almost decided to leave the Provincials, even though jobs were impossible to get, but then I was transferred. Next I was in the Kootenays for six years, where I guess I began to comfortably fill the uniform, guarding bridges, trying to figure out what would burn next, doing the regular patrol things.

189

*Rescue work was just part of the job for BCPP constables. Here Constable W.H. Richmond struggles over the ice in the Skeena River near Terrace to retrieve a body adrift on the floes.*

*For the highway patrol in the early days, there weren't many highways to patrol. More typical was this twisty mountain road near Nelson.*

Policing that area compared to being a border guard was such a massive relief.[18]

Meanwhile, even as the BC government attempted to keep out destitute immigrants, labour unrest was growing. In his annual report for 1935, Commissioner McMullin recognized that it had been a turbulent year:

> It perhaps would not be amiss to mention here in a general way the noticeable efficiency with which all ranks handled the various disturbances which cropped up during the year. At Corbin, Vancouver, New Westminster and on Vancouver Island, there were demonstrations in connection with labour troubles, and I cannot speak too highly of the manner in which our men conducted themselves on these occasions. Without brutality, but firmly and tactfully, each situation was faced and handled in the most efficient manner. True, there were some clashes between the police and picketers, but there was no recourse to firearms nor was any person fatally injured.[19]

The labour clashes prosaically summarized in McMullin's report were bloodier than any before in British Columbia, particularly a coal miners' strike in Corbin. In early April, the town's largest mine reopened after a strike and then a lock-out, and management requested protection for workers choosing to go back to work. Fifty additional Provincials were brought in. On April 17, 250 striking miners and their wives gathered in front of the mine manager's office, threatening to demolish both him and the scabs returning to work. Provincials were barely able to control the mob.

The mine manager, frightened that strikers would break through the police cordon, ordered someone to drive a tractor with a heavy snowplow attached down the street toward the crowd. A number of Provincials apparently rode on the tractor as well. This scare tactic failed tragically when a rock from a striker's slingshot knocked out the driver. The massive machine careered out of control, mowing down men and women unable to flee from its path. Strikers thought that the tractor was driving over people on purpose, and a bloody battle broke out. Thirty-two civilians and sixteen police officers were injured, some severely. Subsequently, twenty-two strikers were prosecuted and convicted on charges ranging from creating a disturbance in a public place to assaulting a police officer and assault occasioning actual bodily harm.

In the aftermath, mine management decided to close the Corbin mine permanently. The strikers and the men who had been trying to return to work no longer had a company to fight over. Many miners became destitute, as there were few jobs in the economically barren Crowsnest area and Corbin employees were shunned by other managers. A resolution sent to Attorney General Gordon Sloan by the Corbin strikers accused their former employer, the Provincial Police and the government of a premeditated attempt to terrorize strikers with fascist terror tactics. The incident received much attention then and in subsequent years. The severely injured policemen received none. Many of them had been employed as specials so they did not receive much government aid. Those permanently injured became forgotten men.

Provincials looking back on those unsettled times remember that policing picket lines changed with the Corbin tragedy: the police became the enemy. Previously most strikers had recognized policemen as fellow workers having to do a job: they would verbally harass and threaten the police, but they would not attack them. After Corbin, however, Provincials felt much more vulnerable and apprehensive when they went out on labour patrols.

Chaotic conditions prevailed in most of BC in 1935. In the spring, many men in relief camps decided that exchanging a shovel for food and shelter was no longer enough. At a March meeting in Kamloops, about sixty delegates, representatives of the men still in camps and of the transients evicted from them, met with representatives from the communist-supported Relief Camp Workers Union to organize a general walkout. Then on March 31, the Communist Party held a mass meeting organized by Tim Buck, the party secretary, in the arena in Vancouver. The event attracted almost 6,000 people. Youngsters dressed in white with red sashes around their waists and the red stars and soviet emblem embroidered on their sweaters, paraded to the sound of kettle drums. They escorted Buck and E. Cumber, a representative of the Relief Camp Workers Union, and other speakers to the platform where they decried work camps as "slave compounds." Cumber spoke of the forthcoming strike of relief camp workers, and Buck predicted that "in the near future Canada would be governed by the Communist Party, men modelled after the type of Stalin, and not men of the type of Hilter and Mussolini."[20]

On April 4, hundreds of men left the federal camps scattered throughout the interior to converge on Vancouver. BCPP undercover agents reported that before they left an area, some reliefers planned on "paying back" suppliers who had been providing minimal food to the camps and pocketing large profits on their contracts. The occasional supplier was cornered, slapped around and threatened. The Provincials usually found the assailants among the men on the move and took them in. But the cases seldom went to court because the victim seldom wanted the publicity.

Provincials who patrolled the spread-out procession heading to Vancouver recalled the order, the lack of thefts, the small amount of violence.

"What do you think would happen now in the 1980s if we had comparable conditions?" one former NCO mused.

> All those men, many of them hungry, all worn out from years of just surviving. People had a different humour then or a different something. The marchers in 1935 were generally a good-natured bunch, they shared every-thing, amused each other, set up jokes, sang songs. They also protected each other, both from us and from the bullies in their ranks. Most of us sympa-thized with them, treated them courteously, requested rather than ordered. Agitators did not have an easy time stirring them up—most were pretty independent individuals. When we policed them, most of us were smart enough to try and keep them co-operating. Hard to explain, the differences between those times and these. It would be much more violent now.[21]

He commented that they policed preventively, using the BCPP short-wave network to keep track of suspected agitators. When detectives learned of plans for a demonstration in a town en route, they usually could locate the marchers expected to appear at it. Provincials with trucks picked up those men, often fifteen or thirty at a time, and drove them 70 or 100 miles down the road while another constable in the town met the train, intercepted the speaker and suggested that he remain aboard. They arrested a few suspected dissidents but the charges and subsequent sen-tences were usually minor.

Official nervousness increased as hundreds of men neared the coast. Was Vancouver about to become a battleground? Extra Provincials and specials as well as an RCMP mounted troop arrived to reinforce the Vancouver police force when the relief camp marchers arrived in town. As a show of strength, and to exercise men and horses, the Provincials and the RCMP marched through the streets every day, accompanied by their mounted patrols. However, civic authorities stressed that they expected the reliefers to be able to police themselves and that they hoped police action could be avoided. Though both senior forces were on hand to assist as necessary, all police were clearly aware that Mayor Gerry McGeer had the authority to decide when and how much policing was required. Attorney General Sloan could order Commissioner McMullin to take over, but he stressed to McGeer that he did not anticipate transferring control of the situation from the civic authority.

As the men from the relief camps arrived to join the unemployed in Vancouver, they organized themselves into a four highly disciplined divisions of approximately 400 men each. The large majority moved into Skid Road, just above the wharfs used by freighters, where accommoda-tion and food were cheapest. While the funds lasted, each man received two 15-cent meal vouchers and one 15-cent lodging ticket daily in exchange for assisting with fund-raising tag days or other assigned tasks. At first, tag days raised enough money to feed and shelter the reliefers. But after a few weeks, donations from sympathizers dried up. The men became restless; disagreements among them increased. Disappointment, frustration and anger grew. In May, all governments refused financial assistance and a riot ensued. Mayor McGeer read the Riot Act and most dispersed, but a few hundred demonstrators took possession of the Vancouver museum and library building and the Hudson's Bay store. They left the store the next day, but they settled into the library for six days. Commissioner McMullin counselled McGeer to take action. The three police forces combined in an impressive show of strength, and the demonstrators left the library voluntarily.

Conditions grew unstable as the reliefers became increasingly destitute. The leaders decided if the government would not send help to them, they would encourage the unemployed to go to Ottawa and live on the lawns until something was done. The On-to-Ottawa trek began in early June. Every freight leaving Vancouver had a roof full of transients as over 1,300 men headed east. The trekkers maintained tight discipline as they rode across BC on the freights, and Provincials reported few incidents of law breaking. A constable who supervised the overnight stay in the Kamloops Exhibition livestock barn recalled how tired and cold the men were when they arrived.

> It's hard riding on top of railway cars. Many of them were so young while others were old weary men. Some were obviously highly educated, all were courteous. They were appreciative of the soup kitchen provided for them and policed themselves re smoking and cleanup. As a community, we were somewhat nervous about being the overnight stop for so many. Part of the Provincial mounted troop had been brought in to back up police resources. Kamloops was vulnerable to damage if things got wild, but they remained well-behaved. Nor were there any other problems. Extra guards had been put on quite a few bridges, both along the CNR lines and the CPR as reports had come in from the undercover fellows that some railway bridges and the Connaught Tunnel were to be blown up. But nothing was.[22]

Prime Minister R.B. Bennett ordered the RCMP to stop the transients at Regina and not to allow any to continue east. Riots ensued there, resulting in the death of a Mountie, numerous serious injuries and many arrests. Many of the reliefers headed back to BC much angrier than when they had left.

As the men wandered through the province, some became more surly and threatening than before. Inspector MacDonald in Penticton ordered over 100 reliefers transported to an isolated point on the Hope–Princeton highway by truck on July 21, 1935: "My reason for sending the men over the Hope Princeton trail was to prevent a riot and possibly save life," he explained in a radiogram to Commissioner McMullin.

> Received information that the strikers had arranged when they got all together at the last camp on the way to Princeton to attack the police, beat them up and take control. While we were in the camp, they were quite boastful about what they were going to do once they got control. Of course they were not aware we knew of their intentions. Tacks were placed on the road at the last camp on the way to Princeton to stop our cars. Sergt. Gammon got 22 punctures. But fortunately, there were no men there to attack us. The majority of the men have recently returned from Regina and do not belong in this province. I was also informed that it was their intention to set fire to the camps. In fact in one bunk house while we were there they broke two lamps and put coal oil on the floor. I consider our actions saved a good deal of trouble as well as expense. The men were determined on going to Vancouver. This was the shortest route, the trail is good and they were supplied with food for the journey.[23]

During the same spring, when the Powell River Pulp and Paper Company locked out its newly organized union employees in mid-May, the Longshoremen's Union declared a strike in BC and declared Powell River paper shipments "hot." Tons of the giant paper rolls, due to be shipped through the ports of Vancouver, New Westminster and Powell

*During the Depression, the police were called out frequently to patrol demonstrations in front of the legislature in Victoria.*

River to newspapers in international markets, were left stacked on wharfs and in warehouses. When non-union men were hired in an attempt to move the paper past picketing strikers onto ships, the strike broadened. Violent confrontations occurred among longshoremen, their sympathizers and "scab" labourers in Vancouver and New Westminster. Civic officials, already stretched thin policing the reliefers, agreed that policing the docks would be done by the RCMP and BCPP forces.

Two hundred Provincial Police and specials lived on a CNR ship on the waterfront for almost seven months, taking round-the-clock shifts on the docks. Commissioner McMullin later reported: "that they were able to do so without a single clash in the territory allotted to them is some evidence of their firmness, tact and tolerance."[24]

When he heard McMullin's report, one Provincial who had guarded the waterfront commented:

> It had to have been luck more than tact and tolerance. Sure, we were lectured daily about self-control, but when fifteen of us lined up to stop hundreds of them from rushing the docks to pulverize the scabs, there was a lot of luck involved. I remember how my stomach would knot up sometimes. Thinking about it now, I do not really understand how we managed to hold that line, day after day, night after night, without any of us being seriously injured or killed. It got rough sometimes. Probably the commissioner was surprised, too. When we had originally been sent to the Beatty Street armouries as a permanent emergency force, one of the things we were taught was how to slow march, which is used at funerals. After all, there was a good chance that some of us would be killed. When I recall the animosity and the massive numbers we often faced then, it is amazing that all of us survived.[25]

Attorney General Sloan kept a close watch on Vancouver, particularly when the strikers began to return from Regina and moved into Skid Road along with the longshoremen. Aware that the returning reliefers might join in the wharf conflict and that more unions were considering going out in support of the longshoremen's strike, Sloan ordered the BCPP to be prepared to take control of Vancouver, emphasizing to Commissioner McMullin that it would be done only as a last resort and on short notice.

However, the civic force continued to maintain control, though strikers became increasingly belligerent that fall. Harassment of the public and the police increased and some strikers began damaging stores. One former Provincial who was on the municipal police force at the time recalled how he was posted outside the Hudson's Bay store, directed to check all people and to stop any who were not shoppers.

> It was a ludicrous job. I could not have stopped any group without shooting

them and that was against the rules. So my partner and I had to stand there and be shouted at all day. One guy stood and spit at me for a while. Only at my feet, luckily, or my self-control would have exploded, even if it had of meant my job. But I was lucky. That same day, two constables at Woodwards were injured, one had a bad head injury after being smacked with an iron bar and another had taken a brutal kick in the groin.[26]

In late October 1935, the longshoremen went back to work and Prime Minister King transformed the relief camps into farming and forestry camps run by the Department of Labour rather than the military. Residents received $15 a month, part in cash and part in forced savings. Many reliefers decided to return to the camps rather than face a homeless, hungry winter. Many others chose instead to wander around the province, looking for a day's work, attending meetings and surviving as best they could in hobo jungles.

Conditions improved somewhat in the following two years. Then, early in 1938, the relief camps in British Columbia started closing, welfare money to municipalities was cut back and once again the unemployed trekked to Vancouver. An estimated 6,000 unemployed men gathered in the city and on May 11, 1,200 of them took occupancy of the post office, the Hotel Georgia and the Vancouver Art Gallery. After ten days, the 300 protesters in the Hotel Georgia withdrew. But the post office and art gallery occupants refused to leave. Finally authorities decided to evict them forcibly if necessary. When threatened with tear gas, the protesters at the art gallery left peacefully but protesters remained in the post office until the RCMP officers, backed up by the BCPP and Vancouver police, lobbed tear gas into the federal building. Thirty-nine people, including five police officers, were injured and twenty-two protesters were arrested. In the aftermath, hundreds of people protested the action by demonstrating at the legislature in Victoria and thousands gathered at a large protest rally in Vancouver. A Provincial reported that the demonstrators were quite orderly but many individuals were "spoiling for a fight."

Employment opportunities began to improve and massive demonstrations by unemployed people ended. But even as men found work, policing confrontations continued. Throughout BC, Provincials had to intervene in an increasing number of labour conflicts. The disputes became more and more violent, particularly in logging camps and mines along the coast, which necessitated expanding the BCPP marine department. A former PML crew member recalled:

> Often the only way into a mine or mill was by boat, which made it difficult to estimate who had arrived in a certain area accurately. It was easy to take a couple of boat loads of men in to a strike situation in the middle of the night.

It's easier to maintain secrecy along a waterway than anywhere else. Then when we went in, expecting to find thirty men in a dispute, we might suddenly be faced with sixty or seventy. For instance, when the union was attempting to make the lime plant at Blubber Bay, close to Powell River, into a closed shop and was also protesting the use of Oriental labour, we were ordered in. About 100 paid agitators arrived to get the so-called scabs the night before we arrived. Quite a fiasco . . . six of us had been sent in to try and cool things down. It was rough, we were so outnumbered. I was knocked over and had the caulk boots put to me — had punctures from those boots all over my chest and legs. I also lost some teeth, but I wasn't too bad . . .

But I was lucky. If it hadn't been for Andy Williamson, another constable, seeing them drag me into that shed, they might have killed me. A big man, he apparently got to me, picked me up under one arm and used his riot stick with the other hand to belt the men attacking us down like nine-pins. Lucky for me, as by then I was not conscious. Forty more policemen arrived shortly after that from Vancouver, and there were massive arrests on charges of unlawful assembly, bodily harm, assault. After I got out of hospital, I was twelve weeks in Vancouver, attending the trials.[27]

Many Provincials recalled similar incidents as they explained how much people changed during the Depression and how policing evolved.

Issues became much more confused. By the end of thirties, not only were most people irresponsible to driving and alcohol laws — they obeyed them most of the time but felt little guilt if penalized for an infraction — quite a few now perceived policemen as bullies who went around swinging nightsticks. In the smaller places, things didn't change for the individual constable but in the larger places, policing had changed a lot. And we all feared that we were about to be dragged into another war; that made conditions unsettled, too.[28]

Commissioner McMullin turned seventy in 1938, and decided that after being at the helm of the BCPP for fourteen years, he could finally take his long-delayed retirement. The past seven years had been professionally difficult and personally wearing, and his health was failing. The long years of the Depression were almost ended but, as he knew, even greater challenges would soon face the Provincials: Europe would soon be at war again.

# CHAPTER NINE

## "Please accept my resignation"
## 1939–1943

THOUGH REPORTS FROM EUROPE grew increasingly ominous in early 1939, and constables pondered what they would do if war was declared, their main concern was keeping vulnerable residents safe from the raging spring runoffs. Rivers sometimes rampaged without warning, washing out bridges and roads. On March 24, at midnight, moving ice demolished the tiny community of East Pine in the Peace River country.

When the weather warmed rapidly, tons of ice on the Pine and Murray rivers thawed, cracked into chunks and started downriver much too quickly for the narrow channel. People, buildings and animals were suddenly in grave danger as blocks of ice jammed together to form a dam and block the river. Eventually the dam ruptured, and a torrent of water and ice blocks rushed forward like forty bulldozers in a line, levelling or carrying away whatever was in the path.

When the Dawson Creek Provincial Police office received word of the disaster, Constable Jack Watt and Game Warden Oscar Quesnel managed to make the fifty-mile trip to East Pine in three hours. They travelled the first thirty miles of soggy snowdrifts by car, then transferred their emergency supplies to a horse-drawn sleigh for the rest of the way. When they arrived, none of the buildings remained standing. Mounds of ice glistened in the sunshine and the only sounds they heard were of ice grinding and water flowing.

Constable Watt fired three shots to find out whether anyone had survived, and shouts came back from across the river. Using floating ice blocks as a bridge, he crossed to the few survivors who were staggering out of the trees. Clad in wet nightwear, they were cold, exhausted and glad to be alive. The schoolteacher, his wife and baby and a young family who had run the general store had been trying desperately to keep a tiny fire going for hours. They had fled from their cabins through hastily enlarged chimney holes, even as ice piled up against the doors and windows. The storekeeper and his family had spent most of the night on a barn roof, before fleeing again at dawn when it became obvious that the barn was going to go as well.

Watt and Quesnel linked the weary survivors together with an alpine-style rope lifeline and guided them on the perilous journey back across the moving ice. The Provincials then wrapped them in blankets and soon had them drinking hot soup beside a roaring fire. Then they began to search for the eight other people who had lived in East Pine. But no more survivors were ever found, only three bodies, including one of a three-year-old boy that had to be chipped out of the frozen river.

When McMullin retired and Parsons became commissioner, he revised the BCPP district borders. Policing thirty-six municipalities under as many separate contracts meant that some districts had become unwieldy. However, as British Columbia's geography defined divisional borders and each region required certain policing methods, Commissioner Parsons and his newly appointed assistant commissioner, John Shirras, did not change the boundaries of the five main divisions or two sub-divisions.

"A" Division consisted of five districts – Victoria, Duncan, Nanaimo,

*Police search the ice jams for bodies after the East Pine flood.*

Courtenay and West Coast—and included two motor branches and six police boats, including the PML 14, a floating detachment with cells and a courtroom. The division was divided into nineteen detachment offices, which policed Vancouver Island, the surrounding ocean and five municipalities.

"B" Division was responsible for over 27,000 square miles in southern British Columbia, from the Coquihalla Pass to Penticton and Oliver, then to Trail, Grand Forks and the Crowsnest mines outside of Fernie. Four districts of Boundary, Grand Forks, East Kootenay and West Kootenay contained nineteen more detachment offices.

"C" Division covered 65,000 square miles and its wide rivers and towering mountain ranges presented enormous transportation difficulties. It included much of the Okanagan and part of the Selkirks and Rockies as well as the Cariboo. Quesnel, Barkerville, Bridge River, the Chilcotin to Tweedsmuir Park, the Fraser Canyon to Yale, the Nicola Valley, Kamloops, Vernon, Kelowna and the upper Arrow Lakes were policed under its seven districts, divided into twenty-eight detachments. Eleven municipalities contracted the services of the BCPP.

"D" Division was a massive area extending from north of Prince Rupert to south of Ocean Falls, including the Queen Charlotte Islands and the immense Tweedsmuir Park. Its three districts had fourteen detachments including two police boats, the PML 7 and the PML 8.

"E" Division covered the lower coast and the lower mainland. It had the greatest population and therefore the largest concentration of BCPP personnel and equipment. It was divided into six districts which were divided again into twenty-five detachments, including the Mounted Troop, seven vessels, two motor branches, and a Criminal Investigation Branch.

The Peace River sub-division, which bordered Alberta and the Northwest Territories, and the Fort George sub-division, which went north from Prince George to the Yukon, divided BC's extensive northern interior territory between them. Because of the region's small population and extreme weather conditions, much of the work there involved rendering assistance in emergency situations, often in isolated spots.

Commissioner Parsons knew each area of British Columbia well. When he joined the Provincials in 1912, he had been posted to Kitselas on the Skeena River, then had been transferred to Terrace. He was promoted to chief constable of the Peace River district in 1914. Later, he served in Kamloops, then South Fort George and in 1923, he was promoted to inspector of the Prince Rupert district, then transferred to take charge of the Vancouver Island district. As the commissioner liked to explain, he had been stationed in every division except for "B," where he had served temporarily twice.

Born in England, Parsons had served with the City of London Artillery. In 1904, he had joined the South African Constabulary for a brief period, then immigrated to Canada. A large man with military bearing and dry British humour, he was an internationally respected writer about police affairs, his best-known work being *A Handbook for Constables*. He was an advocate of international policing, particularly some form of alliance between Canada, the United States and Mexico, a concept that had been under discussion for some years. The new commissioner was acquainted with many police officials and political administrators outside of BC, and stayed abreast of innovative policing techniques. He took pride in the BCPP's reputation of speedily incorporating new methods.

One of Parsons' first responsibilities was to organize protection and ceremonial guards for the Royal Tour in May 1939. The Provincial Police joined the RCMP, municipal police forces from Vancouver and Victoria and CN/CP railway police in providing both security and crowd control for King George VI and Queen Elizabeth. Security had to be exceptionally thorough in light of the deteriorating international situation and the increased possibility of royal assassinations. In British Columbia, police feared that agitators and dissidents might create disturbances around the royal visitors. As well, the geography of the province was a challenge: protection had to be arranged at every vulnerable railway bridge and crossing, a massive feat when compared with guarding trains on the flat prairie.

Because the king and queen travelled out to Vancouver on the Canadian Pacific Railway, then returned east on the Canadian National line in order to visit the maximum number of communities, both rail routes had to be secured. The joint policing was a tightly planned and co-ordinated effort. Colour-coded passes were issued to everyone — dignitaries, journalists, policemen and suppliers of food to the royal train. Enthusiastic Provincials lobbied their officers for "front-line" guard duty. Flags and bunting hung in every town and village, flower baskets decorated telephone poles, storefronts and even barns along the routes were painted. Crowds gathered to cheer the royal couple and children waited impatiently on every train station's platform en route, waving Union Jacks at the sound of the steam engine's whistle.

The royal visit was just the start of extraordinary duties that year. The Japanese Crown Prince visited a few weeks later and although his stay in BC was brief, the BCPP was his official escort while he was in Canada. There was considerable concern about his safety. Besides the increased risk to all royals, the war between China and Japan had created much bitterness within the Chinese–Canadian community. As well, anti-Oriental attitudes persisted, particularly in BC. But the six Provincials who accompanied the prince and his entourage on the train trip from Vancouver to Halifax encountered no difficulties. They maintained tight security, shielding the prince from strangers on station platforms and bringing in prearranged safe food.

Then from May through October 1939, some Provincials had a unique tour of duty at the San Francisco World's Fair. They guarded BC's massive "Gold Display," a collection of mining paraphernalia and nuggets valued at half a million dollars. Immaculate in their khaki uniforms and Stetsons, Provincials also acted as good will ambassadors, answering questions about British Columbia and its display. The teams rotated every six weeks, primarily to keep BC's "ambassadors" sounding enthusiastic, but also to allow more members a turn at the popular duty.

When the world went to war and the Defence of Canada Regulations under the War Measures Act were enacted on September 3, 1939, the Provincials again had many new responsibilities. Parsons reported at year end:

> The registration of enemy aliens was, of course, the first duty and data compiled by this Branch over a number of years immediately became of paramount importance. Many of our branches were appointed by the Regis-

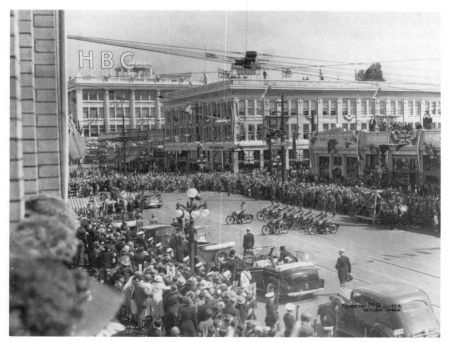

*BCPP were out in force to escort King George V and Queen Mary when they visited the province in 1939.*

trar-General in Ottawa as registration points . . . Trespassing and loitering in
prohibited areas and the control of publications required attention. Then the
clause in the Defence of Canada Regulations, providing for the safe-guarding
of information useful to the enemy, communication with enemy agents,
photography, etc., had to be given attention. The control of explosives,
ammunition, and firearms was a salient feature of the regulations that needed
much of our time.

In the first months of the war we were literally flooded with information
from all classes of people who had heard statements they considered to be
subversive. All these statements had to be investigated and tracked down. In
many cases, of course, evidence did not justify prosecution. There was also
a large number of complaints concerning the activities of alleged enemy
aliens . . . gratifying to know that we were in a position to take our place along
with the Defence Forces and that our work was of vital importance to the
National defence.[1]

Enforcing defence regulations quickly strained BCPP resources, especially since many Provincials resigned to join military units. One of
Commissioner Parsons' principal concerns was shortage of qualified men,
particularly radio and marine officers, whose special services were needed
by the Armed Forces. In the early months of the war, Parsons travelled
throughout the province, emphasizing to the men how crucial their
services were for the defence of the British Columbia. Many agreed to
remain with the force for at least a year or two.

All Provincials began working longer shifts in order to accommodate
war duties as well as maintaining regular policing. Crews aboard the
motor launches began tracking as well as checking out all unidentified
boats as they watched for suspicious activities along the coastline. Radio
operators monitored all shortwave signals, searching for unidentified
stations. As well, scrambled military messages were sent daily over the
Provincial Police shortwave network. Though national security was a
federal matter, Commissioner Parsons assured his federal counterpart that
the BCPP was available to assist the RCMP on request. The BCPP and
the RCMP "E" Division, headquartered in Vancouver, immediately began
pooling knowledge and responsibilities, their co-operative investigation
techniques having developed during the thirties. The Provincial Police's
Criminal Investigation Branch helped to locate suspected subversives and
eighteen Provincials at various locations were officially appointed as
registrars of enemy aliens; costs to the BCPP of temporarily holding aliens
and providing guards for them was paid by the federal force.

A large segment of the population, all British Columbia's German-
born and Italian-born residents, were registered when Canada declared
war against their native countries. Those suspected of supporting the Axis

cause and any men who had ever been suspected as subversives—quite a number because of the mass "suspect" categorization during the Depression—were interned. In the winter of 1939–40, some internment camps were unprepared for housing inmates and were without adequate food, heat and supplies. The internees, many of them long-term Canadian residents, suffered from the disorganization. As well, once they were interned, their Canadian-born offspring were shunned by some of their neighbours. It was an era in which people comfortably called Italian Canadians wops, Chinese Canadians chinks and German Canadians krauts.

Aliens considered dangerous or undesirable were deported and the BCPP often acted for the RCMP when a deportation was ordered. When a request to pick up a German-born rancher from Vinsulla arrived at

*Sergeant Harold Raybone, left, and Constable Frank Grimshaw shovel confiscated firearms into the Strait of Juan de Fuca from the deck of PML 14.*

Kamloops Provincial Police district headquarters, two Provincials drove out.

They lived up in the North Thompson Valley, up in the mountains above Vinsulla. When we arrived, we showed the deportation order to the German and his Canadian wife and then explained that they had to decide what they were going to do. They could be given no time. We had to stay with them, then take him back to Kamloops with us and provide escort for him on the night train. So they had to decide immediately whether the whole family would go or whether the wife would remain.

Pretty tough country up there for a woman with young children, especially in the winter. Some could survive but she wasn't the type. And as the man had committed armed robbery and served a jail term since coming to Canada, there was no possibility that he would be let back in at the end of the war — it eliminated the possibility of him becoming a citizen. Actually, it was funny that he hadn't been deported when he was released from jail, many were. But maybe he got to stay because apparently he had fled Germany in the political upheaval in the early thirties. His wife decided to go with him even though he kept saying, "I'll be killed as soon as I put foot in Germany."

I went down to the one-room schoolhouse to get the children while my partner helped the man drive his cattle to a neighbour's pasture and to make arrangements for the chickens and dogs. Within a short time, the woman had the little bit of stuff they were taking loaded up and we started off. The German said, "There goes my little home in the West." In the morning, he had been a rancher with an organized little spread, a charming young wife and two happy little tow-headed kids. By suppertime, chaos.

The wife went across to Halifax then did not leave with him. She and the children returned briefly to Kamloops. The public trustee got a pretty good price for her for the ranch so at least she had something.[2]

Alien Registration meant that all naturalized German and Italian Canadians over eighteen had to formally identify themselves and provide all pertinent facts about their families to a registrar. Their Canadian-born children were not registered unless there were extenuating circumstances. After Japan signed a treaty for mutual defence with the Rome–Berlin Axis on September 27, 1940, all residents of Japanese descent were registered also. As "aliens," these people were supervised by both RCMP and BCPP personnel. They had to report in once a month, unless the officer they were reporting to changed the time period. They were not allowed armaments, explosives, radio transmitters or photography equipment, except by special permission.

Many German, Italian and Japanese Canadians had lived in Canada for years, having arrived as infants, and substantial numbers did not even know their parents' mother tongues. Yet the fact they had relatives in the old country made them suspects. In 1939–40, registering and reporting was such a difficult emotional process for many long-term residents that some Provincials attempted to ease the pain by calling on them instead. In most areas, the Provincial acting as the registrar knew his region's residents well and treated them according to their past reputations. Consequently, those first registered "aliens," all too aware of the consequences to them if an Italian or German saboteur was caught, were the first to notify him if they saw a suspicious stranger around. Unfortunately, the constables' workload grew steadily—by early 1940, each Provincial's workday was about twelve hours—and special consideration for individuals became the exception rather than the rule.

Shortage of manpower was Commissioner Parsons' most urgent problem, aggravated by the fact that military recruiters depleted the pool of men available. More Provincials resigned in order to enlist. Some were so anxious to get overseas that they paid $100 to buy their way out of their three-year contract, while others served out their terms, then declined to renew. The loss of experienced Provincials left a void. Though Douglas House trained the BCPP probationers more thoroughly than new members had ever been previously, it could not provide the one-to-one lessons the senior men had traditionally provided. "Learning all the theory is necessary but it is the apprenticeship which trains men," an officer explained.

> When I joined up, something called savvy was learned from fellow policemen, especially from the men who had served ten years or so. They had begun to understand people pretty well and were gruffly patient and kind to just about anyone. They were pretty adept at keeping us from getting too big for our britches, too. That training was invaluable. Good policing needs some mature perceptiveness and I guess they taught us that. So when a lot of them went to war, we lost some of that as well. Fewer men telling us not to get puffed up by the power of being a policeman.[3]

Along with wartime duties, Provincials policed more residents as British Columbia's population expanded rapidly. Workers involved in the numerous war-related industries arrived as did many military personnel and the camp followers. Though additional people meant more crimes were committed, it also meant more long and complicated rescue missions. For instance, when the *Great Northern V*, an ocean tug and scow with three men aboard, was reported missing out in the Pacific somewhere between Estevan Point and Quatsino in late December 1939, Provincials began a hazardous marine search. The PML 14, which normally patrolled the area, was in Victoria for a long overdue safety inspection, so Constable

R. Winegarden from Zeballos detachment joined in the search by plane. Meanwhile, every boat in the area scoured the rugged, foggy coastline.

The airplane pilot eventually sighted a man, but on a stretch of shoreline where it could not land. Constable Winegarden, accompanied by a civilian volunteer, worked his way in a small boat through the waves and dangerous reefs to the marooned man. It turned out to be Hugh Skinner, crewman on the *Great Northern V* and son of the missing skipper. He was frantic about his dad. He explained that when their boat sank and the engineer drowned, he managed to get his injured father ashore, far up the coast. But he could not carry him out. As they were without food, water or fire, Hugh had left his father by a waterlogged cedar root and gone for help. That was five days earlier and the young man was exhausted by the time his rescuers arrived. They started back up the coast to find the elder Skinner, but there was a strong tide running and the launch could not handle the sea so they had to return to port.

The December storms and fogs foiled several rescue attempts until finally, on January 3, Corporal J. Howe, Constable E.W. Lockwood, and two experienced volunteers, William Ilkstead and Schuyler Ilkstead, succeeded in landing on a point twelve miles from the skipper. It took them another day to hike through thick bush and along the rocky coastline to reach Captain Skinner, barely alive after eighteen days huddled under the massive root. A large fire soon had the patient and his rescuers warm, and it served as a beacon for the plane to drop medicine and supplies. Two people were credited with saving Skinner. His wife insisted that he was

*PML 14, the flagship of the BCPP fleet, patrolled the west coast of Vancouver Island and adjacent waters. Its facilities included a jail cell and a courtroom.*

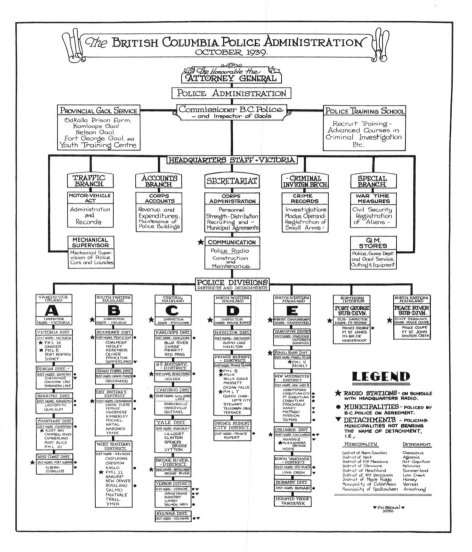

*This chart illustrates the organization of police administration in BC in 1939.*

still alive, and Constable Lockwood, who had been a New Brunswick fisherman before joining the BCPP, had agreed with her, saying that a man could survive such storms. They had kept up the search, despite the experts' opinion that Skinner had to be dead.

When reminiscing about their careers, many former members of the BCPP said that perseverance was a necessity for policing, perhaps the most important factor. Long hours of effort often showed no results at the end of the day or week, but eventually something would occur that made all the work worthwhile. This was particularly true in labour disputes. Commissioner Parsons emphasized to his men, as McMullin had before him, that they were not to have opinions about who was right or who was wrong in a strike. Their job was to prevent conflict and property damage, and preferably to take no action except to stand guard.

Although the province's labour problems had decreased, miners and management at the Pioneer Gold Mine outside of Bralorne had been in conflict for some time. On February 13, 1940, a group of miners seized the lowest levels in the mine and the government decided that the best way to prevent violence was to saturate the area with Provincials. One former member who was a young man at the time recalled:

I was sent into the Pioneer Gold Mine in early March 1940, where a rotating strike had been going on since fall. Originally there were seven of us in there for about ten days, then I was sent back to Kamloops when the situation appeared to have improved. But it quickly built again and this time ninety-eight men were sent into Bridge River for two weeks. There were considerable undercurrents of tension but no conflicts.

We were billetted in the bunkhouses with the strikers—even played poker with some of them one night. Found out later it was the same night that they had dished out clubs and pick handles! We all expected violence after that. But it remained peaceful, though there were still miners down in the mines who wouldn't come up and management remained afraid of sabotage. So part of our job was to see that no more went down.

I was sent down to police the 500-foot level, that was where I did my eight-hour shifts. Five hundred feet down, all by myself. The power was off so we had to climb down and climb up fifty-foot ladders. My job was to listen and to watch for movement, as once you are underground, you can hear all below, but it remained calm. I wrote letters in the weak light of my lantern to pass the time while I was down there. Quite a place, underground... The miners who had remained in the mine were down at 2,400 feet. One of our officers, Woods-Johnson, climbed all the way down there to talk to them and eventually agreement was reached.

When the explosiveness of the situation was considered to be ended, we were sent back to our regular detachments. Ninety-eight men, about a quarter of the force then, was a lot of men to have had in one place. Hard on the men in the detachments, particularly with war regulations and extras.[4]

Military personnel were moving into British Columbia at a rapid rate. Many industries — shipbuilding, spruce lumber production, heavy water distillation and gunpowder manufacturing, for example — were designated critical to defence and had twenty-four-hour guards posted on their facilities. As well, Home Guards, usually World War I veterans, patrolled all road and railway bridges necessary to the transportation system. In the event of anything suspicious, they notified the nearest Provincial Police office.

When a call came into the Revelstoke detachment from a guard at a nearby railway crossing, a constable was sent out.

The old guard explained that he had seen a guy walking about a short way down the road, which was strange as it was not a walking area, so he had called to him to please identify himself. Instead, the man had run off. I started searching the area where the guard had seen him plunge into the bush and after prowling about for quite some time, located a man sitting under a tree, far back from the road. When I spoke to him, he said nothing, absolutely nothing, yet he obviously could hear.

I didn't like the look of him, he was a pretty hard character, so I searched him and found a map of western Canada. Then I realized with a start that the printing someone had added to it was in German lettering. I took him into the office and he continued to remain silent. We locked him up and started investigating. Sure enough, he was an escaped prisoner from Alberta. Eventually he talked. He could speak a little English but with a real heavy German accent. He explained that he had originally been on a submarine, then became a prisoner of war in Canada when the sub had been blown up in the Atlantic. We sent a wire off to the prisoner-of-war camp saying that we were arranging guarded transportation for him back to the camp. They hadn't even known he was missing![5]

For some Provincials, the war occasioned some extraordinary experiences. When three American B-26 airplanes on their way to Alaska went down somewhere between Dawson Creek and Watson Lake on January 13, 1941, Constable Jack Purdy from the McDams detachment went searching for them with Russ Pater, a bush pilot. Purdy happened to be at the airport putting his wife on a plane to the outside. He was feeling lonely and reluctant to have to go back to McDams without her, so Pater invited him along for the search.

211

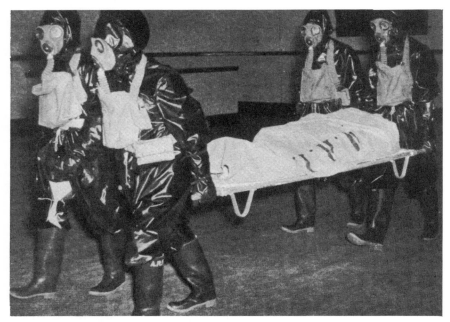

*Provincials trained thousands of Air Raid Protection (ARP) volunteers during World War Two.*

*These members of the force were the top-ranked pistol-shooting team in the province.*

The two men searched the white wilderness for quite a while without sighting anything. Then, west of Smith River, some distance outside of Fort Nelson, they spotted the B-26s in a shallow valley on top of a mountain just about at the timberline. There they were, three great silver birds, all in the same valley, each about two miles from the other. As darkness was approaching, Pater landed at a trapper's cabin about fifty miles away. At dawn the next day, they were able to land about three miles from the downed aircraft. When they snowshoed over, they found most of the men in good shape. Only two people were injured in the crash. Purdy took a piece of cowling and shaped it into a toboggan to drag the injured men back to the rescue plane. "Fortunately we had a very mild stretch of weather at that time so we got them all out," he later recalled. "Pater took the injured men and went for help and the weather held until we were out. Couldn't have made it in a blizzard. The planes stayed there and it became known as The Million Dollar Valley. I understand the US Air Force eventually took the motors out but they left the fuselages. Apparently fuel capacity calculations had been wrong."[6]

During the first year of war, much consideration had gone into policing the postwar period as the war was expected to last months, not years. But by late 1940, many people had stopped believing that it was going to be a short war, including Commissioner Parsons and Attorney General Wismer. Though Parsons agreed with international police experts' forecast of postwar chaos if Depression conditions and unemployment occurred, and he continued his long-term planning, he knew his main problem in the next three years was going to be manpower. The Allied troops suffered some defeats and the war effort became the dominant concern in BC, almost everyone was involved somehow in supplying the forces or protecting the home front. Many men and women volunteered for emergency rescue training programs. The part-time training was made compulsory for men between eighteen and forty-five in the spring of 1940, initially for a period of one month. After Japan joined the Axis forces, the compulsory training was extended to three months. The Provincials had participated in the emergency measures training program from its inception, assisting the military with recruitment and training. In October 1941, the Air Raid Precautions of the Civilian Protection Branch, better known as the ARP, came completely under BCPP administration.

Over 10,000 civilians around the province were trained on ARP equipment, such as anti-gas clothing, respirators, fire scoops, stretchers and other emergency gear needed in case of attack. For many, the training was what crystallized the reality of war for them. "Raised my bile," one man recalled. "It was an unreal experience, yet suddenly I understood what soldiers did, what bombs did."[7] After the course, volunteers were formed into homeguard units, mainly involved in enforcing security.

Also, as more Provincials resigned to join the armed forces and the shortage of qualified specials grew, Commissioner Parsons organized a volunteer Police Reserve, which, at its peak, had 2,000 men trained for emergency policing duties.

Panic swept British Columbia on December 7, 1941, when Japan bombed and sank the American naval fleet at Pearl Harbor, then the next day attacked Hong Kong. The Allied forces declared war on Japan. As it became known that Japan's campaign against Hong Kong had resulted in the death or internment of 2,000 Canadian soldiers, many British Columbians became convinced that Japan could win the war for the Axis, and that the west coast was Japan's next target. Their anxiety and anger focussed on the province's Japanese communities at Steveston, New Westminster, Vancouver and Prince Rupert, most of whose residents were of Japanese descent. These Canadians had few options for protecting their interests. Though born in Canada, they had no MP or MLA representing them as they had never been allowed to vote.

Tempers rose and letters to the editor became increasingly vindictive against all British Columbians of Japanese origin. By the end of the year, big yellow balloons had appeared in many fraternal clubs and military messes, complete with a donation can and a sign saying, "Slap A Jap, donate a nickel, support the war effort."

During the same period, the government of BC was in chaos. A general election on October 21 had rejected Premier Pattullo's government: fourteen members had been defeated, including Attorney General Wismer, mainly by candidates from the CCF (Co-operative Commonwealth Federation, a coalition of progressive socialist and labour groups). The delegates at a Liberal party convention on December 2 voted for a coalition government with the Conservatives. They nominated John Hart as the coalition premier, and their decision was ratified two days later in the legislature. During December, as the war intensified, the coalition government worked at appointing a cabinet acceptable to all its members, a slow process. Premier Hart held the attorney general's portfolio in the interim. Finally, in mid-January, the new premier designated the powerful R.L. (Pat) Maitland as attorney general.

Meanwhile, members of the Standing Committee on Orientals, a committee of civic and RCMP representatives set up in early 1940 by the federal government,[8] advised that something be done quickly. Two days after Pearl Harbor, Prime Minister Mackenzie King ordered the arrest of all persons suspected of sympathizing with Japan. And despite earlier offers from fishermen to volunteer their boats for coast defence, all BC fishermen of Japanese ancestry were ordered to dock their boats. To fulfill the government's initial directives, additional RCMP members, the BCPP marine constables and teams from the navy joined the four RCMP responsible for all security investigations in the province. They directed that the 1,100 fishing boats tie up at cannery wharfs, then removed engine rotors to immobilize the boats. Each owner co-operated and there were no protests. Most owners and crews were detained temporarily because authorities worried about their intimate knowledge of the coast: fishermen made ideal spies. In addition, some fish boats registered to Japanese Canadians were rumored to be financed by relatives living in Japan and some fishermen had sons and daughters going to school in Japan. While officials pondered for a couple of weeks, Provincial constables guarded the fishermen temporarily imprisoned in the cold cannery buildings.

During December, official and public impatience with Ottawa's lack of action intensified. Commissioner Parsons and Premier Hart judged the public mood to be growing more volatile. They also agreed with the military that the four-man RCMP security investigation team could only do so much. Though all police forces co-operated, their role was unofficial and limited except when the RCMP requested assistance for specific tasks.

Commissioner Parsons did not believe that Canadian-born or natural-ized citizens of Japanese descent would necessarily help repel an invasion by Japan. He also believed that if rioting started, all Oriental residents were at risk: many people proudly proclaimed their inability to tell a Chinese person from a Japanese one. Also he recognized that some Chinese factions in BC might be waiting for an opportunity to settle old scores left over from the Sino-Japanese war by implicating innocent people.

No evidence of sabotage was ever found. When directed to bring in all possible subversives sympathetic to Japan, the RCMP had ordered thirty-eight men apprehended out of a population of over 22,000 people of Japanese ancestry. Fourteen nationals had been arrested in Vancouver, New Westminster and Steveston and an additional twenty-four at various locations; most were temporarily held in Provincial police cells. Though both governments agreed that those numbers hardly added up to a security risk, some BC officials questioned RCMP security investigation methods and their choice of contacts in the Japanese communities. However, co-operation between the forces remained strong. RCMP Assistant Com-missioner C.H. Hill agreed with Commissioner Parsons, and the municipal and provincial politicians, that massive disorder threatened the Vancouver region. They judged the risk would increase with each Allied defeat and each Japanese victory.

A former Provincial recalled:

Right after Pearl Harbor, we requested the Japanese communities to take precautions as we expected the crazies to start attacking individuals. Amaz-ingly, despite the general horror and anger after Pearl Harbor, there were very few actual incidents against the Japanese in British Columbia. Don't forget that a Japanese was immediately recognizable, different from Italians or Germans, which added to their risk. As well, the Japanese had always been a dignified people, inscrutable, joined in general community things but still stayed separate. From our viewpoint a crime involving Orientals was always the hardest to solve and the most frustrating . . . people had not trusted them easily.

The Allied forces were having a tough go of it then, a high casualty rate and many parents and wives in BC were being informed that their son or husband had died in battle. People become a little less reasonable then, sometimes grief unbalances people. Still, although there were many threats of violence against the Japanese which added another factor to the policing of them, incidents were few.

The sound of an airplane made everyone jumpy. Fear was real. I guess we all felt more nervous, aware of our vulnerability to attack in a way that we hadn't before . . . Feelings against the Japanese ran high.[9]

Fears about the adequacy of internal defences and questions about the loyalties of Japanese residents were voiced throughout the province. Rabid letters to newspapers demanded something be done. "Come on, Ottawa, wake up, or do you need a few Jap planes to sound 'Reveille' with bombs?" asked one letter in the *Vancouver Sun*.[10] Another, published in the *Province*, said:

I am appealing to someone in authority to see that every Japanese, Man, Woman and Child, in BC be interned without delay. Once a Jap always a Jap, whether born here or in Japan. Undoubtedly their natural trait of treachery so clearly demonstrated to the world on December 7th would be repeated here in BC in case of the war closing in on us . . . Japanese-owned property, businesses, cars, boats, etc. should be confiscated and the owners placed in an internment camp well out of harm's way.[11]

"If this coast is to be made secure against Japanese aggression from within," another writer argued, "the Japanese must be totally excluded from our coastal waters, from our woods and mills and from any activities in connection with the preparation of food consumed by ourselves or our allies, for in all these vocations there are ample opportunities for their treachery."[12]

As the new year arrived, worried individuals gathered at fraternal lodges, union halls and churches to express their fears and to consider solutions to "the Japanese question." Many British Columbians voiced concerns about the vulnerability of railways being built by Japanese crews, others became positive local Japanese Canadians could be pressured into sabotage by threats against their relatives in Japan. Many recommended that Japanese Canadians be kept in total isolation immediately. Only a weak chorus of voices dissented and questioned how people born in BC could be treated so badly. They pointed out that the RCMP had ordered the arrest of fewer than forty individuals after long-term investigations. They stressed that over two-thirds of those of Japanese ancestry were Canadians by birth. Few listened.

A conference on the Japanese Problem in BC was held in Ottawa on January 8–9, 1942. Commissioner Parsons attended at Premier Hart's instruction, along with Minister of Labour George Pearson and members of the Standing Committee on Oriental Problems in BC: Mayor Fred Hume, Lieutenant Colonel Macgregor MacIntosh and A.W. Sparling. Though all delegates were knowledgeable about the situation, opinions about internment as a solution were split. Some representatives from the federal government, the RCMP and the military opposed the move to intern all male Japanese nationals between eighteen and forty-five, approximately 1,700 people. But other representatives from the same groups, and all the representatives from BC, voted for it. The conference could not decide what to do about Japanese Canadians. What were their rights, particularly if they had been registered at birth as dual citizens?

For five days, Prime Minister King and his cabinet considered the diverse opinions from the convention. On January 14, 1942, they tightened controls on all British Columbians of Japanese ancestry. A dawn-to-dusk curfew was imposed; ownership or use of shortwave receivers or transmitters was prohibited; the freedom to drive or travel in vehicles was severely limited. They also established a "protected zone" 100 miles inland from the coast and ordered the removal all male Japanese nationals between eighteen and forty-five.

On February 26, the federal government ordered the removal of all persons of Japanese racial origin from the protected zone, "in the public interest and for efficient prosecution of the War."[13] Almost 22,000 people, many of them elderly people and children, were to be moved away from the coast, deported to the interior of BC and to other provinces.

On March 2, 1942, RCMP Commissioner Stuart Wood wrote to the Officer Commanding, RCMP Vancouver:

> There are a few points that occur to me in connection with the movement of Japanese which I wish to bring to your attention.
>
> In the *New Canadian* dated the 25th of February, there is a plan for total evacuation which contains some good suggestions and, no doubt you have these points in mind, or will bring same to the attention of the Commission.
>
> Bearing in mind how fickle public opinion is and our rather bitter experience in connection with the internment policy relating to Italians and Germans, we should guard against being accused of harsh and illegal

methods in connection with the Japanese. Municipal Forces may be inclined, due to pressure of public opinion to prosecute members of the Japanese race—whether enemy aliens or not. —Consequently, I think this situation should be brought to the attention of the Commission, and an effort made to see that no illegal or unjustifiable action is taken. Publicity should be given to the fact that the only penalties for non-concurrence with the Orders of the Minister, dated the 26th of February, is internment, and before such action can be taken, the necessary evidence must be placed before the Departmental Committee or the Registrar of Enemy Aliens. The Japanese should be advised, through your contacts, of their rights in connection with internments or any prosecutions that might follow as a result of the Minister's order. Furthermore, they should be advised in regard to obtaining relief for their families, should such be necessary, due to the male head of the family being transferred to the interior. . .

I am particularly anxious that there should be no justification in the future for the accusation against the Force that members of the Japanese race or their families have been left without adequate provision for their maintenance. It is essential that no great hardship should result, due to police action.

The lengthy instruction then went into specifics. Wood pointed out that "violent protests against the Japanese entering their area" could be expected from the interior of BC. He explained his concerns about camps located near vulnerable points and he authorized the hiring of special constables.

Bear in mind that these guards are there solely for the purpose of guarding the railway property. British subjects of the Japanese race once outside the protected area should be regarded as free agents to move about as they see fit. . .there is no intention in the Government Order to herd these people, once they have complied with the regulations; nor should there be any persuasion or compulsion to compel British subjects of the Japanese race to remain in the employment or camps which the Government is providing.[14]

Commissioners Wood and Parsons had known each other well for years because of their shared interest in international and technically innovative policing. Wood knew that criteria he set for his men would become Parsons' instructions to the BCPP as well. He concluded his lengthy letter: "Mr. Maitland has assured me that he will instruct his Provincial Police and Municipal Police Forces to co-operate and assist in carrying out the Minister's Order relating to the Japanese, dated the 26th of February, 1942, based on Order-in-Council P.C. 1406."[15]

The BC Security Commission, headed by BCPP Assistant Commissioner John Shirras, RCMP Assistant Commissioner Frederick Mead and

BC industrialist Austin Taylor, was officially created on March 4, 1942, after both the RCMP and the Department of National Defence had pleaded their inability to take full charge of the evacuation. The BCSC became responsible for the movement of all Japanese nationals and Japanese Canadians to redistribution centres and then to permanent resettlement locations for the duration of the war. It was also empowered to confiscate personal property. The BCSC reported to the Department of Labour, which took over its functions and staff when the commission was formally dissolved on February 5, 1943.

The uprooting proceeded methodically. The RCMP handled most of the work in Vancouver and New Westminster and the BCPP organized the exodus from Vancouver Island and the coast. The Japanese made no group protests and most maintained an outward dignity and self-control. Many had sold their possessions at fire-sale prices; all remaining property and possessions were confiscated except for what they could take with them in suitcases. Most families owned comfortable homes, valuable businesses or a fishing boat or two. They had to abandon much of this, property worth millions of dollars, and almost none of it was ever returned.

Provincials remember many women weeping quietly, even as they proceeded efficiently and politely to organize their families for the devastating move. One NCO said:

We had the unfortunate job of rounding up the Japanese in the Campbell River area and there were quite a number – business people and fishermen. Real nice people, some were personal friends. It was a heartbreaking hard thing to have to go round, knock on the door and say, "Pack a suitcase." They all knew before I came, of course, even that I then had to order them to be down at the wharf at a certain time the next day.

I'm the first one to say how heart-wrenching it was for them but one has to remember what Japan was doing then and how they treated people...Compared to that, these people received almost gentle treatment. They had to stay for a while in the temporary camp at Hastings Park where, sure, it was crowded and uncomfortable. The camps in the interior were spartan, too. Outhouses, lack of privacy. The families I knew then came from comfortable, well-kept homes but. . .

It was war. There were so many boats and inlets. Some of our Japanese residents had been trained originally as Japanese military officers. Had the Japanese landed, what would have been the reaction of the Japanese here? They lost a lot of property, no question. It was a disaster but it was a sign of the times.[16]

The Japanese were transferred from Hastings Park to various locations. Many families were separated: the father went to work on railway projects in BC or on road projects in Ontario, while the mother, children and elders went to live in former ghost towns in the Kootenays or to the shanty towns hastily constructed to accommodate them. Others were sent to sugar beet farms in Alberta. A small percentage, the most wealthy residents or those with sponsors elsewhere in Canada, were allowed to choose where they would go, provided they moved at their own expense. They had to sign papers guaranteeing that they would never be an expense to the government and they also had to find towns that would allow them to take up residence, not an easy task.

In a report on June 9, 1942, Minister of Labour Humphrey Mitchell reported on "Japanese Movement Pacific Coast" to Justice Minister St. Laurent. The total number of individuals to be moved totalled 23,480, of which 14,091 were women and children. There were 6,584 Canadian-born people, 7,012 naturalized Japanese Canadians, 9,868 Japanese nationals and 16 United States citizens. The number yet to be evacuated as of May 28, 1942 was estimated to be 12,101. The detailed report specified plans developed and progress made, reporting that 2,635 people were still housed at Hastings Park, and identifying where people had been placed. In summation: "Road camps will accommodate, say 6,000, Interior towns—4000, Sugar beet fields—3600, Special permits—1400, Bridge River, etc., self-supporting—1000, Miscellaneous—200, Nicola—350, Indian schools—4000, leaving plans still to be worked out for, say—2930."[17] Canada now had official numbers for residents of British Columbia with a Japanese heritage, numbers that became pawns in the international war as well as ammunition for BC's racists.

At the request of the RCMP, the Provincials assumed almost all responsibility for policing the Japanese nationals and citizens as they were transferred to the interior. Theoretically, most of the banished were free to do what they chose unless they accepted government help; then they had few rights as all decisions were made without consulting them.

The women, children and elders required almost no policing as they set up homes, schools and social organizations in the makeshift communities organized by the BCSC. The Provincial who had patrolled the border area in the west Kootenays, where some deported families rebuilt ghost towns, recalled that he had not had any complaints or made any investigations there, nor did he know of any other Provincial who had been called to police an internment community. Another Provincial agreed:

> I was at Hope as they were throwing up the shacks at a valley that became Tashme, fourteen miles out of town. Stark, cold and foggy, it became home for 2,300 of the deported, coming mainly from Vancouver, I think. Interesting how quickly they organized into a working community. Though the women were self-effacing, they were incredibly capable and determined.

*Charged with defending British Columbia, the BCPP force was equipped with radiotelephones and other equipment.*

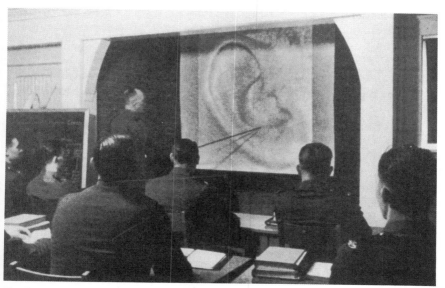

*Probationers take instruction in Portrait Parle at the BCPP training school in Victoria. Portrait Parle was an identification system that stressed the differences between individual physical features.*

221

They created a world for their children and parents quickly. I was never called out – they had no need of a policeman – but I visited twice before I transferred. So civilized compared to Hope! The first time, an ancient elder welcomed me, his tiny wife served me tea. Dignified, gracious, he let me know the community had no need for me. But not directly, mind you, that was not their way. I tried to find out if there was any help they needed from me or any problems but he replied, "Oh, no, thank you – isn't that an interesting cloud above the mountain? – did you have a good drive in?" The second time, I was invited into the school, then watched a soccer game for a while before again having tea. So I know little about the people of Tashme. Mind you, perhaps I was numb then. A brother had been killed in France, another one was missing. I needed to go and fight but knew what it would do to my mother and wife. But the enemy was not those people at Tashme.[18]

One former Provincial assigned to police Japanese Canadian work crews pointed out that the situation made so little sense, it became a joke between the crews and their guards. The men had been removed from the coast to prevent them causing trouble, only to be put to work along the railway tracks where they had an excellent opportunity to create havoc through sabotage if they were so inclined. The constable never experienced any work-camp strikes personally though he knew that there had been some. "It was the only power left to the deported men. Whenever they protested, something would most likely be resolved, such as visiting rights to their families or poor work conditions."[19]

The Japanese nationals and citizens endured the uprooting and internment; then, after the war, they had to endure the government's attempt to "repatriate" them – i.e., deport them to Japan. Most remained in British Columbia, and many eventually returned to the "protected" area to rebuild their worlds, both personally and economically.

Even as the Japanese were removed from the coast, British Columbians' fear of attack grew and officials continued to organize defence plans. Every city, town and village considered the best way to move people in case of attack. Civil defence planners mulled over the options, sometimes to the amused frustration of the Provincial Police officer delegated to sit on the committee. One recalled trying to explain to a group of well-meaning citizens on Vancouver Island why it was not feasible to plan on taking boatloads of evacuees up Bute Inlet and overland to the Cariboo country. He pointed out that the rugged terrain was almost impassable, but they listened to him with glazed eyes. "So I smartened up and shut up. After all, there were few viable options and I had no better plan, so not making too many objections to theirs was important. Coming up with some sort of plan made them feel better and we all needed that then."[20]

One defence project that had caught the interest of the public and certainly had the full attention of the Provincials unlucky enough to be running detachments in the construction area, was the Alaska Highway. Because transportation was crucial to defending the North, the United States planned to use military forces to build the road. By the time final negotiations were completed between Canada and the US, there were already close to 1,000 US Army troops in the area around Pouce Coupe. Staff Sergeant T. Duncan described the situation to Commissioner Parsons:

> They continue to arrive daily in Special Trains during this week...Owing to the heavy traffic between Dawson Creek and Fort St. John, that part of the road will be impassable for cars because of the depth of the ruts...Also 80 trucks owned by civilians have been engaged for hauling gasoline from Dawson Creek to Fort St. John and Fort Nelson.
>
> I have been having Constable McKay on duty at Dawson Creek from 8 a.m. until midnight or later to assist the Constables at that point in patrolling the town, owing to the number of troops in that area and trucks, etc., running all night and trains arriving at all hours. Additional manpower is required immediately.[21]

Commissioner Parsons arrived to assess the turmoil. He concluded that the whole area from Prince Rupert through to the Peace River country needed additional policing. Each detachment required more manpower, preferably experienced men, and quickly. Since the massive amount of equipment coming in was vulnerable to saboteurs, he proposed that all regular members of the CNR Investigation Department be gazetted as special constables to help guard the track. Parsons reported that almost 2,000 American soldiers, not including their support staffs, were going to be working on the roadbed. Along the Skeena River, American troops would be stationed at Woodcock, Tyee and Port Edward. As well, 500 civilian road construction workers were being hired in eastern Canada and were expected to arrive shortly. More Canadian troops were also expected in the area; they were being brought in to guard both the highway construction and the CNR line between Jasper and Prince Rupert. Canadian bases at Prince Rupert, Terrace and Prince George were all expanding. Policing the influx was going to be a massive job.

Additional Provincials were transferred in, but many of them were inexperienced, unsure how to control the boom-town atmosphere that the construction of the Alaskan highway created in northern BC. When American and Canadian military police became increasingly unable to keep control of the troops, attacks and harassment of civilians, theft of military supplies and general brawling became common. After Dawson Creek residents complained loudly to their MLA, Commissioner Parsons pointed out that six BCPP and thirty-six regular soldiers serving rotating duty as US Military Police had no hope of enforcing order among the thousands of troops and construction workers in the Dawson Creek area. And Dawson Creek was not an isolated case. Terrace, Prince Rupert and Prince George also needed more experienced policemen.

As the troops and civilians stationed throughout the Alaska Highway construction area created growing havoc in their off-hours, it became evident that something had to be done. Bootleggers, gamblers, prostitutes and thieves were arriving daily to help amuse the restless, well-paid workers. Commissioner Parsons and Attorney General Maitland considered the options and decided that some kind of joint action was necessary. They requested a meeting with the American and Canadian military authorities and the RCMP. At this meeting, the Americans suggested imposing martial law would solve the problems but the others disagreed. Instead, it was arranged that a US Army Provost Division would be brought in and Commissioner Parsons would temporarily transfer in twelve additional Provincials, senior men adept at crowd control. As well, the RCMP would increase their manpower, as they were responsible for the supervision of aliens and subversives. Co-operation and long hours on the job worked: the joint force soon had the situation under control and some of the undesirables shipped out. At the same time, another method of policing was also used. The bawdy houses in the Prince Rupert, Prince George and Peace River districts were inspected so often that most of the madams closed up their establishments and left.

"I learned so much from that NCO in the first week," recalled one junior constable as he explained how the experienced Provincials not only helped to regain order, they also demonstrated how to police effectively in such situations.

> It's pointless to be told about, or to read about, projecting authority. Knowing how to express oneself to gain authority can only be learned through watching an expert do it. It was amazing how quickly we learned the timing and the tone of voice which captured attention, once we had the older blokes there. I stopped feeling like an overworked mark and started being proud of being a Provincial again.[22]

Sometimes an incident amused members of both forces so much that it became widely publicized. One evening, four American soldiers went to a community dance in Prince George and became annoyed when the musicians ignored their requests to play more fast numbers. As the slow tunes played, the soldiers disappeared. A short time later, they returned to the dance hall, just as there was a loud explosion. The stage tipped forward and the musicians were blasted into the dancers. Luckily, no one

# CHAPTER TEN

# "Who knows what the government will do next?"
# 1943–1949

THE WAR AFFECTED ALMOST EVERYONE. Worry about the men overseas, mourning for those already lost, nervousness about invasion, gas rationing, inflation and housing shortages were daily pressures. People gathered around the radio to listen to Churchill, King and Roosevelt, thankful when the Allied forces won battles, devastated when they lost. They continued planning for "after the war," but they no longer expected it to be soon. Wartime workers enjoyed their prosperity, even as they worried that Depression conditions might return when the war ended.

Personally, Provincials were finding it increasingly difficult to look after their own and their families' needs as inflation ate into their salaries. Competition for housing became a nightmare. One constable recalled having to move his family three times in three months because landlords took advantage of the skyrocketing prices and sold the property he was renting. Food and clothing were expensive and in short supply. The shortage of manpower meant constables worked longer and longer hours. On top of regular policing duties, Provincials chauffeured doctors to emergency calls when requested, supervised the gas rationing, checked out aliens or reports of subversive behaviour, searched for black market kingpins and helped to keep juvenile boys in line. The commissioner warned the legislature that though most Provincials willingly worked long hours because of wartime conditions, they would expect set hours of work, adequate equipment and good benefits once the war was over.

Regular policing was becoming more complex because of the seriousness of the crimes being committed, he explained in his 1943 Provincial Police report. The increased number of indictable offences, time-consuming to investigate and to prosecute, also indicated a "less safe" province.[1] He suggested two reasons. First, the vast wealth created by having so many military personnel and construction workers in BC attracted organized underworld criminals; second, the values of the generation raised since World War One were radically different from those of their parents.

However, law-enforcement techniques were more efficient as new technical developments produced increasingly conclusive evidence. For instance, when minute particles of fibre were found on a suspect's car after a hit-and-run incident, the threads were matched to the victim's coat in the laboratory, and the driver was successfully prosecuted for manslaughter. Ballistics had become a much more exact science, and laboratory assistance and expertise allowed police to use stomach contents, broken glass, stained clothing or fingerprints as evidence.

It was not only the police who were using more sophisticated methods. Lawbreakers also used improved technology: crooks at two North Vancouver shipyards forged brass identification tags and National Registration certificates in a massive payroll fraud. When management reported to Provincial Police that some of their 14,000 employees were getting paid for a shift they had not worked, detectives started looking into it. It took them several months, but eventually eighteen people were apprehended. Investigators discovered that the con men actually had two scams going. In one, a man using the forged credentials of an off-work employee showed up at the pay wicket and claimed the absent man's wages. In the other, a worker entered the yard for his own shift and punched in on the time clock. A few minutes later, he left with the outgoing shift but only pretended to punch out. Later in the day, he re-entered with the next shift, again pretended to punch, then left with his own shift a few minutes later and actually punched the clock. Thus he was credited for a full day's wage by the clock, even though he had worked less than ten minutes. As well as pressing charges against the eighteen involved, management changed its time clock procedures.

Some Provincial policing was still done under primitive conditions, although the advent of the airplane changed that to a degree. One case Commissioner Parsons included in his 1943 report was a murder he considered interesting because of its unique circumstances.

Rex vs. Poole, Steven (Murder) — On January 11th, 1943, word was received from Fort Ware on the Upper Finlay River that an Indian woman had died under circumstances pointing to murder. The only way of reaching Fort Ware at that time of year was by plane and as weather was bad, Sergeant

*During World War Two, the larger police boats were armed with machine guns. At the sound of an aircraft, the Provincials on board donned their helmets and prepared to fire.*

*Striking loggers were part of the increasingly troubled labour scene following World War Two. Police were called in routinely to patrol the strikes.*

G.H. Clark of Prince George was unable to reach Fort Ware until January 30th.[2]

On arrival, the sergeant learned that on January 8, Margaret Poole had gone to visit with a native trapper and his wife who lived a distance down the river. Her husband, Steven Poole, a non-native, joined them for supper, dancing and drinking. About 9 p.m., the couple left to return to their own cabin, followed by Tommy, their ten-year-old son. When the sergeant questioned him, Tommy said his father had started to beat his mother with a rifle butt, and when he tried to interfere he was knocked out of the way. Poole then removed most of his wife's clothing, making it appear she had frozen to death. That evidence confirmed the message a trapper had sent to the police after seeing Margaret's battered body two days later.

As the weather was closing in fast, Clark decided to go back out on the plane to bring in a magistrate and coroner. He left behind a special constable, directing him to try to locate Poole out on his trap-line. Clark expected to fly back in the next day. However, on the return trip when the plane landed for fuel at Findlay Forks, a cylinder cracked, stranding the group there until a replacement part arrived on February 15. Then the weather closed down and it was not until March 2 that Magistrate/Coroner W. Harris, RCAMC Captain J.C. Dawson, Sergeant Clark, Constable G.P.W. Russell and Indian Agent R. Howe reached Fort Ware. Captain Dawson performed an autopsy on Margaret Poole's exhumed body and Coroner Harris held an inquest. Poole was charged with the murder of his wife and committed for trial.

One of the group later embellished Commissioner Parsons' report, recalling it had been a memorable trip. It had been almost midnight when, after the autopsy, the murdered woman was returned to her grave. The wind and wolves howled as they carried the thawed body back up the hill through the blizzard, scraped snow out of the hole dynamited for her first burial, and placed her in it again. Someone said a few words, then they hurried back to the cabin and spent the night in crowded discomfort. The next day, the weather closing in fast, they had all squeezed aboard the plane for the trip out: two policemen, the prisoner and his two children, the coroner, the doctor and the Indian agent. They had to sit with arms and legs entangled in order to fit everyone on board—which became unpleasant when the children got airsick. "One just had to sit there and get splashed and try not to vomit oneself. It was a rough trip."[3]

Some Provincials tried to keep their law enforcement practices sensitive to the situation. One man recalled that when he first went up north, he was a young constable with little experience who thought that if a law was broken, the person responsible had to be brought before a court.

It wasn't long before I realized that law had to apply to circumstances. For instance, take someone shooting a moose out of season who desperately needed the food. I soon realized that although there is a law about when to shoot moose, which usually works well, there was no way it should be applied to some cases up there, when people were hungry, needing meat, and moose were plentiful. That law then made no sense.[4]

Another former Provincial remembered policing railway workers in Revelstoke,

where winter was seven months long and the snow usually seven feet deep. They drank a bit, not much else to do. But policing in a railroad town is rather a funny thing because if a railroader got convicted of drunkenness, he was fired. So you didn't want to convict a railroader because you didn't want to see him lose his job. They would get into some pretty good fights and I would have to put them in jail. Then in the morning, I'd ask, "You still feel as tough?" When they would say "No," as they always did, I'd tell them to go home. We charged very few.[5]

Not all Provincials were sympathetic. In every group given power over others, there are a few who abuse it. When such an infringement was discovered, the Provincial received reprimand or censure, just as he did for infractions of personal behaviour. Each year, the commissioner summarized the number of discipline actions required, penalties ranging from fines to the occasional dismissal; but not all incidents reached that stage.

We natives, meaning the ones who looked Indian, sometimes got rough treatment. I looked white and passed for it when I was with the Shore Patrol [Canadian Navy police]. We were in Prince Rupert for a time. Most of the Provincials I worked with—we worked out of the Provincial offices—were pretty good guys. But not all. I particularly remember one guy in Prince Rupert, an NCO. Rough. Always called a native woman klootch or squaw, a man siwash or buck. You knew that when an Indian broke the law around him, that one had never looked the other way.[6]

The Provincials appear to have had considerable latitude in choosing when to enforce some laws or when to look the other way. As promotions were not tied to the accumulative charges a constable laid, there was no pressure to charge people for misdemeanors, except as a last resort; a Provincial who pressed too many was considered not to be controlling his patrol well. Although more BCPP procedural rules were instituted annually, some Provincials continued to shape them to suit their specific responsibilities. "When a new rule came down that all vehicle accidents with an aggregate damage over $25 were to be reported, which was every small bang, I found I had to decide whether to be a patrolman or a bookkeeper," explained a highway patrolman stationed on a main highway and responsible for all vehicle accident reports in the area.

I would find my desk heaped with reports each time I came back from a patrol—everyone began reporting all accidents. I used to methodically sort through the pile, take out all those which were borderline, insignificant fender-benders, then file them in the furnace. I was sheepish about that until I was commended for having significantly cut down on the serious accidents. By not getting overwhelmed with the massive quantity of little ones and the related paperwork, I spent much more time

*Dogs were a regular part of the BCPP investigative team.*

patrolling. I was on the highway most of the time and I was tough on drunk or careless drivers.[7]

Rescues became more complicated each year. Provincials took people out of burning houses, or found them on mountainsides after they got lost skiing or hiking or after a plane crash. They dragged occupants out of flaming cars or from cars balancing on cliffs, pulling the specially designed rescue sleds up steep slopes. Crews on PMLs and waterfront patrolmen saved over-optimistic swimmers, capsized sailors or fishermen and downed pilots. "Rescues went with the job," said one Provincial, who had been highly commended for rescuing residents from a burning building. "For every headline, there were probably a dozen other incidents which never received any publicity but where the officer involved had taken greater risks than we had."[8]

As the end of the war neared, experts agreed that tough times lay ahead. They expected when the troops came home and the war industries ground to a halt, the massive unemployment would generate labour confrontations and increased crime. Commissioner Parsons and Attorney General Pat Maitland were also concerned about the force itself. Although the BCPP was an efficient and respected force, it had too many men with less than five years' experience. Yet they knew even more Provincials had to be hired to cope with the population boom. Douglas House was training more probationers each year, and Parsons hoped that many former members would return. Along with the attorney general, he began formulating incentive packages for veterans to rejoin the BCPP.

The war on the European front ended on May 8, 1945, and on the eastern front on August 16, 1945. Provincials braced themselves for unsettled times. Many military veterans chose to take their discharge in British Columbia, which quickly reached, then surpassed population growth projections. However, Commissioner Parsons' aggressive rehiring campaign had results, and most former Provincials returned to the BCPP. As predicted, some who rejoined left again within their first year, explaining that they could not tolerate returning to the same pre-war problems of inadequate salaries and working conditions. Others, particularly those with radio and navigation skills, were lured away by private business to make twice the money for fewer work hours. The veterans who stayed bluntly warned the administration that a Provincial's lot would have to be improved quickly if they were to remain.

Commissioner Parsons lobbied the government for higher pay for his men, pointing out that keeping pace with inflation was difficult for all Provincials, and almost impossible for a constable with a young family. He also instituted an innovative, fairer system of promotion, based on personal qualifications as well as on recommendations. The first ten eligible constables, chosen alphabetically, received invitations to sit for advancement examinations, a series of written tests plus oral interviews. Usually at least half of those declined, either because they were content where they were and did not want to change locations, or because they did not want to write exams. Besides, a promotion did not necessarily mean more money. Seniority was reflected in salary within each rank, so that a long-serving constable sometimes got more than his NCO. To get the desired number of applicants, another batch of letters went out inviting the next ten on the list to apply. When ten acceptances were accumulated, those men went to Victoria.

During the first two days, written examinations tested the individual's knowledge of the Criminal Code, federal and provincial statutes and municipal policing, and his theoretical knowledge about all aspects of police work. Then a candidate appeared before three BCPP inspectors who questioned him on policing and general matters. They asked for his personal opinions on issues; then the candidate was expected to give a short speech.

A former inspector who frequently sat on the Examining Board explained why the inquiry was so broad:

> We asked the candidate quite a variety of different questions, mainly to ascertain his stability and mental outlook. . . a man can become a nuisance with a fast or hardened dogmatic view of things so if you put enough questions to him, you could see his reactions, whether he was anti-Catholic or might be quarrelsome.
>
> Then we did not publish a list of those who had failed, we published a list of those who had passed. Those men knew that they could not be overlooked. If a man was in Dawson Creek or Revelstoke or Powell River and he was next on the pass list to be promoted to corporal, he knew that it was just a matter of time until he would be made one. They wrote exams to go to corporal and to sergeant, then a few were invited to write to see if they qualified as a potential officer.[9]

Being adequately trained to police became increasingly critical after the war, when there seemed to be a general animosity toward laws and law enforcers. The former inspector explained why restlessness grew among veterans as they tried to readjust to civilian life.

> They had become used to living in a world filled with action and fear, waiting and boredom. But military life was also without many of the everyday problems. They were fed and clothed.
>
> You gave orders or you took orders. Everything is clear-cut in a military

system. Sure, they had witnessed and participated in barbarous scenes, some had become hardened. Many found it difficult to blend back in their old lives. We were called to quite a few violent domestic squabbles. Also, it was lucky that employment was not too hard to find. The men who had been in the camps during the Depression, then had served overseas, they had no patience left.[10]

Sometimes the events occurring on a Provincial's patrol turned into a legend shared with other policemen in off-patrol hours. One man, explaining how they policed loggers on a week's holiday from isolation, retold a friend's story:

> Those guys worked incredibly hard, in dangerous conditions. Any chance they got, they went on a drunk. On one occasion, eight loggers and four men from a tugboat crew rented rooms at the seaside hotel. They gathered in their adjoining rooms on the second floor and consumed prodigious quantities of booze. Then they decided that the hotelkeeper was too slow supplying them with firewood and they began to break up wooden chairs and burn them. When the manager heard about that, he came rushing up with firewood. They declined it, saying that they preferred furniture and, not to worry, they would pay for all damages.[11]

The hotelkeeper radioed for help, and the nearest police vessel started down the coast. By the time the Provincial arrived, he discovered a space heater sitting on the damp soggy ground by the front door, still smoking. The loggers had burnt all the wooden furniture in their rooms and heaved the heater out through a window. The Provincial was popular with the loggers, probably because of his reputation for being willing to take off his uniform, declare himself off duty and take on challengers with his fists, so the inebriated men were delighted to see him. When he arrived upstairs and interrupted the noisy party, he had no trouble collecting sufficient funds to cover all the hotel's damages. After all, he was Joe, the cop who had even whipped that bully, Sven. He persuaded the loggers to go to bed and escorted the other four back to their big tug to do the same. Everything quieted down, and as the men had not slept the night before, he thought that the party was over.

The Provincial stayed in the area and went to call on a friend around the point. When he came back in the middle of the night, having decided to tie up to the hotel wharf and supervise the partyers' departure the next morning, he found the tug almost up on the beach, where the crew were securing a towing hawser around the hotel. Laughing in drunken merriment at being caught, the men undid the hawser and took the tug back to the wharf, where they settled in for the rest of the night. In the morning, after giving the foursome an ear-blistering lecture about what they could be charged with, the corporal ordered them to load up the loggers and head for camp. He followed them for a distance down the strait.

Policing that would be unconventional now was acceptable then. On occasion, Provincials took the initiative to solve problems themselves. One man remembered that after the war, equipment remained in short supply, particularly motor vehicles.

> I used a motorcycle to patrol North Vancouver but I was recognizable a good distance off, I really needed a car. But the only way you could get one in those days was to go and seize one from a bootlegger. Well, by gosh if we weren't fortunate enough to find a guy bootlegging outside a supper club. So we collared him, collared his booze and collared his Chev. And that's how I got a highway patrol car. Though it had to go through the court, of course, that Chev became a BCPP vehicle.
>
> Bootleggers' cars were automatically confiscated, then when the case was proven, the car became government property. Then sometimes, it ended up being turned back over to us. I guess that was one of the innovations of a very different time period. The Provincial Police was a well-equipped force but sometimes we helped the government figure out the means of equipping us. It was a good little Chev, much better in winter rains than a motorcycle...
>
> Three of us patrolled the North Vancouver district then. Big territory, we weren't responsible for the city, but Capilano had 20,000 residents, Deep Cove and Lynn Valley each had 18,000. So there was one policeman to 19,000 residents, not counting all the crowds which came over from Vancouver on Sundays and holidays. Fairly usual odds then... hardest and most time-consuming duty was searching for lost hikers or skiers.[12]

When the force celebrated its eighty-eighth birthday on November 17, 1946, it had a strength of 445 officers, NCOs and men. British Columbia had almost a million residents by then. The BCPP policed over forty municipalities as well as all rural areas and unincorporated settlements. In some of the larger cities such as Burnaby, Chilliwack, Prince George, Nanaimo, Port Alberni, Trail, Kamloops, Vernon and Kelowna, the adult crime rate had gone up approximately 35 percent in the past year and the rate of juvenile delinquency was increasing even faster.

To help recognize how valuable the BCPP was to the province, the government developed a BCPP Long Service and Good Conduct Medal and awarded it to forty-one men in 1946.[13] One man explained:

> The medal recognized twenty years of service to the BC Provincial Police, the last ten of which had been served without any censure or reprimand. In those times, particularly in postwar years when what medals a man had the

236

right to wear told much about him, medals meant something. Now the only award which catches public recognition is a vast sum of money. We were different then, we did genuinely appreciate being honoured. Medals said something. For instance, when Bill Stewart received the King's medal for bravery... [14]

On June 13, 1944, Constable W.B. Stewart at Keremeos had received an abrupt telephone summons from a local merchant, asking him to come at once. The constable found the distraught merchant on the street in front of his store. Bailey, the merchant's son-in-law, was in the upstairs suite, threatening his estranged wife and mother-in-law with a revolver. After asking the merchant to phone the Penticton Provincial detachment for assistance, Stewart, who knew Bailey well, cautiously climbed the stairs and entered the living room. He was unarmed. As Stewart attempted to reason with him, Bailey appeared to listen but then, without warning, fired twice at the constable. Stewart fell to the floor with one bullet in his groin and another through his leg. He knew that reinforcements from Penticton

*Attorney General Pat Maitland at 83 Mile House on a tour of inspection of outlying police districts. He is flanked by Constable Thomas Moore, left, and Constable D.D. McIndoe. The photographer is BCPP Commissioner T.W.S. Parsons.*

would take at least forty minutes to arrive, so, despite his injuries, he continued to try to calm Bailey. The armed man repeatedly threatened to kill the women as he ranted and paced the floor. Sometimes he appeared to be listening as Stewart assured him that he was sick and that they could get a doctor who would help him as soon as he put the gun down. But when Bailey looked out the window and saw the Penticton police car winding down the long approach to Keremeos, he fled, taking the women as hostages and leaving Stewart, still bleeding, lying on the floor.

Bailey loaded his hostages into a car and started driving west along the Similkameen River. Shortly after, the Provincials followed in an unmarked car. A few miles out of town, they met the two women running along the road. They reported that Bailey had abruptly stopped the car, announced he was going to shoot himself, then walked down to the river and disappeared from sight. Provincials and civilian volunteers cautiously searched the river, unsure if they were looking for a dead man or a dangerous one, but darkness fell without any sign of the fugitive. Residents of Keremeos bolted their doors and slept with hunting rifles close by. The next day searchers found Bailey on a small island with a self-inflicted head wound. He recovered and was sentenced to eighteen months in Oakalla.

Constable Stewart's recovery from his wounds was much slower. His long police career, which had begun in 1912, was ended. For his bravery, he was awarded the King's Medal, the highest police award in the British Empire and one that was rarely presented.

Within the force, postwar restlessness increased. Policing became more difficult, but proposed improvements to wages, benefits and working conditions were not made. Attorney General Pat Maitland, a strong supporter of the BCPP as well as a powerful individual in BC's unstable coalition government, died of a heart attack in 1946, and many Provincials feared that the changes he had promised would be delayed indefinitely. However, Commissioner Parsons assured members that changes would be made. To help emphasize that and to emphasize the need for change to Gordon Wismer, the newly appointed attorney general, he ran an essay contest, a popular method then for employers to learn employees' opinions. He received entries from almost one-quarter of the force. One hundred and five individuals commented on the topic "How Best Can Conditions of Service in the British Columbia Provincial Police Be Improved?" Their concerns were, in order of priority, salaries, housing, promotions, transfers, hospitalization, superannuation, personnel, hours of work, training, travelling expenses, police unions and office accommodation.

About unions, Parsons was unsympathetic. "I must express strong opposition to the question of 'unionism' in relation to police work," he told

Wismer. "The place for policemen, devoid of 'side,' must be the 'middle of the road' and so accessible to all." The commissioner was more sympathetic on the issue of wages. "Returning to the question of salaries, it would seem that as all ranks of the Provincial Police of British Columbia are of high calibre and perform duties exactly similar to those of the RCMP in six Canadian Provinces so there should be no differences in pay and allowances. But this would be expensive."[15] Commissioner Parsons outlined the additional budget necessary to bring all salaries to the RCMP level, a 10 percent increase. But instead of increasing the policing budget as expected, the coalition government directed the attorney general to find a method to cut policing costs.

Though public rumours about a possible RCMP takeover surfaced occasionally, most Provincials dismissed them as inconceivable. At government levels, however, there continued to be debate over the value of a strong national police force as compared with the benefits of provincial forces with policies tailored to their own populations and geographic territories. Commissioner Parsons and Deputy Commissioner Shirras began considering the issue in late 1946, concerned that of the BCPP strength of 431 men, 190 had less than six years' service. As well, during the past year, 21 probationers had left before completing their initial three-month course. At the same time, concerns about national security continued to grow. As the Royal Canadian Mounted Police Act had been amended in 1940 to allow the RCMP to contract for policing with any province or municipality with the prior approval of the lieutenant governor-in-council of any province, the legislation for the Dominion government to assume provincial policing was already in place. The Act also provided that any member of a provincial force who qualified to join the RCMP at such a takeover would receive recognition of his prior service. The discussions did not result in any action, however, and the BCPP budget was increased.

Members of the force remained blissfully unaware of what was happening in Victoria. Most of them were content to be Provincial policemen. As one man said:

> Sure, as with any group, we lobbied for a little more money and better benefits and working conditions, but we were a proud, capable force. Strong esprit de corps, despite the fact we were so spread out. British Columbia is an interesting place to police, so much variety. Most of it [policing] was pretty usual, except for the Doukhobors. And perhaps we had more union-related battles than other provinces.[16]

Yet it was the Doukhobor and labour policing costs that particularly worried Wismer, as it did many members of the coalition government.

He had gained first-hand knowledge of both issues in his previous term as attorney general and apparently believed they related to his defeat in the 1941 election. Over the years, the Doukhobors, primarily the Sons of Freedom sect, remained a unique policing problem. Though individual Sons of Freedom considered to be the instigators of burnings and bombings had been charged and jailed regularly over the years, the burnings, bombings and nude parades had not stopped. Former members of the force recalled that whenever they relaxed their vigilance in the Kootenays, the number of incidents increased again. Kootenay residents complained to the government regularly as schools went up in flames and they had to cross all bridges nervously. One oldtimer, a former shopkeeper in Nelson, recalled:

> The lads could only do what they could and it was pretty unlikely that the Provincials would ever catch someone striking a match or tucking another bomb under Verigin's tomb. The Sons were a close-knit bunch, different, sort of like olden day serfs. You never knew what they were thinking, sometimes wondered if they ever did as individuals, they were all bound so closely into communities. One good thing, at least the Douks were pretty careful not to cause injuries, though they were nerve-wracking.[17]

He added that everyone there knew that the MLAs and MPs from the

*Highway patrolmen in Duncan after escorting a motorcade publicizing the completion of the highway from Port Alberni to Victoria.*

Kootenays continued to bicker about whose responsibility the Doukhobors were, particularly when the RCMP detachment, which had been established to search for subversives during the war years, was withdrawn.

Provincials who patrolled the Doukhobor region recalled it as one of their most frustrating experiences, difficult and dispiriting. During the early years of the war, when many terrorist leaders were serving jail terms, things had been relatively quiet. Then the burnings started again, along with hunger strikes in the Freedomite community to protest national registration. One such hunger strike ended when Attorney General Maitland ordered other Doukhobors, supervised by the Provincials, to force-feed the strikers. After the war, fighting intensified between factions of the Sons of Freedom and dynamite explosions again echoed through the night. In 1947 alone there were ninety incidents of bombings and burnings. As well, terrorists sprayed Mary Nazaroff, a Freedomite, with gasoline, then set her on fire. She died three days later, and police arrested fifty-one men and fourteen women. They were subsequently convicted and jailed on minor charges, but no one was ever tried for her murder. Even after those individuals were jailed, the furor continued unabated.

The BC government, in the hopes that the Doukhobors themselves would have advice on how to achieve peace, set up another Royal Commission to inquire into the Doukhobor question. On October 14, 1947, Judge Harry Sullivan began hearing evidence from the Sons of Freedom as well as from the Orthodox and Independent Doukhobor sects. While the hearings were under way, some individuals not suspected to have been involved in burnings requested Provincials to arrange for their stories to be heard also. But few had any recommendations on how to end the demonstrations. Even as witnesses were heard, the burnings and bombings continued, culminating in a massive explosion that destroyed the Grand Forks Doukhobor Co-operative, a dry cleaning business and an insurance company's offices.

Judge Sullivan concluded the commission in early January 1948. Expressing his disappointment that the commission had not gained the confidence of the Doukhobor people, he concluded:

> The first part of my job, to ascertain the cause . . . is easy. The answer is, that these shootings and bombings, fires and murder, and attempted murder, have been due to crime and insanity, and the work of certain agitators who prey upon their simple, credulous countrymen for power or money, or perhaps both. And I think the situation should be cleaned up, using every bit of force necessary for the purpose, before I go any further into these minor matters . . . to improve conditions of the law-abiding people among you. I know that most of you are law-abiding.[18]

Sullivan pointed out that many Independent and Community Doukhobor leaders concurred with his decisions.

Despite the fact that four MLAs and two MPs attended most of the hearings and agreed that the situation had to be cleaned up, it was not until two years later that Attorney General Wismer ordered the arrest of two men; apparently there had been numerous federal-provincial debates in the interim. Provincial Police Staff Sergeant W.J. Hooker supervised the apprehension of "Archangel" Michael Verigin and his secretary, Joe Eli Podovinikoff, without encountering any difficulties. However, the fires and nude parades continued before, during and after their lengthy trials. Both men were sentenced to two years. During this period, the need for more BCPP manpower in the Kootenays increased.

"Doukhobors Have Exhausted Public Patience," an editorial on April 28, 1949, stated.

> In reinforcing the Provincial Police at the scene of the disturbances and in securing emergency assistance from the RCMP, Attorney General Wismer appears to have done all that lies within his power at the moment, and it is to be hoped that this show of force will have salutary effect. At the best, however, it can bring only a temporary sense of security to the district, leaving a permanent solution to the problem of law enforcement still to be found. Under existing laws that may not be easy.[19]

Provincials who policed the Doukhobors agreed with that summary. The laws did not adequately cover the situation, they explained; it was a political question unresolved for thirty years. Some years after the BCPP had been disbanded, most of the confrontations stopped. Tough new laws were passed; as well, the most aggressive Doukhobors grew old, and subsequent generations became more integrated into the surrounding culture. By the 1950s, there were many fewer individual Doukhobors willing to obey their leaders blindly.

In November 1947, Commissioner Parsons retired and Deputy Commissioner John Shirras became head of the force. He had many connections with police and security forces across Canada and the US from having served during the war as head of the alternate BCPP headquarters in Vancouver, and as an initial director of the BC Security Commission. In a letter to all members, the new commissioner pointed out that as he had policed in almost every district, he understood the range of conditions Provincials coped with and the importance of recognizing those differences. Shirras assured the men that he would continue to improve working conditions and that he would decentralize administration of the force. Such a reorganization would allow better liaison, and encourage more efficient response to BC's wide variety of policing requirements. He acknowledged that policing was changing and that security continued to be of prime importance for the safety of Canada. He assured the men that he had high expectations for the BCPP and great pride in their abilities.

Shirras chose Inspector Roger Peachey as his deputy commissioner and immediately put him to work reorganizing the force. Basically an administrative move to make the districts more autonomous, it actually had little effect on the Provincials in the field. Members of the force, particularly in isolated regions, continued as they had for decades. They acted as boundary riders, coast guardsmen, fishing overseers, fire wardens, collectors of revenue and statistics, and general handymen for other branches of government, as well as policemen. One former member recalled:

> We were never too knowledgeable about what was happening at Headquarters. Other than the monthly General Orders, which were mainly updates on cases, suspects, legal changes, commendations, transfers, disciplines—sometimes a dismissal, complete with all details—we didn't hear much. We were kept pretty busy and communication was still much different then than it is now. We didn't chat with other detachments; telephones were only for business.[20]

For instance, reorganization made no difference to the constable at the Masset detachment. Located on the tip of the Queen Charlotte Islands, he was a one-man show. He had radio contact with the outside world, but vessels could only dock when the tide was right and the weather often made flying to Masset impossible. The population there was approximately 300 whites and 600 Indians; the constable's work load was light but varied. He explained that he issued licences, registered births, deaths and marriages, searched for lost fishermen and occasionally had to duck a stray bullet.

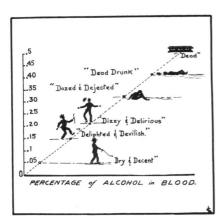

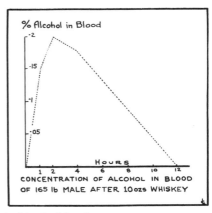

*Charts used to establish the amount of alcohol in the blood.*

It was a hard place, I was there twenty-two months. The rains, the Indians, the tides — everything depended on the tides. You just put in time, someone had to be there. Biggest difficulty was that no one would go out with you when there was trouble on the reserve, because the few merchants all made their livelihood from Indians. The reserve was three miles out and I'd get a call around two or three in the morning, "There's shooting out here." So I would go, my wife would lie in bed awake, wondering if I was going to get back home.

The taxi driver would loan me his car but he'd never drive me, he'd say, "I don't want to be seen driving you. Take wide corners, though. They've been saying, 'We're going to get him tonight'."

The Indian agent wasn't allowed to go and the magistrate was frail, at least seventy-five. So I'd go alone. But other than when they got into knockout, I respected most of the Haidas. They lived well, had their own sawmill, fished, made good money. They are a fine people, masters in the water, beautiful to watch.

One January night, I saw a fire burning across Masset Inlet, maybe five or six miles away. I thought someone had been shipwrecked so one of the Haida fishermen agreed to take me across in his 60-foot seine boat, though it was blowing pretty bad and the waves were man-high. We got about 300 yards from shore and couldn't go in any closer. But we could see a figure huddled by that fire. "I'll take the rowboat in," the owner said, instructing his brother to take the wheel and declining to take me. "No point you coming with me — you'd be no good to me anyway." So he went to shore and picked that guy up and brought him back. Sometimes we had not been able to see his boat, the waves had been so high. His fingers were frozen into a curve from hanging onto the oars and they were white from the knuckles down with frostbite. He said, "It's all right. I've had them that way before." Refused to take anything for the rescue or for taking his boat out in such weather. A proud and capable people.

Mind you, the same guy, if he'd been drinking, get out of his way. Of course legally they weren't allowed to drink so that made for problems, too, as they would bring in boatloads from Prince Rupert, eighty miles away, or made their own, rough and raw. And then they'd fight. When I was there, the problem was that there were still two Haidas, two social standards. There was the "real" Haida and the "slave" Haida, the offspring of people brought back from raids many, many years before — the Haida had been quite warlike in their earliest days. When they were all sober, they all lived together without problems but when they got drinking, then it would come out. "You're not real Haida — you're slave!" Then the trouble would happen and I would have to go out there by myself where they were shooting at each other and take the rifles away. Had to walk a very fine line...

But the hard part was just living in Masset. Cold damp quarters, right on the edge of the swampy forest. The building had a police office and cell in one corner, then living room, bedroom and kitchen. A cistern filled with rainwater out the back, from which little wrigglers would spurt out of the tap into the glass when you went for a drink sometimes. No doctor, no hospital and we had a small baby. And I hated boats and water, never been around them before until I was transferred to Masset. Got used to the boats somewhat but I never did like being on the water.[21]

Policing one end of the Queen Charlotte Islands was quite different from the other. Masset was quiet, compared with Queen Charlotte City, which attracted loggers, fishermen and Indians on weekends. During the peak seasons, the Masset constable occasionally went down to help out, usually going by boat to Port Clements. The Provincial from Queen Charlotte City would meet him there, then they would travel across the muskeg for thirteen miles on a narrow plank road.

It used to be crazy. We'd regularly go through the dance halls, breaking up fights, bouncing men around. But he'd never arrest anyone because he only had room for two prisoners and there would be a hundred raising hell. He was so tall, we'd go in, he'd pick out the worst fights, we'd break those up and then we would go and check out the hotel. It didn't have any doors on the rooms – the owners had put up doors more than once but they got ripped off so they finally just left them off. Then we'd go and play a bit of cribbage before we went back to the hall and did it all over again. Crazy. I was so glad, and so was my wife, when we finally got transferred.[22]

The isolated policing necessary at Masset and Queen Charlotte City, comparable to what policing had been fifty years earlier, differed radically from most Provincials' duties and daily routines. As the BCPP was policing forty-three municipalities by the end of 1948, most Provincials served in densely populated areas, part of an efficient policing team. Commissioner Shirras took pride in maintaining the force's reputation for integrating technical advances quickly and for innovative training. The wartime shortages having ended, the BCPP buildings, vehicles, vessels and equipment were upgraded rapidly, despite some legislators' concern about the increasing cost of policing.

One situation that again required more policing manpower was labour confrontations. During 1948, there had been much bitter competition for members between rival unions, particularly in the logging industry. A few men would split off from a powerful union such as the International Woodworkers of America and form a new union, then aggressively seek new members. These splinter groups often called small wildcat strikes, usually illegal under labour legislation because of organization or the numbers involved.

One Provincial recalled that violence seldom occurred in the conflicts between unions, but the potential for outright battle was always there:

> I remember one out by Oyster Bay, started by a splinter group, strictly wildcat. In those days, it was either '48 or '49, there were actually few union members and organizers sometimes attempted to sign up new members pretty roughly. But the union members who worked this area were IWA. So when the other bunch came along—I forget what they called themselves, just outlawed commies, I guess—the IWA moved in from Port Alberni. I had been there earlier in plain clothes, then when the fighting started as the workers went into the bush and the splinter group tried to stop them, I went back to where our guys were stashed at Oyster Bay and jumped into my uniform and we went back there because it was building.

*Complete mobile two-way radio unit concealed in the trunk of a police car.*

We were the thin brown line. I can remember standing in the middle of the road, the ocean across the sand on one side, the dense forest on the other. Maybe a dozen of us, I guess, under Inspector Jack Thompson. The splinter group had set up a bit of a lean-to on the beach as a headquarters across the road from where the loggers would come out of the bush. Three busloads of IWA guys, about 120 men, arrived from Port Alberni to support the crews. They massively outnumbered the gang of rabble on the beach. Inspector Thompson commanded, "We'll line up right in the middle of the highway, making a thin brown line." Then he stepped out and in his best ex-British Horse Marine voice, called to the IWA, "Now, gentlemen, this is as far as you go!"

Everyone stopped. The inspector explained in no uncertain terms that we were here to maintain law and order, and that there was no need for any violence and we were going to see that there wasn't any, adding, "I would ask you all to keep calm and to have your leader step forward, please. I will talk with him further and with the leader of the other group and then if you wish to have a joint discussion, I will be happy to supervise it."

So the man in charge of the IWA types, a sensible man, stepped forward and he and the inspector had a chat, then he turned back to his group and said, "All right, boys, we'll cool it." By this time, the opposition had started fading away. They knew they'd be massacred if they started anything. So by the time the crews came out of the woods, and there were quite a number of them so it could have been quite a battle, there wasn't a picket in sight.

Dangerous? Yes, somewhat. We did the best we could but you had to use common sense, twelve of us, we couldn't have stopped them. They had come prepared for trouble. For instance, as the IWA guys left, an arm came out a window of the last bus and suddenly the lean-to on the beach exploded into flames. Guess someone had used his molotov cocktail. When we were on the road, I had said to the guy next to me, "Listen, if that mob rushes us, don't try to be a hero. Let them get through and get the guys who started it all and push them into the sea." I said, "I don't intend to get my head knocked in to protect this scum. If they start coming at us, let them go." We couldn't have stopped them anyway, the twelve of us spread out along the road.[23]

In Commissioner Shirras' annual report for 1948, he summarized the disastrous year. Not only had the Doukhobor radicals and union agitators created enough havoc to require additional policing, but it had been the worst flood year since the 1894 disasters. The spring had been unseasonably cold, then temperatures soared. Detachments at Prince George, Princeton, Kimberley, Grand Forks, Fernie and Kamloops reported rivers overflowing their banks, endangering all nearby residents, livestock and buildings and isolating whole areas by taking out bridges.

The disaster spread fast. Provincials at the Hope detachment reported hourly on the Fraser River's incredible rise and government authorities knew that diking throughout the Fraser Valley would not hold. They ordered emergency evacuation of some areas. But even as evacuation began, the brown torrent filled the riverbanks and flooded over, sweeping homes, barns and animals downstream. Large sloughs covered the cultivated fields, smothering next month's crops, drowning thousands of hens and hundreds of cows. As the rich agricultural region provided most of the vegetables, milk, butter and eggs to coastal cities, food shortages resulted. Communication ceased as telephone and telegraph poles washed away, roads became impassable and railway bridges were washed out.

The BCPP shortwave system became the main communication network. Provincials worked around the clock, rescuing stranded individuals, answering medical emergencies and preventing looting. They also had to mediate among interest groups, as people fought over what to dynamite. Blowing a dam would protect one area but only by flooding another. Tempers grew hot as the water kept rushing down from the snow-covered mountains. On June 5, the hottest day yet, the rushing flood waters of the Fraser River combined with a high tide from the Pacific Ocean, and the disaster spread. Water was forced back even farther into the flooded regions; then, when the tide turned, it sucked the river far out into the ocean and dead livestock and debris began washing up on beaches as far away as Vancouver Island. The BCPP and all emergency personnel enforced strict health regulations, prohibiting swimming and instructing

*Cleaning up after spring floods in Penticton, 1942.*

some residents to get typhoid inoculations. Food rationing began as shortages grew acute.

By September, Provincials reported a return to normal conditions. Temporary bridges, replaced rail tracks and new telephone and telegraph lines were finally in place. Dikes, barns and houses were rebuilt, many of them on higher ground. The costs to the province had been astronomical.

As British Columbia entered 1949, its administrative costs continued to grow faster than its revenues. In a June election, the Liberal–Conservative government, which had been in power since 1941, was re-elected with an overwhelming majority. However, the coalition was riven by internal disputes, particularly over spending priorities and the escalating debt. One of the issues dividing Liberals and Conservatives in the cabinet was the police question.

The cost of policing was a growing concern. Most provincial politicians believed that British Columbia was not receiving an equitable share of the federal dollars raised through income tax. All agreed on the necessity of expanding police services and upgrading police equipment. The BCPP marine fleet required new vessels and Provincials were also taking to the air. Experts agreed that, in some cases, using planes was the most cost-efficient form of law enforcement because of BC's rugged terrain and vast area. One plane, a de Havilland Beaver, had been purchased and more were required. However, some MLAs began to question why the province was paying these costs out of its own pocket when it could hire the federal police force for less.

Rumours began to circulate in Victoria and the lower mainland that the cabinet was debating the pros and cons of contracting out the province's policing to the Dominion government. News reporters questioned sources and decided the rumours were the usual stale news, that a change of policing was unlikely in the next few years. The few Provincials who heard the rumours also dismissed them, sure it was the same old speculations surfacing again. After all, everyone knew that legislators were protective about provincial autonomy and the BCPP's role in maintaining it.

## CHAPTER ELEVEN

# "And I was suddenly a Mountie"
# 1950

"**P**OLICE CHANGE HINTED," the Vancouver *Province* announced on February 28, 1950, as did the Victoria *Times*: "BC law enforcement may be taken over by RCMP." Those papers as well as the Victoria *Colonist*, the Vancouver *News Herald* and *Vancouver Sun*, reported again the next day, but information was scanty. The *Colonist* reported:

> British Columbia's Provincial Police, oldest territorial police force in Canada, may hand over its duties to Royal Canadian Mounted Police within a few months. Reports of the changeover are well founded, Ottawa advice indicated last night. It is understood that preliminary and informal discussions between British Columbia and Federal justice authorities have begun. An official request for the move is expected soon. If the change is made, it will bring the number of provinces policed by the RCMP to seven . . . Commissioner S.T. Wood of the RCMP said yesterday that he had not heard of the proposal. "No comment," said Attorney General Gordon Wismer.
>
> The Federal force, it is said, charges about $1,500 per man for this work. Provincial constables receive from $2,400 to $2,700 and corporals some $3,000 annually. The difference in pay, it is understood, would be met by the Federal Government . . . Whether or not the recent bid for certification of British Columbia Police under the Industrial Conciliation and Arbitration Act had any bearing on the proposed change could not be learned.
>
> If the move is carried through, it is understood that most Provincial Police officers would be enlisted in the RCMP . . .[1]

That same afternoon, Attorney General Gordon Wismer issued a release to newspapers throughout British Columbia announcing that Commissioner Shirras had retired and Deputy Commissioner Roger Peachey, a member of the force since 1920, had been promoted to command of the BC Provincial Police. He gave no reason for Shirras' retirement. He also announced that Inspector Cecil Clark, who had joined the Provincials as a clerk in 1916, was the new deputy commissioner. On March 7, the attorney general introduced a bill in the BC legislature, seeking blanket authority to make an agreement with RCMP and the federal government for the changeover. The amendment to the Police Act bill quickly passed first reading and Wismer left for Ottawa, empowered by the government to negotiate a policing contract.

The proposed change in policing generated immediate reaction on Vancouver Island and in the lower mainland. Editorials and letters expressed disbelief and puzzlement. "This province takes great pride in its police and with good reason," stated an editorial in the *Colonist*.

> It is a public pride built up . . . on [BCPP] reputation for just and impartial law enforcement, tempered by those somewhat rare attributes, courtesy and kindness.
>
> The news that a surrender of provincial jurisdiction is in the cards will come as a surprise to British Columbians, for there seems little room for belief that the province could be policed better by the RCMP. On the contrary, whatever the calibre of the RCMP as a force, it is doubtful indeed if it could do as good a job as a provincial force staffed by fine young men who know and understand their territory and, what is equally important, directed by seniors who from personal experience are familiar with every inch of the province and its local problems.
>
> There is a remoteness about centralized Federal police control that could be disadvantageous to the country west of the Rockies. Those at top executive and administrative levels could not be cognizant enough of the conditions and needs of British Columbia to be able to give them anything but arbitrary rulings based on the inflexibility of policy that is largely inescapable under any Dominion-wide system.
>
> It would be interesting to know what influenced the present negotiations and who made the overtures. If thoughts of economy are behind them, it is difficult to see how the British Columbia taxpayer could be the gainer in the long run, since a Dominion share of the cost could be met only by taxation in another form. British Columbia is efficiently and on the whole inexpensively policed now, and its Government would be ill-advised to surrender provincial jurisdiction for problematical returns.[2]

Most Provincials who heard the reports recalled that they put little stock in them, deciding it was another chapter in the ongoing saga of federal-provincial discussions about policing costs and responsibilities. When questioned about the application for union certification, only a few even knew about it. A former constable who was approached by the union said:

> They [BCPP members trying to organize a bid for certification] had a long way to go before they would receive much support. There was maybe about fifty men or so involved, mostly men with less than ten years. I guess certification had some good points but I never could have voted for it. Mind you, they certainly had the right to look into it and I guess they were, which would have shook up the bunch at Headquarters. But I don't think it would have gone anywhere. We were pretty independent blokes, most of us preferred the right to look after our own needs. . . In any event, I don't think it influenced the takeover. I think Wismer had to sell us out to keep the coalition government together. The feds had wanted to do all policing across Canada for years so there was probably a standing offer. They paid BC lots of dollars when they got to absorb us.[3]

BCPP Headquarters was suddenly alive with rumour. Some argued that a takeover was imminent. Others claimed the force could not be eliminated without creating a public outcry, forcing the matter to be put to the electorate. Provincials dismissed the notion that the RCMP could provide cheaper policing. The amicable relationship between members of the two forces kept them well-informed: they knew the Mounties had a higher pay scale, received more benefits and were much more expensively equipped.

The progression from rumour to fact, and the public's reaction, were chronicled in newspapers around the province. Editors and the public expressed concern about the secrecy, the rationale behind the negotiations and the lack of a referendum on the matter. Though all agreed that the RCMP were a respected force, there appears to have been little public support for the proposed change. Neither was there much understanding about how fast such a change could be made in a legislature with a large majority and a weak opposition.

The Act to Amend the Police and Prisons Regulation Act came up for second reading in the legislature on March 19, and Attorney General Wismer spoke for more than an hour. He informed the legislators that the province would save $1,700,000 by switching to the federal force. He acknowledged that he did not know why Ottawa would consent to subsidizing so large a portion of the policing bill. He speculated that Ottawa's concern about guarding northern Canada was due to the spreading fear of communism. Wismer paid tribute to the Provincial Police and traced their history from BC's earliest days, even as he announced their demise:

> I am of the opinion for esprit de corps, for efficiency, for community spirit and for fairness to accused persons, they had created a great tradition. At the

*Attorney General Gordon Wismer, the politician who negotiated the demise of the BCPP.*

same time, it is the duty of the government to see that policing is carried on as economically as possible without loss of efficiency. With such huge expenditures for public works, care of the aged, sick and infirm in British Columbia, it is the duty of the government to economize wherever possible. . .[4]

Opposition Leader Harold Winch attacked the proposal, concerned about the tentative changes and the method to be used: passage would give the cabinet power to make the policing agreement without ratification by the legislature. Winch spoke at length, as did other members of the Opposition, protesting and demanding that a full study be conducted into what policing method was best for the province. They decried the misuse of the parliamentary system, pleading for further discussions and more information. But the Opposition only had seven votes. The coalition government had thirty-nine.

The editor of the *Colonist* agreed with the Opposition's arguments and objected to the unnecessary secrecy.

> Listening to Attorney General Wismer present the police transfer bill for second reading in the British Columbia Legislature yesterday one would be hard put to discover wherein lay the Government's real argument. Is it "economy," or "national security" or the mere fact that six other Provinces have done it "this way"? Not one of those reasons supplies its own mandate, or affords any reason why the British Columbia Legislature should not have the transfer agreement spread in front of it when ready. That is the place where agreements which are to last forever should be examined and discussed. Nor, in a speech of more than one hour, did Mr. Wismer supply one reason why the Legislature should be asked to ratify such a step sight unseen.[5]

On March 30, 1950, An Act to amend the Police and Prisons Regulation Act was given final assent in the legislature.

The amendment, written in bureaucratic legalese, gave the government broad options. Its core, Section 38, stated:

> [The provincial government] may from time to time enter into an agreement or agreements with the Governor in Council whereby the duties and powers, or a part of duties and powers assigned by and under this Act or any other Act to the Provincial Police Force, shall during the currency of the agreement or any agreement in substitution thereof be assumed and carried out by the Royal Canadian Mounted Police, and the members of the Royal Canadian Mounted Police may exercise all the powers and hold all the offices conferred by or under this or any other Act upon the Provincial Police Force and members thereof.[6]

Despite protests from the Opposition and the public, the majority of MLAs authorized cabinet to do as it thought best about policing in British Columbia. When they voted for the amendment, Wismer had the right to make all negotiations about policing without having to answer any further questions.

On April 30, he returned from meetings in Ottawa. "Switchover To RCMP Forecast By Midsummer — Attorney General Wismer said yesterday, 'if a satisfactory deal can be worked out. Talks were most satisfactory... but changeover details were not complete.'"[7]

Most Provincials expected that the changeover, if it happened, would be a lengthy process. Many members still scoffed at the idea. A large number did not even realize that it was a legal possibility. Policing in BC continued as usual during the next few months, and the issue seemed to have disappeared. A few Provincials on Vancouver Island were called in for a medical exam; they were told it was to update BCPP records.

The end came without warning. On August 9, 1950, nine senior BCPP officers received letters from Attorney General Wismer.

> We have now completed the agreement with the Federal Government for the policing of this Province by the Royal Canadian Mounted Police. As must be apparent to you, it was impossible to disclose the details of the agreement until both of the high contracting parties had signed it. Both Governments felt that in the interests of national security, and for other reasons, it was essential that the arrangements should be made. One of the difficulties we met with was the fact that the Royal Canadian Mounted Police only required eight commissioned officers to police the Province, and also that their regulations compel retirement on completion of thirty-five years of service (including war service), or on attaining the age of sixty years...[8]

The letter told the nine officers that as of August 15, 1950, they would be struck from the rolls. The long BCPP careers of Commissioner Peachey, Deputy Commissioner Cecil Clark, Inspectors R. Harvey, C.K. McKenzie, H.H. Mansell, F.W. Swanson, and Sub-Inspectors A. MacDonald, W.J. Thomson and G.A. Johnson ended abruptly. The attorney general stressed that the RCMP commissioner had made it clear that there was no objection to anyone on the grounds of inefficiency, or otherwise, and that he had the highest regard for the integrity and ability of the officers.

That left eight BCPP officers and the rest of the force. Most of the men were offered jobs in the RCMP by a brusque letter from the attorney general. He informed each man that agreement had been reached and bluntly explained the terms. If they qualified to become members of the RCMP, which he assured them that most did, they would continue policing in BC and could expect that any RCMP training would be modified in accordance with each man's age and physical condition. Wismer then outlined the much greater benefits received under the RCMP pension plan, plus other benefits, and detailed the grants that would be made until March 31, 1952, to compensate for any differences. After again briefly stating that the change was desirable in the interest of national security and for other reasons, Wismer thanked the recipient "on behalf of the Government of British Columbia for your efficient and loyal services in the past."[9]

The agreement had been signed and sealed. It was now up to the province to determine how much manpower they were delivering.

Under the detailed new policing agreement, the RCMP would police British Columbia, covering all eventualities for both the present and future. The lengthy document specified responsibilities and costs, giving the time factors of the contract as well as the conditions. It specified that the attorney general of BC had the right to add more duties, subject to agreement about additional costs. However, in all matters relating to the enforcement of federal laws where Doukhobors were concerned, the minister of justice had to be consulted, and no RCMP action could be undertaken except with the joint permission of the minister of justice and the attorney general. Although the contract period was from August 15, 1950 to August 14, 1956, either party could cancel it on one year's notice. The RCMP would maintain at least 545 officers and men in British Columbia.

*Provincials were flown into isolated areas where they were left to complete their patrol by dogsled and snowshoes.*

In exchange, British Columbia agreed to pay the Dominion Government $775,000 each year, based on $1,400 per man, subject to review every three years. This amount included the transportation and maintenance of RCMP prisoners. Within the first year, the Dominion government agreed to purchase or lease all suitable BCPP buildings and equipment.

Some provincial policing autonomy was built in, as the officer commanding of the RCMP in BC was contracted to act under the direction of the attorney general "without reference to the Senior Officers of the Force at Ottawa, except where Federal Statutes other than the Criminal Code of Canada or Federal Police duties are concerned."[10]

The contract outlined how municipalities with current provincial contracts for BCPP policing would continue paying the amount agreed upon per policeman. Since that amount was normally above the $1,400 the Dominion was charging BC, the difference was to be paid to the sub-contractor, the RCMP. Most municipalities were particularly irate about that clause. They had had no say in the transition, so some considered that their contracts with the provincial government had been illegally sold to the federal government. But the cost of equipping and starting their own local police force was prohibitive. All contracted municipalities were policed initially by the federal force, in many cases by the same men who had been policing them.

The agreement also specified that the attorney general could request an increase or a decrease of manpower, and could request that new detachments, above the 124 guaranteed by the agreement, be opened at a cost of only $1,700 per detachment. This was another bargain. British Columbia's population was expanding at a rapid rate. For an attorney general trying to budget in inflationary times, when the cost of land, buildings and equipment was escalating, this must have been an appealing clause.

At one minute after midnight on August 15, 1950, the British Columbia Provincial Police ceased to exist. Ninety-two years had passed since James Douglas, Matthew Begbie and Chartres Brew had participated in its origin. There was no formal goodbye, no fanfare, no ceremony.

Why did the government of British Columbia choose to contract out its policing mandate?

The cost of policing was increasing each year, both because of population growth and the seriousness of crimes being committed. Some Provincials were demanding parity with the Mounties in wages and benefits. Concern about national security was persistent. But it is entirely possible that the BCPP got torpedoed for reasons of political expediency.

In the postwar years, faction fighting in the Liberal–Conservative coalition had intensified. Despite its large win at the polls in 1949, the coalition government was shaky. (In 1952, the neophyte Social Credit party would defeat most of the coalition candidates.) When Attorney General Pat Maitland died in 1946, the cabinet split over the appointment of Gordon Wismer as attorney general. The Conservative cabinet members had hesitated to appoint Wismer, the man who ran Vancouver's Liberals, to such a powerful position, and many trade-offs had apparently been necessary. His appointment remained a thorn in the side of some Conservatives. By 1950, the fighting in cabinet had broadened as Conservatives and Liberals argued about the provincial debt, social services and railway policy.

As the government blundered along and decisions were delayed by arguments, the Liberals knew that they must placate the Conservatives. Wismer and his cohorts decided to try to achieve that by reducing provincial policing costs. The federal government was willing to subsidize policing in order to develop a national police force, and its purchase and lease of BCPP property and equipment would generate provincial capital. Both factions apparently agreed with the attorney general's proposal. No coalition MLA spoke against the transfer during the legislative debate. Wismer's strategy worked: the legislated demise of the BCPP was achieved quickly and, as the critics pointed out, with no assessment of long-term consequences.

For the Provincials themselves, there was chaos when the changeover was made. A former Provincial explained:

> I'd been away on holidays during the takeover. Even though I was an officer and knew it was in the works, I hadn't expected it to happen that fast or that way. I walked into Headquarters and people were scurrying all over the place. Another officer said, "Check your desk—if it's a fat envelope, you have the opportunity to join the RCMP. Skinny one, you're gone. Get up there and see which, then if you're staying, see if you can do anything about this paper pouring in here that nobody knows what to do about!" It was a fat envelope, I stayed. And sorted paper.[11]

The large majority of Provincials entered the ranks of the RCMP, exchanged their khaki and green uniforms for scarlet and gold. Of the 502 on the BCPP rolls on August 9, 488 Provincials were offered the opportunity to transfer to the RCMP and almost everyone accepted, at least initially. Quite a large number resigned during the next two years, however, many of them to undertake totally different careers. One man who stayed just over a year explained: "As most of us were married men with families, of course we stayed until we could figure out what we wanted to do. It had not been possible to make that sort of long-term decision between August 9th and August 15th!"[12]

Of the nine officers abruptly released, two accepted positions with the government as official administrators, but the idea received a cool response from the others. The attorney general's offer had pointed out that commissions earned for administering estates plus the former officer's superannuation would equal or perhaps exceed what he had been making in pay and allowances, but the job was unappealing. "Being an official administrator had no challenges," one former officer commented. "Just routine paperwork. It was not quite what I had anticipated doing as I approached the zenith of my years of training."[13]

After the initial confusion, the transition period went relatively smoothly, although many former Provincials found it a difficult time. The BCPP style of policing was distinctive, different from the RCMP style, and they had to adjust to the differences. The RCMP was based on a military organization, whereas the BCPP had been developed as a constabulary and had not changed its essential training style. A perceptive man who served for many years as a senior officer in the RCMP compared the two:

> Quite a difference in the BCPP's basic setup to the RCMP's, you know. In the Mounties, discipline is of a military nature, Orderly Room Proceedings. Police forces have different styles. Whereas some govern their men with thick instruction manuals which need continual updating, the slim, simply worded BCPP manual portrayed our method of policing. Everyone could understand what it said and with what intent. Constables quickly knew all it contained and used it adeptly.
>
> When there are very detailed instructions supposed to cover every situation, a man becomes afraid to make decisions in case he has missed instructions. He worries that his decision might fall on his head because of the system. The Provincial force had almost none of that—not because they were better equipped or better men, but because their system bred a different style of reaction to everyday problems. They were expected to be self-disciplined, and prepared, and able to handle most things without finding a reference to it in a manual or without contacting a senior officer for instructions.[14]

But adjustments were not made only on one side. One former BCPP constable who became an RCMP inspector theorized that as much as the Mounties modified policing in British Columbia, the manpower absorbed from the Provincials caused changes in the federal force as well. The Provincials had had much more experience policing in municipalities, and that experience became part of and helped shape the federal policing style. As well, because most Provincials were initially left in the regions they had worked in before the takeover, they had much concrete advice about the particular residents for the young Mounties who joined them. That type of people-contact was new to some Mounties, especially those who had recently gone through the rigorous but isolated RCMP training, or those who had been transferred frequently. One man remembered:

> One thing that was a bit of a shock to some of the RCMP was the amount of brawling we were used to doing . . . in logging camps and rough towns, with toughs in beer parlours, well, you sometimes have to prove yourself to them on Saturday nights. Dragged the boys out by force as need be and charged each one with being a drunk, that's all. The magistrate might assess damages as well as fining a fellow if he had badly ripped your uniform. But the young Mountie coming in thought it was a major assault against the "Majesty of the Law." Quite amusing—though sometimes a bit awkward. Of course, many of us were so much older, too. It wasn't long before most of the ones from the east took themselves somewhat less seriously.[15]

Another man pointed out:

> Policing changed quite quickly in the fifties — maybe a sign of the times rather than because of the style of policing. For instance, police and parents used to co-operate in an informal sense, the court was only brought in as a last resort — a woodshed justice where most accepted that you deterred crime by the certainty of punishment. It was that way not only for the kids but for anyone. I think that concept changed fast in British Columbia.[16]

The rapid changeover mystified British Columbians, who were unsure about why and how it had occurred. Some were angry that it had been done without going to the electorate, others wondered if perhaps there were not internal scandals being hushed up or if communist infiltration had become a grave danger to the nation. "People stopped us on the street," one former Provincial explained, "partly to make sure we were okay but also to see if we could shed any light on why the government had sold policing to the federal government. We would reassure them, then we would both mainly shrug. Who really knew?"[17] Another man observed:

> You have to remember that it had been only five years since the war had ended and people remained uneasy over possible subversive activities. Most expected arbitrary government decisions and questioned little. The scars and fears of a war are deep. Quite a bit of talk about the reds and the danger of communism.[18]

There were also problems with uniforms, which caused more confusion for the public. Although many Provincials were immediately provided with RCMP uniforms, quite a number of the men were too large to fit into the regular sizes stocked. They had to wait months for custom-tailored uniforms. In the interim, they continued to wear their khaki and green. Some of the men recalled people saying how glad they were that the government had changed its mind and brought the Provincials back.

On the whole, however, there was little public outcry about the demise of the BCPP. Because so many members were left in the same location

*The last commissioner of the BCPP, Roger Peachey.*

for the first year after the transition, the public did not have to get used to new policemen. Rather, they learned to call "their" policemen Mounties rather than Provincials. In later years, some people reminisced nostalgically about the Provincials, but could not pinpoint the reasons. One man, a garage owner, commented that Provincial Police offered a more relaxed policing, perhaps because each man had a lot of independence.

> I was in my early twenties then and had been a hot-rodder earlier so I knew quite a few — not always willingly. But it was a different style. For example, when you were given a speeding ticket, you might be asked questions about your family, then you got a lecture about your value to them. You accepted it, often ended up genuinely agreeing that it was in your best interests, and your family's, to slow down.
>
> Maybe it was more personalized. Most had an innate courtesy, even when they had to be tough. And they could be tough and control things fast when they had to.[19]

Ironically, it was their experience in the BC Provincial Police force that enabled many Provincials to meet the challenge of moving from the BCPP to the RCMP. A former Provincial who went on to serve in the RCMP summed it up best:

> Quite a number of our men from the Provincial force did well in the RCMP; a lot of us became officers, more than could have been statistically predicted. Mind you, we brought a variety of experience with us when we were taken over. Especially valuable was our knowledge about municipal policing as the RCMP had actually been primarily a rural force previously. I had interesting and varied years in the RCMP, and many good men served under me. But I remain proud — I'm glad — to have been able to be part of the BCPP for over eighteen years. The Provincials were quite a group of men.[20]

# Notes

**Author's note:** In researching this book, I interviewed forty-seven former members of the British Columbia Provincial Police and nine other people between September 1983 and May 1991. All interviewees chose to remain anonymous to allow for frank discussion. I conducted extensive archival research during the same period; each collection grew, and some storage and indexing methods have been revised. The citations in my notes and source lists reflect these changes as accurately as possible. The Public Archives of British Columbia, Victoria, BC, is shown as PABC; the Public Archives of Canada, Ottawa, Ontario, is shown as PAC.

## Chapter One

1. Chartres Brew to James Douglas, November 11, 1858, Douglas files, Colonial Papers GR 1372 B-1326, PABC.

2. Sir Edward Lytton to James Douglas, Douglas files, Colonial Papers GR 1372 B-1326, PABC.

3. Richard Moody to James Douglas, December 29, 1858, Douglas files, Colonial Papers GR 1372 B-1326, PABC.

4. F.W. Howay, *The Early History of the Fraser River Mines* (Victoria, BC, 1926), p. 84.

5. *Ibid.*, p. 96.

6. Brew files, May 28, 1859, Colonial Papers GR 1372 B-1310, PABC.

7. *Ibid.*

8. Sir Matthew Begbie to James Douglas, January 1861, Colonial Papers GR 1372 B-1308, PABC.

9. A.N. Birch to W.C. Cox, May 14, 1864, Colonial Papers GR 1372 B-1321, PABC.

10. Mel Rothenburger, *The Chilcotin War* (Kamloops, BC: Ryan, McLean, Alaric, 1976), p. 59.

11. Proceedings at inquest held at Bute Inlet, May 23, 1864; verdict signed by Leslie Jones, Foreman, Colonial Papers GR 1372 B-1321, PABC.

12. Chartres Brew to Frederick Seymour, May 23, 1864, Colonial Papers GR 1372 B-1321, PABC.

13. *British Colonist*, October 14, 1864.

14. *British Columbian*, July 27, 1867.

15. Chartres Brew's tombstone, Barkerville cemetery.

## Chapter Two

1. Brew files, Colonial Papers GR 1372 B-1311, PABC.

2. *Ibid*.

3. Sworn Information from "Louis, Comox Indian & guide," Colonial Papers GR 429, box 1 file 2, 1873, 55/73, PABC.

4. Victoria *Daily Colonist*, May 23, 1873.

5. *Ibid*.

6. Victoria *Daily Colonist*, May 1, 1875.

7. BCPP Correspondence In: GR 429 box 1 file 4, 1875, PABC.

8. Report on Revenue & Expenditures, Sessional Papers, 1878, Legislative Library of BC, Victoria, BC

9. Charles Todd to attorney general, BCPP GR 61 B-2568, PABC.

10. Victoria *Daily Colonist*, December 23, 1879.

11. *The Guardian* (London, England), September 5, 1880, BCPP GR 61, PABC.

12. BCPP Correspondence In: Yale, BCPP GR 61 BCPM GR/OS, PABC.

13. *Ibid*.

14. *Ibid*.

15. BCPP Correspondence In: Clinton, BCPP GR 61 BCPM GR/OS, PABC.

## Chapter Three

1. Summarized from letters to attorney general from Herbert Roycraft, July and August 1884, AG GR 996, PABC.

2. *Ibid*.

3. Herbert Roycraft to deputy attorney general, April 5, 1885, GR 55, PABC.

4. Frederick Hussey to Herbert Roycraft, August 11, 1884, BCPP GR 61 vol. 2 , PABC.

5. Malcolm Sproat to attorney general, AG GR 996, August 24, 1885, PABC.

6. BCPP Correspondence In: letter to Matthew Begbie, date not readable, BCPP GR 55, PABC.

7. Port Moody *Gazette*, October 22, 1885.

8. Victoria *Daily Colonist*, March 2, 1887.

9. Charles Dickie to Cecil Clark, April 28, 1948.

10. *Ibid.*

11. Frederick Hussey to attorney general, AG 429 box 2, PABC.

12. Cecil Clark, *BC Provincial Police Stories*, vol. 2 (Surrey, BC: Heritage House, 1986), p. 141.

13. Constable at Duncan to Frederick Hussey, BCPP GR 55 vol. 3, PABC.

14. Sir John A. MacDonald papers, MG 26A, vol. 325, PAC.

15. *Ibid.*

16. Sam Steele report, July 1888, RG 18 vol. 18 file 247, 1888, PAC.

17. N. Fitzstubbs to Herbert Roycraft, February 1888, AG 429 box 2 file 1, PABC.

18. Herbert Roycraft to N. Fitzstubbs, March 11, 1888, GR 677, PABC.

19. Roycraft reports, AG 429 box 2 file 2, PABC.

20. *Ibid.*

21. N. Fitzstubbs to Herbert Roycraft, October 1888, AG 429 box 2 file 2, PABC.

22. Constable at 150 Mile House to Frederick Hussey, AG 429 box 2 file 5, PABC.

23. Constable Stewart at Nanaimo to Frederick Hussey, BCPP GR 55 vol. 2, PABC.

24. Constable at Rivers Inlet to Frederick Hussey, BCPP GR 55 vol. 2, PABC.

25. Constable D. Anderson's memoirs, *Shoulder Strap*, Spring 1939.

26. Government agent to attorney general, date and location not readable, AG 429 box 3, PABC.

27. *Provincial Police Act*, Sessional Report, 1896, Legislative Library of BC, Victoria, BC.

28. Victoria *Daily Colonist*, May 19, 1896.

29. *Ibid.*

30. *Ibid.*

## Chapter Four

1. Interview with former BCPP member, October 1984.
2. *Ibid.*
3. "Old Timers' Memoirs," in *Shoulder Strap*, Spring 1940.
4. Interview with former BCPP member, October 1984.
5. *Ibid.*
6. Chief Constable A. McLeod in Fernie to Frederick Hussey, August 1902, BCPP GR 1323 B-2047, PABC.
7. *Ibid.*
8. BCPP Correspondence In: BCPP GR 55 vol. 46, 1902, PABC.
9. *Ibid.*
10. *Ibid.*
11. Thiel Detective Agency to Sergeant Atkins in Victoria, BCPP GR 61, 1902, PABC.
12. Martin Robin, *The Rush for Spoils* (Toronto: McClelland & Stewart, 1972), p. 26.
13. BCPP Correspondence In: AG 429 box 8, 1901, PABC.
14. BCPP Correspondence In: AG 429 box 11, 1904, PABC.
15. BCPP Correspondence In: GR 55, PABC.
16. C. Taylor to Frederick Hussey, November 1910, BCPP GR 55 vol. 48, PABC.
17. G. Dinsmore to Frederick Hussey, November 1910, BCPP GR 55 vol. 48, PABC.
18. BCPP Correspondence In: AG 429 box 14, PABC.
19. Interview with elderly resident of Kamloops, October 1984.

## Chapter Five

1. Interview with former BCPP member, September 1984.
2. Fort George report, 1912, BCPP GR 61 roll 35, PABC.
3. Archival files from BCPP GR 55, 1910, reprinted in *Gazette*, December 1, 1976.
4. BCPP GR 55, 1910, PABC.
5. Interview with former BCPP member, May 1985.
6. Interview with former BCPP member, September 1984.
7. Correspondence to Colin Campbell, AG 1323 B-2073, PABC.
8. A. Ross McCormack, "The Industrial Workers of the World in Western Canada: 1905–1914," in *British Columbia: Historical Readings*, p. 487.
9. Interview with miner's daughter, Vancouver, June 1985.
10. Reports, October 1912, BCPP GR 68, PABC.

11. Reports, November 1912, BCPP GR 68, PABC.

12. Lynne Bowen, *Boss Whistle: The Coal Miners of Vancouver Island Remember* (Lantzville, BC: Oolichan Books, 1982), p. 149.

13. *Ibid.*, pp. 175, 176, 177.

14. Reports, December 1913, BCPP GR 68, PABC.

15. Reports, January 1914, BCPP GR 68, PABC.

16. Interview with former BCPP member, September 1985.

17. Hugh Johnston, *The Voyage of the Komagata Maru* (Delhi: Oxford University Press, 1979), p. 78.

18. Interview with former BCPP member, May 1985.

19. Correspondence, BCPP GR 55, PABC.

20. Margaret Ormsby, *British Columbia: A History* (Vancouver: Macmillan, 1958), pp. 379, 380.

21. Correspondence, BCPP GR 55, 1914, PABC.

22. Interview with former BCPP member, October 1984.

23. Correspondence, BCPP 1323 B-2109, B-2118, 1915, PABC.

24. *Ibid.*

## Chapter Six

1. Interview with former BCPP member, May 1985.

2. Interview with former BCPP member, June 1985.

3. Interview with former BCPP member, October 1984.

4. BCPP Correspondence out: AG 1323, B-2146, 1918, PABC.

5. Interview with former BCPP member, September 1985.

6. Public Accounts, Attorney General, 1919, Legislative Library of BC, Victoria, BC.

7. Interview with former BCPP member, May 1985.

8. *Ibid.*

9. Government Records, RG 18 vol. 1966, PAC.

10. *Ibid.*

11. *Ibid.*

12. *Ibid.*

13. David Jay Bercuson, "Industrial Conflict & The Labour Movement," in *British Columbia: Historical Readings*, pp. 452, 453.

14. Interview with former BCPP member, June 1985.

15. W. Peter Ward, "Class and Race in the Social Structure of British Columbia, 1879–1939," in *British Columbia: Historical Readings*, p. 583.

16. 17 RCMP files: RG 18 vol 580 G 445-1919 PAC Ottawa, Ont.

17. *Ibid.*

18. *Ibid.*

19. RG vol. 581, PAC.

20. RG vol. 580, PAC.

21. RG 18 vol. 592, 1919, 1068, PAC.

22. *Ibid.*

23. *Ibid.*

24. *Ibid.*

25. BCPP Correspondence in: AG 1323, B-2182, 1920, PABC.

26. Interview with former BCPP member, June 1985.

27. Martin Robin, *The Rush for Spoils* (Toronto: McClelland & Stewart, 1972), pp. 180, 181.

## Chapter Seven

1. *Vancouver Sun*, May 9, 1921.

2. *Ibid.*, May 12, 1921.

3. *Vancouver Daily Province*, May 2, 1921.

4. RCMP files, RG 18 vol. 3167, PAC.

5. *Ibid.*

6. Interview with former BCPP member, May 1985.

7. RCMP files, RG 18 vol. 3167, April 8, 1923, PAC.

8. *Ibid.*, April 18, 1923.

9. *Ibid.*

10. *Ibid.*

11. *Ibid.*, May 11, 1923.

12. *Ibid.*

13. *Vancouver Sun*, December 19, 1923.

14. *Vancouver Daily Province*, February 1, 1924.

15. RCMP files, RG 18 vol. 3171 file G 501-1-23, PAC.

16. *Ibid.*

17. BC Provincial Police Regulation Constable's Manual, 1924, Legislative Library of BC, Victoria, BC.

18. Interview with former BCPP member, May 1985.

19. Interview with former BCPP member, July 1984.

20. *Ibid.*

21. Interview with former BCPP member, May 1985.

22. Interview with former BCPP member, July 1984.

23. Interview with former BCPP member, September 1983.

24. *Ibid.*

25. Interview with former BCPP member, July 1984.

26. *Criminal Code of Canada*, 1929, Section 464(c).

27. Interview with former BCPP member, July 1984.

28. Report of Provincial Police, 1929, Legislative Library of BC, Victoria, BC.

## Chapter Eight

1. Report of Provincial Police, 1930, Legislative Library of BC, Victoria, BC.
2. Interview with former BCPP member, July 1984.
3. BCPP Papers, GR 68, PABC.
4. Interview with former BCPP member, June 1984.
5. Interview with former BCPP member, July 1984.
6. *Ibid.*
7. Interview with former BCPP member, October 1984.
8. Interview with former BCPP member, May 1984.
9. Pamphlet on Princeton Strike, AG 429, 1933, PABC.
10. Report of Provincial Police, 1932, Legislative Library of BC, Victoria, BC.
11. Board of Inquiry re Spences Creek CPR incident, AG 429, 1933, PABC.
12. Interview with former BCPP member, June 1985.
13. Interview with former BCPP member, May 1984.
14. Interview with former BCPP member, October 1984.
15. Interview with former BCPP member, May 1984.
16. Interview with former BCPP member, June 1984.
17. *Ibid.*
18. *Ibid.*
19. Report of Provincial Police, 1935, Legislative Library of BC, Victoria, BC.
20. Report on Vancouver Arena crowd, AG 429, 1935, PABC.
21. Interview with former BCPP member, October 1984.
22. Interview with former BCPP member, June 1985.
23. Radiograms, GR 55, 1935, PABC.
24. Report of Provincial Police, 1935, Legislative Library of BC, Victoria, BC.
25. Interview with former BCPP member, May 1985.
26. *Ibid.*
27. Interview with former BCPP member, July 1985.
28. Interview with former BCPP member, May 1985.
29. *Ibid.*
30. Interview with former BCPP member, October 1984.

## Chapter Nine

1. Report of Provincial Police, 1939, Legislative Library of BC, Victoria, BC.

2. Interview with former BCPP member, June 1985.
3. Interview with former BCPP member, September 1987.
4. Interview with former BCPP member, May 1985.
5. *Ibid*.
6. Interview with former BCPP member, June 1985.
7. Interview with former BCPP member, October 1985.
8. Interview with former BCPP member, March 1991.
9. *Vancouver Sun*, February 10, 1942. Committee members included Mayor Fred Hume of New Westminster, chairman, Col. A.W. Sparling, Lt. Col. Macgregor MacIntosh, Assistant Commissioner C.H. Hill, RCMP, Prof. H.F. Angus, UBC, and Sgt. J. Barnes, RCMP, secretary.
10. Interview with former BCPP member, July 1988.
11. *Vancouver Sun*, December 23, 1941.
12. *Vancouver Daily Province*, December 23, 1941.
13. *Ibid*.
14. Order-in-Council PC 1486, AG 429, 1942, PABC.
15. RG 18 vol. 3563, file ll-19-2-9, March 2, 1942, PAC.
16. Interview with former BCPP member, July 1985.
17. RG 18 vol 3563, May 28, 1942, PAC.
18. Interview with former BCPP member, September 1986.
19. Interview with former BCPP member, June 1985.
20. *Ibid*.
21. Reports on Alaska construction, AG 429, 1943, PABC.
22. Interview with former BCPP member, May 1985.
23. Interview with former BCPP member, September 1984.
24. *Ibid*.

## Chapter Ten

1. Charges are divided into summary convictions and indictable offences. The less serious offences, which under the Criminal Code are tried by a magistrate without a jury, are summary prosecutions. Under the Criminal Code, for all serious offences, which were originally prosecuted as "indictments," written accusations had to be presented to a grand jury. That procedure evolved to the more serious charges being called indictable offences, even though many are now tried by a judge without a jury.
2. Report of Provincial Police, 1943, Legislative Library of BC, Victoria, BC.
3. Interview with former BCPP member, May 1985.
4. Interview with former BCPP member, July 1985.
5. Interview with former BCPP member, September 1986.
6. Interview, February 1991.

7. Interview with former BCPP member, September 1985.

8. Interview with former BCPP member, June 1985.

9. Interview with former BCPP member, July 1984.

10. *Ibid.*

11. Interview with former BCPP member, September 1984.

12. Interview with former BCPP member, June 1985.

13. Long Service and Good Conduct Medals presented in 1946, at the only such ceremony, were received by Commissioner T.W.S. Parsons, Deputy Commissioner John Shirras, Inspectors Robert Owens, Roger Peachey, Cecil Clark, Richard Harvey, F. Swanson, C.K. McKenzie and H.H. Mansell, Sub-Inspectors J. Russell, G.J. Duncan, Staff Sgts. G.A. Johnson, A. Macdonald, W.J. Thomson, Sgts. Carl Ledoux, C.G. Jacklin, W.J. Hatcher, R.S. Nelson, G.H. Clark, Thomas Herdman, S. Service, W.J. McKay and L.A.N. Potterman, Corp. T. Backler, Det. Const. J.A. Williams, Constables G.C. Sharpe, R.C. Barrington-Foote, J.M. Green, M. Martin, R.H. Hassard, J.A. Quesnel, C.J. Gurr, P.R. Hutchinson, Peter Kelsberg, C.J. Waddel and W. Smith, Chief Clerk E. Patterson, Assistant Chief Clerk T. Kennelly, Senior Clerk C.V. Embleton, Assistant Chief Clerk G.D. Mead, Armorer R. Marshall, Superintendent G.A. Hood of the Motor Licence Department and Assistant Superintendent J.P. Hannah. (Hood and Hannah were awarded the medals for service before their transfer to the new Motor Vehicle Department.)

14. Interview with former BCPP member, July 1984.

15. Ministry of the Attorney General, file P291, Records Management Branch, Victoria, BC.

16. Interview with former BCPP member, September 1984.

17. Interview with former BCPP member, November 1987.

18. Simma Holt, *Terror in the Name of God* (Toronto: McClelland and Stewart, 1964), pp. 105–106.

19. Victoria *Daily Colonist*, April 28, 1949.

20. Interview with former BCPP member, July 1984.

21. Interview with former BCPP member, September 1984.

22. *Ibid.*

23. Interview with former BCPP member, July 1984.

## Chapter Eleven

1. Victoria *Daily Colonist*, March 1, 1950.

2. Victoria *Daily Colonist*, March 21, 1950.

3. Interview with former BCPP member, May 1986.

4. Victoria *Daily Colonist*, March 20, 1950.

5. Victoria *Daily Colonist*, March 28, 1950.
6. Sessional Records, 1950, Legislative Library of BC, Victoria, BC.
7. Victoria *Daily Colonist*, April 30, 1950.
8. AG 429 file 5, 1950, PABC.
9. *Ibid*.
10. RG 2, series 1 vol. 1823, PAC.
11. Interview with former BCPP member, July 1984.
12. Interview with former BCPP member, September 1984.
13. Interview with former BCPP member, May 1985.
14. Interview with former BCPP member, August 1984.
15. Interview with former BCPP member, May 1985.
16. Interview with former BCPP member, February 1985.
17. Interview with former BCPP member, June 1985.
18. Interview, August 1987.
19. Interview with former BCPP member, August 1984.

# Sources

## Books

Akrigg, G.P.V. and Helen. *British Columbia Chronicle 1847–1871*. Vancouver: Discovery Press, 1977.

Akrigg, G.P.V. and Helen. *British Columbia Place Names*. Victoria: Sono Nis Press, 1973.

Barlee, N.L. *Gold Creeks & Ghost Towns*. Summerland: Hancock House, 1970.

Begg, Alexander. *History of British Columbia*. Toronto: William Briggs, 1894.

Berton, Pierre. *The Last Spike*. Toronto: McClelland and Stewart, 1971.

Berton, Pierre. *The National Dream*. Toronto: McClelland and Stewart, 1970.

Bowman, Lynne. *Boss Whistle: The Coal Miners of Vancouver Island Remember*. Lantzville, BC: Oolichan Books, 1983.

Broadfoot, Barry. *Ten Lost Years*. Toronto: Doubleday, 1973.

Cail, Robert. *Land, Man and the Law*. Vancouver: University of BC Press, 1974.

Clark, Cecil. *BC Provincial Police Stories*. Surrey, BC: Heritage House, 1986.

Clark, Cecil. *Tales of the British Columbia Provincial Police*. Sidney, BC: Gray's Publishing, 1971.

Dunn, Joyce. *A Town Called Chase*. Penticton, BC: Theytus, 1986.

Fort Nelson Historical Society. *History of Fort Nelson*. Fort Nelson, 1958.

Friesen, J. and H.K. Ralson, eds. *Historical Essays on British Columbia*. Toronto: Carleton Library No. 96, McClelland and Stewart, 1976.

Goodchild, Fred H. *British Columbia: Its History, People & Industry*, London, UK: Allen & Unwin, 1951.

Gosnell, R.E. *A History of British Columbia*. Vancouver: British Columbia Historical Association, 1928.

Granatstein, J.L., et al. *Twentieth Century Canada*. Toronto: McGraw-Hill Ryerson, 1983.

Griffin, Harold. *British Columbia: The People's Early Story*. Vancouver: Tribune Publishing, 1958.

Hibbens, T.N. *Guide to the Province of British Columbia for 1877–8*. Victoria: Ministry of Agriculture, Canada, 1877.

Hill, Beth. *Sappers: The Royal Engineers in British Columbia*. Ganges, BC: Horsdal & Schubert, 1987.

Holt, Simma. *Terror in the Name of God: The Story of the Sons of Freedom Doukhobors*. Toronto: McClelland and Stewart, 1964.

Howay, F.W. *British Columbia: The Making of a Province*. Toronto: Ryerson Press, 1928.

Howay, F.W. *The Early History of the Fraser River Mines*. Victoria: Archives of British Columbia, 1926.

Howay, F.W. and E.O.S. Scholefield. *From the Earliest Times to the Present*. Vancouver: S.J. Clarke, 1914.

Hutcheson, Sydney. *Depression Stories*. Vancouver: New Star, 1976.

Hutchison, Bruce. *The Fraser*. Toronto: Clark Irwin, 1950.

Jenness, Diamond. *The Indians of Canada*. Ottawa: Supply & Services Canada, 1977.

Johnson, Anthony. *Sketches of Pioneering in the Rocky Mountains*. Toronto, 1905.

Johnston, Hugh. *The Voyage of the* Komagata Maru*: The Sikh Challenge to Canada's Colour Bar*. Delhi: Oxford University Press, 1979.

Johnstone, Bill. *Coal Dust in My Blood: The Autobiography of a Coal Miner*. Victoria: BC Provincial Museum, 1980.

Kelly, Nora and William. *The Royal Canadian Mounted Police: A Century of History*. Edmonton: Hurtig, 1973.

Kilian, Crawford. *Go Do Some Great Thing: The Black Pioneers of British Columbia*. Vancouver: Douglas & McIntyre, 1978.

Large, R. Geddes. *The Skeena: River of Destiny*. Sidney, BC: Mitchell Press, 1973.

Lindo, M.A. *Making History: An Anthology of British Columbia*. Victoria, 1974.

Liversedge, R.C. and V. Hoar. *Recollections of the On-To-Ottawa Trek*. Toronto: McClelland and Stewart, 1973.

Mayne, Richard C. *Four Years in British Columbia and Vancouver Island*. London, UK: J. Murray, 1862.

McGregor, Donald A. *They Gave Royal Assent*. Vancouver: Mitchell Press, 1970.

McKelvie, B.A. *Pageant of British Columbia*. Toronto: T. Nelson, 1955.

Morice, A.G. *The History of the Northern Interior of British Columbia*. Toronto: William Briggs, 1904.

Norris, J.M. *Strangers Entertained: The History of Diverse Ethnic Groups*. Vancouver: Evergreen Press, 1971.

Norris, J.M. and M. Prang. *Personality & History in British Columbia: Essays in Honour of Margaret Ormsby*. Vancouver: BC Studies, 1977.

Ormsby, Margaret. *British Columbia: A History*. Toronto: Macmillan, 1958.

Paterson, T.W. *Encyclopaedia of Ghost Towns & Mining Camps of British Columbia*. Haney, BC: Stagecoach Publishing, 1979.

Pethick, Derek. *British Columbia Disasters*. Haney, BC: Stagecoach Publishing, 1978.

Pethick, Derek. *Men of British Columbia*. Saanichton, BC: Hancock House, 1975.

Phillips, Paul. *No Power Greater: A Century of Labour in BC*. Vancouver: The Boag Foundation, 1967.

Potterton, Lance A.N. *Northwest Assignment*. Kelowna: Mosaic Enterprises, 1972.

Ramsay, Bruce. *Ghost Towns of BC*. Vancouver: Mitchell, 1963.

RCMP Veterans' Association. *92 Years of Pride*. Kelowna, 1983.

Riley, Bill and Laura Leake. *History and Events of the Early 1920s: A Mounted Policeman's Bird's-Eye View of the Old Cariboo Country*. New York: Vantage, 1980.

Robin, Martin. *Pillars of Profit*. Toronto: McClelland and Stewart, 1973.

Robin, Martin. *The Rush for Spoils*. Toronto: McClelland and Stewart, 1972.

Rothenburger, Mel. *The Chilcotin War*. Kamloops: Ryan, McLean, Alaric, 1976.

Rothenburger, Mel. *We've Killed Johnny Usher*. Vancouver: Mitchell Press, 1973.

Scott, David and Edna Hanic. *East Kootenay Saga*. New Westminster, BC: Nunaga Publishing, 1974.

Shelton, W.G. and University of Victoria students. *British Columbia & Confederation*. Victoria: Canadian Centennial Project, 1967.

Skelton, Robin. *They Call it the Cariboo*. Victoria: Sono Nis, 1980.

Steeves, Dorothy G. *The Compassionate Rebel: Ernest E. Winch and His Times*. Vancouver: The Boag Foundation, 1960.

Tuchman, Barbara W. *The Proud Tower: A Portrait of the World Before the War, 1890–1914*. Toronto: Macmillan, 1966.

Turkki, Pat. *Burns Lake & District*. Burns Lake: Burns Lake Historical Society, 1973.

Wade, Mark S. *The Cariboo Road*. Victoria: The Haunted Bookshop, 1979.

Waite, Donald E. *The Fraser Canyon Story*. Maple Ridge, BC: D. Waite Photo Center, 1974.

Ward, W. Peter and Robert A.J. McDonald. *British Columbia: Historical Readings*. Vancouver: Douglas & McIntyre, 1981.

Wheeler, Marilyn. *The Robson Valley*. McBride, BC: The McBride Robson Valley Story Group, 1979.

Williams, David R. *The Man For A New Country: Sir Matthew Baillie Begbie*. Sidney, BC: Gray's Publishing, 1977.

Williams, David R. *Trapline Outlaw: Simon Peter Gunanoot*. Sidney, BC: Sono Nis, 1983.

Williams, Nina. *Cattle Ranch*. Vancouver: Douglas & McIntyre, 1979.

## Journals

Bescoby, T. "Society in the Cariboo during the Gold Rush." *Washington Historical Quarterly*, July 1933.

Bilsland, W.W. "Atlin, 1898–1910." *BC Historical Quarterly*, 1958.

Boutilier, H.R. "Vancouver's Earliest Days." *BC Historical Quarterly*, 1946.

Campbell, B.R. "The Kootenay Mail." *BC Historical Quarterly*, 1951.

Emmott, N.W. "Policing the Rails," in *Canada West*, 8, 1978.

Hacking, N.R. "Steamboating on the Fraser." *BC Historical Quarterly*, 1946.

Holmes, M.C. "Commissions of Inquiry." *BC Historical Quarterly*, 1945.

Ireland, W.E. "The Annexation of 1869." *BC Historical Quarterly*, 1940.

Ireland, W.E. "The Evolutions of the Boundaries of BC." *BC Historical Quarterly*, 1939.

Lamb, W.K. "Judge Begbie. Memoirs & Documents." *BC Historical Quarterly*, 1941.

"Leonard Norris, 1865–1945" (Obituary of BCPP constable, Notes & Comments). *BC Historical Quarterly*, 1945.

Lugrim, N. deBertram. "Policing BC: The Chilcotin War." *Maclean's*, February 1, 1935.

"Moral Reform Notes." *Methodist Recorder*, 1904.

Ormsby, Margaret. "Frederick Seymour: The Forgotten Governor." *BC Studies*, 1974.

Ormsby, Margaret. "Some Irish Figures in Colonial Days." *BC Historical Quarterly*, 1950.

Ormsby, Margaret. "T. Dufferin Pattullo and the Little New Deal." *Canadian Historical Review*, December 1962.

Owen, Frances L. "Amid the Clouds with a Pack-Train." *The Boy's Own Paper*, 1928.

Pettit, Sydney. "Judge Begbie in Action." *BC Historical Quarterly*, 1947.

Raymer, S.E. "The *Komagata Maru* and the Central Powers." (Notes & Comments), *BC Historical Quarterly*, 1942.

Reid, R.L. "The Inside Story of the *Komagata Maru*." *BC Historical Quarterly*, 1941.

Saywell, J.T. "Labour & Socialism in British Columbia." *BC Historical Quarterly*, 1951.

*Shoulder Strap*. Magazine of the British Columbia Provincial Police, published semi-annually, 1938–1950.

Waites, K.A. "Responsible Government and Confederation." *BC Historical Quarterly*, 1942.

West, Willis. "Staging in the Cariboo." *BC Historical Quarterly*, 1948.

## Newspapers

*British Colonist*
*British Columbian*
*Cariboo Sentinel*
*Daily Colonist*
*Inland Sentinel*
*Kamloops Sentinel*
*Merritt Herald*
*Vancouver Daily Province*
*Vancouver Sun*
*Victoria Gazette*

## Government and Unpublished Materials

British Columbia Provincial Police display pamphlet, P.G. Paterson, curator, June 1984.

Farr, David M. "The Organization of the Judicial System of the Colonies of Vancouver Island and BC, 1849–1871." MA Thesis, University of BC, Vancouver.

Gough, Barry M. *The Power to Compel: White-Indian Conflict in British Columbia During the Colonial Period, 1849–1871*. Department of Indian Affairs Information Services, Secwepemc Cultural Educational Society, 1972.

Government of British Columbia
    Attorney General's department, record of expenditures, 1920.
    Game Conservation Board report, 1918, 1919, 1920.
    Public Accounts, list and salary of BC Provincial Police, 1901, 1910.
    Sessional Records: acts, bills, ordinances relating to policing.
    Superintendent of Police Annual Report to Attorney General, 1895, 1924–49.
Government of Canada. Treasury Board Authority & Regulations. Kamloops, BC: Secwepemc Archives, South Central Tribal Council.
Hutch, Fredrick John. "The British Columbia Police Force (1858–1871)." BA Thesis, University of BC, Vancouver.
Johnson, Arthur J. "The Canadian Pacific Railway & BC, 1871–1886." MA Thesis, University of BC, Vancouver, 1936.
Provincial Archives of British Columbia
    BC Provincial Police (GR55): general records, correspondence to and from Superintendent of Police, area records.
    Attorney General (GR996): correspondence relating to policing.
Secwepemc Cultural Education Society. *British Columbia Papers Concerned with the Indian Land Question, 1850–1875.* Victoria: Government Printer, 1875.
Shuswap Nation Tribal Council. "One People with One Mind, One Heart and One Spirit," 1989.
Tolmie, J. Ross. "The Orientals in British Columbia." BA Thesis, University of BC, Vancouver.

## Reference Bibliographies

Artibise, Alan. *Western Canada since 1870.* Vancouver: University of BC Press, 1978.
*Dictionary Card Catalog of the Provincial Archives of BC.* Boston: G.K. Hall, 1971.
Edwards, M.H. and J.C.R. Lort, *A Bibliography of British Columbia.* Vol. II: *Years of Growth.* Victoria: University of Victoria, 1975.
Granatstein, J.L. and Paul Stevens, eds. *Canada since 1867: A Bibliographical Guide.* Toronto: Hakkert, 1974.
Granatstein, J.L. and Paul Stevens, eds. *A Reader's Guide to Canadian History: Confederation to the Present.* Toronto: University of Toronto Press, 1982.
Jamieson, Stuart. *Times of Trouble: Labour Unrest and Industrial Conflict in Canada, 1900–1966.* Woods Task Force on Labour Relations, Study No. 22, Ottawa, 1968.

Lowther, Barbara. *A Bibliography of British Columbia, vol. I: Laying the Foundations, 1849–1899*. Victoria: University of Victoria, 1968.

*Publications of the Government of BC, 1871–1947*. Victoria: King's Printer, 1950.

*Royal Commissions of the Government of BC, 1872–1942*. Victoria: King's Printer, 1945.

# Index

281

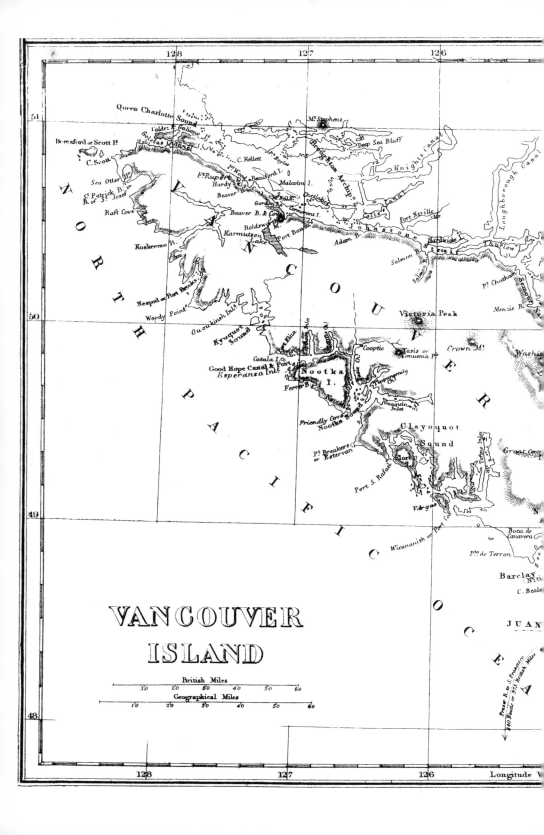

# VANCOUVER ISLAND